The International Eliade

SUNY series, Issues in the Study of Religion
―――――――――――――――

Bryan Rennie, editor

The International Eliade

Edited by
Bryan Rennie

State University of New York Press

Published by
STATE UNIVERSITY OF NEW YORK PRESS, ALBANY

© 2007 State University of New York

All rights reserved

Printed in the United States of America

No part of this book may be used or reproduced in any manner whatsoever without written permission. No part of this book may be stored in a retrieval system or transmitted in any form or by any means including electronic, electrostatic, magnetic tape, mechanical, photocopying, recording, or otherwise without the prior permission in writing of the publisher.

For information, address State University of New York Press, 194 Washington Avenue, Suite 305, Albany, NY 12210-2384

Production and book design, Laurie Searl
Marketing, Anne M. Valentine

Library of Congress Cataloging-in-Publication Data

The international Eliade / edited by Bryan Rennie.
    p. cm. — (SUNY series, issues in the study of religion)
Includes bibliographical references and index.
ISBN-13: 978-0-7914-7087-9 (hardcover : alk. paper)
ISBN-13: 978-0-7914-7088-6 (pbk. : alk. paper)
    1. Eliade, Mircea, 1907-1986. 2. Religion—Philosophy. I. Rennie, Bryan S., 1954–

BL51.I63 2007
200.92—dc22
                                  2006021935

10 9 8 7 6 5 4 3 2 1

Cover photograph of Eliade by Jeff Lowenthal. © *Jeff Lowenthal*

Contents

Acknowledgments — vii

Bryan Rennie, Introduction:
Themes in the International Eliade — 1

I. THE SACRALIZATION OF TIME

Michel Meslin, The Sacralization of Time in the
Thought of Mircea Eliade — 15

Pablo Wright and César Ceriani Cernadas, Cosmological Bridges:
Suspicion and Recollection in the Realities of Myth — 23

II. THE INTERPRETATION OF HISTORY

Ulrich Berner, Mircea Eliade and the Myth of Adonis — 37

Brigitte Ouellet, In Search of a Methodology: Eliade's
Hermeneutical Approach in the Study of Ancient
Egyptian Texts — 47

Joseph Muthuraj, The Significance of Mircea Eliade for the
Study of the New Testament — 71

III. THE INTERPRETATION OF INDIA AND ELIADE'S "TRADITIONALISM"

Liviu Bordaş, The Secret of Dr. Eliade — 101

Natale Spineto, Mircea Eliade and "Traditional Thought" — 131

IV. HISTORY AND HISTORICISM

Philip Vanhaelemeersch, Eliade, "History," and "Historicism" 151

V. THE HISTORY OF RELIGIONS

Katrine Ore, Gender Perspectives in Eliade's History of Religions 169

VI. THE DIALECTIC OF THE SACRED AND CREATIVE HERMENEUTICS

Chung Chin-Hong, Mircea Eliade's Dialectic of Sacred and Profane and Creative Hermeneutics 187

VII. MYSTICISM AND THE ORTHODOX TRADITION

Wilhelm Dancă, The Origin of the Concept of *Mysticism* in the Thought of Mircea Eliade 209

VIII. ELIADE'S FICTION

Okuyama Michiaki, Camouflage and Epiphany: The Discovery of the Sacred in Mircea Eliade and Ōe Kenzaburō 229

Mircea Eliade, Men and Stones 247
Translated by Mac Linscott Ricketts

Works Cited 281

List of Contributors 305

Name Index 311

Subject Index 315

Acknowledgements

As is always the case with any edited volume there are many people to thank and to acknowledge. Firstly all the contributors must be thanked. Their new, previously unpublished work is a genuine addition to scholarship on Eliade and their patience in the unfortunately protracted process of publication is much appreciated. Also, although I cannot name them here, I am very grateful to those would-be contributors whose work does not, for one reason or another, appear in this volume.

Acknowledgment is also due to all of the staff at the State University of New York Press whose help was invaluable on this project. The executors of the Eliade Literary Estate, David Brent and Sorin Alexandrescu gave timely permission to publish the new translation of Eliade's play, "Men and Stones," and it appears here with their permission. The photographer, Jeff Lowenthal, made the front-cover image of Eliade available. I must, of course, thank my wife, Rachela Permenter, for tolerating my constant distraction because of this and other publishing projects. However, finally and most sincerely I must thank all those scholars who have remained interested in "the Eliade case" despite the frequent but fallacious repetition of the claim that it offers nothing more to be learned.

Bryan Rennie
Westminster College, PA
August, 2006

Introduction:
Themes in the International Eliade

Bryan Rennie

THE DEVELOPMENT AND INTENTION OF THE VOLUME

Mircea Eliade was undoubtedly an international figure. Born and educated in Romania, he traveled and studied in India, Italy, Germany, and France. He taught at the University of Bucharest, the Sorbonne, and the University of Chicago. His academic writing has been translated into all major European and some Asian languages and his literary fiction has likewise been widely translated. One of his novels *Nuntă în Cer* (*Marriage in Heaven*) won the Elba-Brignetti prize for the best foreign novel in Italian in 1984, and he was nominated for the Nobel Prize in literature in 1979 and 1980. He carried on a lifelong correspondence with scholars of the history of religions on several continents, including Raffaele Pettazoni, Stig Wikander, Georges Dumézil, and Gershom Scholem. He received the French Legion of Honor in 1978 and honorary degrees from (among others) the University of Washington, the Sorbonne, Lancaster University, Boston College, Universidad de San Salvador, Universidad de la Plata, Ripon College, Calcutta, and Yale. However, despite all this recognition, criticism and assessment of Eliade in the anglophone West rarely takes international opinion into account, or considers Eliade's career and oeuvre as a whole. Ironically enough, this may be partly Eliade's own doing: he insisted that the Chicago journal, *The History of Religions*, be published exclusively in English. This collection of essays is an attempt to address this state of affairs and to introduce the English reader to some of the international opinion on Eliade.

None of the present contributions specifically address the question of Eliade's political past, on which the reader can consult "Mircea

Eliade: Further Considerations," in the second edition of the Macmillan *Encyclopedia*.

In some ways, this anthology began in 1996 at a session on "The Reception of Mircea Eliade in the United States" at the national conference of the American Academy of Religion. The papers offered at that session became the nucleus of an earlier anthology, *Changing Religious Worlds: The Meaning and End of Mircea Eliade* (Rennie 2001). However, it became obvious that there were many contributors from outside the English-speaking world with much of importance to say. The present volume began to take shape after two symposia on Eliade held at the eighteenth Congress of the International Association for the History of Religions in Durban, South Africa, in August 2000. Several contributors (Ulrich Berner, Chung Chin-Hong, Mircea Itu, Michiaki Okuyama, Arvind Sharma, and Bryan Rennie) attended those symposia. Others sent papers in advance for consideration and discussion. Other papers have been added since that time and some papers, sadly, omitted due to severe strictures of space.

I am aware of the self-selecting nature of any group of scholars who choose to write on Eliade and I attempted to mitigate this effect in the call for papers, which stated that "the publication will not be a *'festschrift'* for Eliade ... [but] a balanced consideration of Eliade's significance. Given the currently divided state of evaluations of Eliade, I specifically invite contributions from scholars whose assessments are negative and those who are positive." Given that specification, and the fact that I have not selected papers on the grounds of their position in respect of Eliade, I can only report that the assessment was generally favorable.

A NOTE ON THE ORGANIZATION

The themes of the papers determine their organization. The sacralization of historical time can, in many ways, be seen as an overarching theme, homologous to the interpretation of specific historical contexts. Thus, I begin with Michel Meslin's critique of Eliade's conception and follow his chapter with that of Pablo Wright and César Cernadas, which poses a radical counterpart to Meslin's "hermeneutics of suspicion." The interpretation of specific historical contexts and the utility of Eliadean categories in such interpretation provide the common theme for the next group, consisting of Berner, Ouellet, and Muthuraj. These headings provide permeable boundaries, many of the chapters touching on more than a single theme. Bordaş, for example, touches on both the Indian influence and the equally important question of the influence of "traditional" thought on Eliade and connects to the following section on "traditionalism." Thus, Bordaş should be read together with Natale Spineto, under this heading, and, since Spineto also touches on the question of (a)historicism central to Philip Vanhaelemeersch's chapter, Spineto should be read with Vanhaelemeersch on this point. Several other chapters, notably those of Ouellet, Spineto, Chung, and Muthuraj also touch on the question of history and historicism. Katrine Ore's chapter on gender perspectives in Eliade's history of religions stands on its own. There are, again, permeable boundaries and contiguities between all the following chapters although they each address their own central issues. I have placed the chapters of Chung Chin-Hong and Wilhelm Dancă each in its own section, although I hope that they naturally follow one from another. The final section on literature, a topic raised by Dancă but focused upon exclusively by Okuyama Michiaki, is the venue for a previously unpublished translation of one of Eliade's works of fiction: "Men and Stones."

A SYNOPSIS OF THE CONTENTS

That the contributors' assessment is generally positive does not mean that their response is uncritical. Michel Meslin, particularly, shows the admirable scholarly insistence upon critical assessment that has manifested itself in those Francophone critics of Eliade who have been the most demanding and the most damning of Eliade. I think, naturally, of Daniel Dubuisson and Alexandra Laignel-Lavastine (*Mythologies du XXe Siècle* and *Cioran, Eliade, Ionescu*—these are, as I say, particularly polemical works and should be considered alongside the responses of Rennie [*Reconstructing Eliade* 165–176] and Ricketts [*Former Friends and Forgotten Facts*]). Unlike the other Francophone authors, however, Meslin does not concentrate upon Eliade's politics or past, but on his understanding of the sacralization of time. Meslin builds upon the criticism made by Raffaele Pettazzoni that "it is not the primitive mythical world that confers significance on the present moment, but rather the world *hic et nunc*, which furnishes the components of any representation of the world of origins, conceived of as alternative and seen in opposition to it" (18). Thus, it is not the "the sacred" that "sacralizes" profane experience, but the latter that provides our conception and understanding of the sacred.

Not for this reason alone does Meslin disagree with Eliade's conception of the sacralization of time. We also see in Meslin's critique the claim that Christian eschatological time is linear (although the reinstitution of the divine prelapsarian condition implied by the redemption and the inauguration of the Kingdom can easily be seen to be a *return* to the paradisiacal time before the Fall, and thus as cyclical rather than linear). Meslin concludes that "[c]learly neither for the historian nor from an anthropological perspective does the sacralization of time as Eliade conceives it appear correct" (21).

While Meslin concentrates upon the historical accuracy of Eliade's analysis of the sacralization of time, Wright and Cernadas adopt a more dialectical approach, more reminiscent of Eliade's own. Using Paul Ricoeur's analysis of the positive and negative poles of hermeneutics, they suggest that a middle path between the two is useful in an assessment of Eliade. In so doing they make important comments on Eliade's insistence that even aberrant religious phenomena such as the Melanesian cargo cults are not irrational, but develop according to their own internal logic. They point out that the structuring of perspective (especially on time and myth) results in a structuring of emotion in any and every culture. They also draw attention to an important aspect often ignored in analyses of Eliade: there is a tension in his work between self-disclosure and the explication of the other. Eliade is himself an object of hermeneutics, and the consideration of "the 'theology' implied in the history of religions as I decipher and interpret it" (*Journal II* 74) is nonetheless revelatory of religious behavior for being subjective. As I suggested in *Reconstructing Eliade* (249), Eliade is not only talking about archaic religions and the other but also about the here and now and about himself. Finally, Wright and

Cernadas's chapter makes a beginning of the explanation of the implication for modern culture of the identification of the sacred and the real pervasive throughout Eliade's work.

Where Meslin comments only on Eliade's concept of the sacralization of time and makes no attempt to assess other components of his thought, Wright and Cernadas give a positive reading, but of only the general applications of his thought. The following writers, while remaining critical of Eliade in some respects, nonetheless recognize the value of his work in more specific applications. Ulrich Berner reminds us that Eliade is probably the most highly polarizing figure in the history of religions, defended as strongly as he is criticized, so that the debate on Eliade has tended to be a kind of worldview controversy between "religious" and "nonreligious" scholars of religion. Berner attempts to go beyond such a one-sided approach to show what the history of religions loses when the Eliadean approach is abandoned totally and what it loses when it follows the Eliadean approach exclusively. He attempts both to verify and to critique a central element of Eliade's theory by taking up an example from the religious history of Late Antiquity; the work of Lucian of Samosata. Berner raises the question of "the effort to understand and describe how religious people see the world" (44) to good effect, and points out that both blind discipleship and unappreciative iconoclasm are basically wrong. He draws salutary attention to the dangers of one-sided oversimplification in the study of religions, for example, the identification of any *singular* religious worldview as *the* worldview of "archaic humanity."

The assessment of an Eliadean approach as useful to the understanding of religious phenomena in specific contexts while recognizing its inherent limitations is made even more forcefully by Brigitte Ouellet. Her chapter on the study of ancient Egyptian texts admits the limitations of an Eliadean approach and gives consideration to detailed criticisms. However, it also defends his approach and emphasizes its utility and applicability to this narrowly specialized field. The essay suggests various contributions to the elaboration of a hermeneutic of Egyptian texts implied by the application of the intentions that govern an Eliadean hermeneutic and, at the same time, indicates changes implied by advances in textual interpretation. It is rare that a specialist such as this takes the time to write on the theories of a generalist such as Eliade, and Ouellet's chapter is a significant contribution because of this. Given the acknowledged paucity of Eliade's knowledge of Egyptology, it might come as a surprise that Ouellet not only finds considerable consonance between "Categories of Eliadean Thought and Egyptian Categories" (53) but puts them to good use in explicating ancient Egyptian religion and responds to the identification of normativity in Eliade's work.

Concerning the utility of Eliade's work Joseph Muthuraj gives a significant insight into the specific utility that added to Eliade's popularity in the '60s and '70s. That is to say, its utility in dealing with human faith in an academic and pluralistic environment. The chapter attempts to follow through Eliade's insights. His understanding of religion is seen as offering much to theology and the study of the New Testament. Historical-critical methodology, which provides the concepts and tools for NT study, has largely ignored questions concerning the sacred. Muthuraj explains that Eliade's achievements help to meet the deficiency created by the historical positivism pervasive in NT scholarship. One important area of study relates to the attitude and approach to other religions in comparison with religious phenomena of early Christian experience. Except among a small group of history of religions scholars in NT studies, oriental religion and philosophy, which formed a major component in the thought world of the NT, have not received the attention they deserve. Eliade criticized the reluctance of theologians to use historico-religious hermeneutics since it raises doubts about "the uniqueness of the Judeo-Christian revelation." According to Muthuraj, and specifically for an Indian NT scholar, Eliade forms a mediating ground between Western and Eastern schools of thought because of his positive estimation of Indian religions and philosophy. Muthuraj argues that Eliade's understanding of myth enables scholars to see the richness of the experience of God by NT authors. Both the impersonal and personal dimensions of the Divine, both "Being" and "God" can be uncovered in this way. Very rarely have theologians or NT scholars looked for inspiration from history of religions scholars and too little work within the field of NT has given serious attention to contributions made by Eliade in the study of religious phenomena. However, Muthuraj hopes that his study will help to open a field of research for NT students and theologians.

The same question that Muthuraj broached—the extent of the Indian influence on Eliade's development—is also dealt with by the Romanian scholar, Liviu Bordaş, who deals with the history of Eliade's stay in India and convincingly describes Eliade's tendency to "mythologize" that history. The myth of Eliade the spiritual initiate is clearly revealed, along with its manifestation in some of Eliade's later fiction. As well as the question of Eliade's Indian experiences, Bordaş raises the question of his "traditionalism," a point considered by the Italian, Natale Spineto. Bordaş and Spineto come to similar conclusions on the issue of traditionalism and neither of them concludes that Eliade was any kind of adherent. Spineto provides a nuanced understanding of the term and decisively concludes that it is inapplicable to Eliade. He shows Eliade's dependence upon his historical context without reducing that debt to a simple duplication of the thought of traditionalists, or a radical dependence upon any one man (such as Julius Evola) with all the political baggage that this would entail. Both Bordaş and Spineto provide excellent examples of the detailed and painstaking archival work being done on Eliade. They refer to much of that work, and Spineto points out that in recent literature on Eliade's intellectual biography one of the areas that has received the most original contributions is this assessment of Eliade's relationship to scholars linked to "traditional thought"; particularly René Guénon, Julius Evola, and Ananda Coomaraswamy. Spineto's presentation examines the relevant documents, summarizes the results, and establishes to what extent Eliade's reading of the traditionalists actually influenced his work. Eliade integrates traditionalist terms and concepts within a different conceptual framework that does not admit the fundamental bases of traditionalism. Spineto aims to show that it is neither possible to consider Eliade's works "esoteric" (as Daniel Dubuisson maintains), nor to assert that Eliade's perspective has a connection to "Christian Kabbalah" (as Steven Wasserstrom has argued).

Together Spineto and Bordaş show the complexity of such issues as Eliade's debt to traditionalism and the danger of coming to hasty and oversimplified conclusions. Where Spineto overlaps with Bordaş on the topic of traditionalism, he overlaps with Vanhaelemeersch on the topic of Eliade's attitudes to history and historicism. Vanhaelemeersch discusses the status of "history" in Eliade but does not reiterate the classic accusation that Eliade denies the idea of history (manifest in Meslin's chapter, for example). Vanhaelemeersch brings more nuance to both Eliade's arguments and to the arguments against him. History is a term that continues to create confusion. Instead, Vanhaelemeersch suggests that we address the issue in terms of the concept of "historicism." As a historian of religions, Eliade does not reject history as do yogins or shamans. What he rejects is a specific way of conceiving the historical character of religion. Vanhaelemeersch contrasts Eliade with the Italian form of historicism (*storicismo*). The historicism of the father of *storicismo*, Benedetto Croce, moves the discussion of Eliade and history to a genuinely philosophical level.

Katrine Ore raises the rightly perennial issue of feminism and gender relations. It is no surprise that she should conclude that "[t]he political aspects so well known to gender studies (women's studies and feminist studies) are missing in Eliade's writings" (193), but en route to this conclusion she has more to say about Eliade's attitudes toward women and the potential for the history of religions than might be anticipated. She points out that Eliade deals with feministic issues and themes, but that he uses them to think about maleness. Ore's chapter focuses on the connections between the first and second waves of feminism (c. 1880–1925 and c. 1960–1990) that meet in a reading of Eliade's books with a gender perspective in mind.

However Eliade's history of religions is understood, its elements of the dialectic of the sacred and the profane and "creative hermeneutics" are familiar. These are the elements analyzed by Chung Chin-Hong, who poses two questions: First, "What does the term *religion* indicate?" Second, "How can religion, thus understood, be interpreted?" Eliade's concepts of the sacred and of hierophany have been criticized as so ambiguous that religion appears not only as an objective reality but also as a phenomenon of subjective consciousness. However, Chung argues, Eliade's dialectic of the sacred and the profane proves this criticism wrong. He presupposes humanity as *homo religiosus* and this is experienced in the world of human life. Thus, the question should not be "What is religion?" but "What is *called* religion?" The concern should be turned from metaphysics to experience. What is important is not what Eliade says about the conscious system of religious studies but how he changes the scheme of the question itself. Eliade's hermeneutics is based on traditional phenomenology: his hermeneutic discourse is not greatly different from phenomenological hermeneutics. When Eliade's attitude is criticized as being antihistorical such a criticism is due to the misconception of structure and phenomenon, sacred and profane, and this misconception is the result of ignoring the fact that what Eliade calls free variation is not imaginative but actual, and the fact that the encoding of symbolic meaning or assessment of symbol is done on the basis of experienced existence. What must be understood is the creativity of Eliade's hermeneutics. In this respect, his hermeneutics is more than phenomenological hermeneutics. Chung sees Eliade's phenomenology as differing from traditional phenomenology by overlapping epistemology and praxiology through phenomenology and hermeneutics. Chung calls this the surplus of phenomenology and sees that surplus as Eliade's contribution to religious studies and as still appropriate for students of religion.

Wilhelm Dancă considers the concept of mysticism in Eliade's work and raises the undeniably important but often neglected question of the influence of Eastern Orthodox theology on Eliade's thought. The chapter attempts to outline the efforts of the young Eliade to understand what religion means, and his debt to the friends and teachers he had before World War II. The mystical perspective of Romanian spirituality influenced the researches of the young Eliade, who wanted to engage Romanian culture in dialog with other, larger cultures. Eliade found the ground of all religions to be the natural experience of the sacred. As a result, when he spoke about Greek, Egyptian, or Indian religions, he emphasized concepts such as "asceticism," "absolute liberty," "plenitude of life," "achievement in itself," "harmony with the universe," and so on. The same things were emphasized when he spoke about Spanish or German mystics.

What Dancă sees as absent from Eliade's researches are moral considerations—as is common to a great many mystics. Considering the character of Eliade's literary writings, Dancă suggests that they represent a metaphysical interpretation of life, which does not include any moral attitude, so he tries to explain Eliade's vision of religion by considering both his academic and his literary work. *Homo religiosus*, according to Eliade, is the mystical human being in his or her natural mode everywhere and from any time. Thus reading Eliade's work, Dancă understands both Eliade's personality and the human condition as open at any time to the revelation of the sacred.

Considering both Eliade's academic and his literary work as he does, Dancă makes an appropriate connection to the concluding section of the anthology. Okuyama Michiaki focuses on Eliade's fiction, pointing out that in the preface to his *History of Religious Ideas*, vol. 1, Eliade announced that he would deal with the camouflage of the "sacred," or rather, the identification of the sacred with the profane, in the final chapter of the work. His term *camouflage* is applied to many examples of "myths in the modern world" to indicate that myths and symbols have not lost their vitality even today. Again, when we listen to Eliade speaking of the relationship between his scholarly writings and his literary ones, we find a preoccupation with the problem of the "camouflage of miracle in history." To the extent that Eliade was engaged in "camouflaging miracle" in his novels, Okuyama is drawn to ask whether his scholarly works might not have absorbed the novelist's prerogative of reading "miracle" into historical fact. This suggested to Okuyama his comparison with the contemporary Japanese novelist and Nobel laureate, Ōe Kenzaburō. Ōe read Eliade and was influenced by his ideas in the course of trying to integrate the experiences of his own life with his own vocation as a writer. Okuyama considers two of Ōe's novels to clarify the connection and reconsider the problems posed by Eliade's fiction.

The quest motif is ubiquitous in Eliade's fantasy fiction and reveals a search both for recovering originary values and for remodeling human life patterns. This motif can be seen in Eliade's play, "Men and Stones." This short work relates a two-man expedition into the caverns beneath the Carpathian Mountains in quest of Paleolithic remains. Professor Petruș, the older academic expert in speleology and the Paleolithic, is accompanied by the younger poet, Alexandru, both, perhaps, representing aspects of Eliade's personality. Written early in 1944, when Eliade was thirty-seven, the year in which his first wife, Nina, was later to die of cancer, the play seems to present a premonition of that loss and an attempt to come to terms with a life rendered futile by death; both individual and collective in the horrors of the ongoing world war. It deals with the processes of creative hermeneutics and the role of the sacred in making sense of life and in making sense of foreign cultures, here represented by Paleolithic "troglobites" and human cave dwellers, who appear in Alexandru's fantasies. As in many of Eliade's works, the theme of the untellable secret, the ineffability of the real, is a constant presence.

Taken altogether, these essays reflect the ability of studies of Eliade to ignite valuable debate and to raise important issues in the study of religion. They also indicate the work that remains to be done. Whatever one feels the value of Eliade's work to be, the consideration and clarification of the questions that it raises can only serve to increase our understanding of religion and of all of the issues raised in its academic study.

I

The Sacralization of Time

The Sacralization of Time in the Thought of Mircea Eliade

Michel Meslin
(translated by Bryan Rennie)

Much has already been written on the work of Mircea Eliade as a phenomenologist of religions, and he himself frequently returned to the fundamental themes of his thought in numerous works. Having read and reread him and having spoken with him often, both in Paris and in Chicago, I believe that I can reliably identify one of the essential poles of his vision of religious affairs. That—alongside the symbolism on which I focused at the time of the solemn homage paid to our friend here in Paris in 1987—is the problem of sacred time, and accordingly, of the value of history. It is well known to what extent time was a central element of his literary work, considering his constant examination of the loss of paradise and the origin of humanity's fall into history. Think only of Stefan, who, in *The Forbidden Forest*, tried by every means possible to abolish historical time "in a desperate attempt to regain the beatitude of childhood and reintegration into the lost Paradise" (Meslin in Tacou et al., *Cahiers de l'Herne* 211). One must bear in mind the recurrence of this theme in Eliade the writer the better to understand the thought of Eliade the historian of religions.

The question raised by this consideration is precisely that of knowing the relationship between the irreducibility of the sacred, which Eliade always defined as a structure of human consciousness, and the sacralization of time. I will, very briefly, restate Eliade's position and thereafter present a few critical reflections.

The problem of time, he wrote, "is among the most difficult in all religious phenomenology ... [because] the actual *experience of time as such* is not always the same for primitive peoples as for modern Western man" (*Patterns* 388, emphasis original). Eliade found this difference in the opposition of sacred time to profane duration, such as the fact that "the primitive's experience of time makes it easy for him to change the profane into the sacred" (*Patterns* 388). Always supporting his claims with examples taken from traditional societies and from Romanian folklore, he delineated a tripartite structure of sacred time: it is, first and foremost, the same time as the time of myth; it is the time of rituals, which repeat events occurring in originary time, *in illo tempore*; it is, lastly, the time of the rhythms of the cosmos where humanity witnesses hierophanies such as that of the sun, the moon, and so on. This hierophanic time is distinct from the duration lived by humanity: periodical, it repeats and reactualizes a mythic act and a mythic model. It can thus be considered an eternal present. The periodic recurrence, the repetition, the reactualization *hic et nunc*, of this sacred time stands in opposition to profane time, that duration that flows beyond all power of humanity to stop. Whence this affirmation:

> We thus find in man at every level, the same longing to destroy profane time and live in sacred time. Further, we see the desire and hope of regenerating time as a whole, of being able to live—"humanly," "historically"—in eternity, by transforming successive time into a single eternal moment. (*Patterns* 407)

To which Eliade adds that humanity is simultaneously haunted by a longing for paradise and a longing for eternity. This time (*le temps*) to which humanity wants to return only takes on its sacred character to the extent that it is completely different from the time (*la durée*) that can only be profane. This is, Eliade frequently affirms, one of the fundamental structures of *homo religiosus*. We are, then, in the presence of a cyclic conception of time, a circular time, that of the eternal return, which gives repetition its religious value. Human existence is no longer based either in our consciousness or in the exercise of our freedom, but by relation to a fundamental origin. This sacred time is woven out of archetypes and repetitions: "Everything begins over again at its commencement every instant. The past is but a prefiguration of the future," he writes in *The Myth of the Eternal Return* (89).

This affirmation becomes a principal leitmotif of his thought. However, it is loaded with implications because it entails that the religious fact—the "sacred" to use Eliade's own term—exists only in a reintegration of humanity into the original perfection, in an extraordinary mythical "flashback" created by this "nostalgia for origins." Rituals of the regeneration of time practiced by certain human societies can reactualize in existential human duration this *Urzeit*, this time of the origins, thus creating a festival time strongly endowed with sacrality. It is, in fact, one of the preferred means by which humanity attempts to escape from becoming. However, it really must be asked whether this *Urzeit* thus made present is only the unconscious memory of a prior paradise, a golden age, a virginal time, a time of childhood—of which the desired return would then only be a kind of regression—or if it concerns a conscious memory created and reanimated through the cultural mediation of myth and ritual. Now, this festival time, this time of excess, marked by the lifting of prohibitions and by rites of sexual and social inversion, like *les plaisirs d'amour*, is but a moment long. This short interval is determined by humanity. Once having achieved this festival time, one returns thence to the normal existential temporal order, that duration that Eliade identifies as profane. Even if one has, during this short interval, put all the rules of daily life into abeyance, it nevertheless begins again. To see sacred time only in this festival return to the origins seems to me very reductionist. Our most immediate experience convinces us that we can no more live in eternity than we can return to the past by going back in time. Even if, during this festival time, people believe that they recharge themselves with energies that are close to divine powers, they do not thereafter cease to have other relations with the divine in quotidian time. The problem, such as Eliade envisioned it, appears to me, then, to be poorly posed: what people do is, through various techniques of prayer, of sacrifice, to render the quotidian time that they have to live favorable to the actions that they undertake, which might apply to hunting, to fishing, to examinations, to the choices made in their lives. Now, all of this takes place in the duration of existence— not in any return to origins.

After having affirmed that this festival time and its rituals have as their goal the abolition of passing time and that they connote a need for a periodic regeneration in which "this coincidence between the 'mythical instant' and the 'present moment' " occurs, Eliade, on the other hand, admits that this need "is a proof that they too cannot perpetually maintain their position in what we have just called the paradise of archetypes, and that their memory is capable . . . of revealing the irreversibility of events, that is, of recording history" (*The Myth of the Eternal Return* 79, 75). I will return to the implications of this phrase, but, to begin with, I would like to point out that the undoubted significance of the fact that this abolition of historical time, or at least of a certain mastery over the passage of time, had appeared to Eliade to be a work equally important to alchemists as the transmutation of metals, as they symbolically recreated in their retorts the primordial and cosmogonic chaos (*The Forge and the Crucible* 169–75).

This distinction of Eliade's between original, mythical time and historical time in fact reiterates the opposition of sacred and profane time and "the heterogeneity of these two times" (*The Myth of the Eternal Return* 36). From this he deduces that the very reality of a gesture, of an action, even of a being, is significant only if it reiterates a primordial event and thus refers to the *Urzeit*. Existence is thus not fully real except from repetition, in the present moment, of an archetype that recovers original time. That which was done the first time is that which is at the source and which sets for all time the model to be followed. If, as he claims, "the cosmogonic myth opens the sacred history" (*Quest* 87) it is only because it contains an exemplary model, which is periodically reactualized in the sidereal time that it sacralizes: "Everything begins over again at its commencement every instant" (*The Myth of the Eternal Return* 89). Even if one adopts such a view of matters, it must be emphasized that this continuous re-presentation of the origin can only be actualized through a tradition that transmits myths, symbols, and rites, and that every tradition is always interpretive. Raffaele Pettazzoni had already pointed out to Eliade that it is not the primitive mythical world that confers significance on the present moment, but rather the world *hic et nunc*, which furnishes the components of any representation of the world of origins, conceived of as alternative and seen in opposition to it. Eliade always rejected this diachronic perspective in the name of his concept of contemporaneity: whenever *homo religiosus* repeats the originary action, whenever he ritually commemorates

> a sacrifice ... [it] not only exactly reproduces the initial sacrifice revealed by a god *ab origine* ... it also takes place at that same primordial mythical moment; ... every sacrifice repeats the initial sacrifice and coincides with it ... through such imitation, man is projected into the mythical epoch in which the archetypes were first revealed. (*The Myth of the Eternal Return* 35)

Actually, this so-called contemporaneity appears to be rather a simultaneity of the reinvoked original event and the ritual enacted in the present.

Still on the subject of the time of the origins another observation is essential. If, as has been said (*Patterns* 397), the time that one can repeat by ritual reenactment is sacred, then these same times cannot be situated outside of the duration of the contingent, because it is humanity that effects the representation that, through the ritual, makes primordial time present once more. Humanity does this intentionally, from a particular perspective, by inserting it into our personal, existential time. It is thus humanity that creates this heterogeneity of time by distinguishing the hours, the days, the periods of fast or feast by our activity. This aspect of humanity can still be seen in the varying rhythms that societies impose that give rise to the discord between the religious, sacral calendars—human in origin—and sidereal, astronomical time. Humanity organizes time, constituting this religious time, lived within quotidian time. For this reason the expression that Eliade employs, "an irruption of the Great Time," (e.g., *Patterns* 396) does not seem to me to take sufficient account of the essential role played here by humanity.

I would now like to consider briefly the conception of historical time that Eliade juxtaposed to sacred time. In a letter of 14 February 1949 to Pettazzoni (*L'Histoire des Religions a-t-elle un sens* letter LXV, 200) after the publication of his *Traité de l'Histoire des Religions* he announced what he has "discovered among the most historically conditioned peoples—a tendency to archetypes, to the trans-historical—and I was impressed to note how many religious acts of any type help humanity (of any type) to transcend history." This is an essential claim which he never ceased to develop in his later work. I do not believe that I oversimplify his thought by saying that, in his eyes, duration, historical time has no other function than to be the continuum in which foundational acts of original time are reiterated by ritual. Here is the only reality, to which initiation gives access by creating a path, a passage from existential duration to sacred, primordial time: "the outstanding reality is the sacred: for only the sacred *is* in an absolute fashion, acts effectively, creates things and makes them endure" (*The Myth of the Eternal Return* 11). The knowledge and recitation of myths, the practice of anamnesis, that is found in numerous traditional societies is intended to restore people once again to a time lived in reference to a paradise of origins and the happiness of constantly renewed beginnings, reveals to Eliade to what extent "existence *in* Time is ontologically a nonexistence, an unreality" (*Images and Symbols* 67). The gods are thus different from humanity in the sense that they enjoy an eternal present, home to happiness without limit because it ignores time (*la durée*).

This has a significant consequence: if humanity is only religious insofar as we orient ourselves to the time of the origins and live in primordial time, then historical time cannot be the place of emergence of new spirituality. The religious is given once and for all and the notion of progress is contrary to the very essence of being human. One can understand why Eliade adopted as his own the idea defended by F. W. Schmidt in his *Ursprung der Gottesidee*: the forgetting of the original Great God is the result of a historical process, which has taken place in the same time as cultural disasters, as the transition from hunter/gatherer, from hunting and the nomadic life to agriculture and a sedentary existence. "The primitive man... by the simple fact that he was making history—lost his belief in one God, and started worshiping a multitude of inferior gods" (*Quest* 48). History is thus nothing but a process of desacralization. Humanity can only know anew this paradisiacal happiness that Eliade himself hoped for

> when humanity, to ensure its survival, will find itself reduced to desisting from any further "making" of history... [and] will confine itself to repeating prescribed archetypal gestures, and will strive to forget... any spontaneous gesture which might entail "historical" consequences. (*The Myth of the Eternal Return* 153–54)

This statement, utopian in its character, reveals Eliade's opinion of Christianity. The very conception of Christian time, eschatologically oriented and ascribing its insertion into time to an all-powerful divine origin, is obviously in opposition to the vision of a cyclical time of eternal return. For Eliade, the religions that recognize the value of linear, irreversible time and that give direction to human history betray the sacred in some way. The most authentic, true religion would be that which would be connected to this primordial time upon which human activity depends and for which humanity has a fundamental nostalgia. That is why Christianity appears to him to be the religion of historical humanity, whom he makes responsible for the rupture of primordial, sacred time.

Christianity is "the religion of 'fallen man'" (*The Myth of the Eternal Return* 162), forever separated from the horizon of archetypes and the repetition of primordial time. Even as he considers Christianity in an analysis that he intends to be historical, Eliade constantly juxtaposes a Christianity that developed over centuries as the "cosmic Christianity" of peasant societies, which appears to him to be the religion of natural hierophanies. However, for him, the man of modern societies is totally desacralized because he "has recognized himself to be essentially, and sometimes even uniquely, a temporal being" for whom "the irreversibility and the vacuity of time has become a dogma" (*The Forge and the Crucible* 175, 176). History is thus, for him, an irreversible process of desacralization, simultaneously a creation of the profane and an expulsion of the sacred from the entire life of humanity. In other words, history is a fall because the existence of historical man can no longer be anything other than that of an individual separated from the sacred absolute. From this the task of the historian of religions appears clear to him: he must disengage himself from history the better to recover the religious values that history is bent upon destroying. Even if this position epistemologically resembles the epochē of the phenomenologists, it would not particularly imply that history can be equated with terror. Eliade has explained:

> [T]he "terror of history," for me, is the feeling experienced by a man who is no longer religious, who therefore has no hope of finding any ultimate meaning in the drama of history, who

must undergo the crimes of history without grasping the meaning of them. (*Ordeal by Labyrinth* 128)

No doubt this pessimistic conception of history's tragic nature of could, sadly, find support in current affairs, but it is not obvious that this is what Eliade always had in mind.

And so? Clearly, neither for the historian nor from an anthropological perspective does the sacralization of time as Eliade conceives it appear correct. It gives too great an impression of the religious existing only in a strict relationship with primordial time, whereas even when we encounter it in primitive culture, it always involves human reinterpretation. It has been said of Eliade that he was actually a romantic. Perhaps, but I think above all that his thought represents a contemporary avatar of a type of Neoplatonism strongly influenced by Hindu philosophy in his conception of time. Sacred time will always, for Eliade, be marginal, if not opposed, to historical, existential time—the time that each one of us lives and in which the acts that we perform are directed toward the future, if not toward progress.

Cosmological Bridges: Suspicion and Recollection in the Realities of Myth

Pablo Wright and César Ceriani Cernadas

INTRODUCTION

In this paper we explore the work of Mircea Eliade, originally entitled *Aspects du Myth* (*Myth and Reality*, 1963) in the light of Paul Ricoeur's analysis of the hermeneutic field. From an anthropological perspective, we are interested in finding points of contact between the work of both scholars and its approach to the universe of mythic production and the sacred. At the same time, we consider that both Eliade and Ricoeur elaborate their work from a perspective nourished by Western intellectual tradition, even though they were interested to different degrees of detail in the ways of other cultures. In this sense, we shall point out how, in the analyses of myths, rituals, and religions, Eliade proposes modern humanity and society as present or implicit interlocutors, living, in their own way, both the sacred and the mythic. We believe this comparison to be key, since it demonstrates the geocultural position from which Eliade carries out his studies.

Firstly, we will make explicit Ricoeur's basic ideas of the poles of hermeneutical work, after which the main ideas of Eliade's aforementioned book will be presented. Once this is accomplished, we shall explore the possibilities of creatively positioning Eliade in the hermeneutical field and, within it, of identifying how it positions itself to undertake the study of myths. Lastly, we propose to reencounter Eliade in his role as a thinker of European modernity, a role shared by Ricoeur—although with important differences in method, interests, and philosophical agenda. By placing these two authors together we also intend to propose a dynamic instance of articulation between the hermeneutical modes of recollection and suspicion as identified by the French philosopher.

DIALECTICS OF SUSPICION AND RECOLLECTION

In *Freud and Philosophy: An Essay on Interpretation* Ricoeur gives a reading of the hermeneutic field, delimiting two fundamental perspectives in the interpretation of symbols: *recollection* and *suspicion*. In the latter, the task of interpretation "victoriously attacks the mystification of false consciousness" (35), which imposes from a "depth" the conditions and masqueradings of the "surface." In "recollection," on the other hand, the task of interpretation emerges as a preparation to better understand that which once came to the senses, that which was already revealed or made manifest (28). The hermeneutics of suspicion interprets what symbols hide, their *archaeology*, whereas the hermeneutics of recollection deals with listening to the message of symbols, to its *prophecy* or *teleology*. In spite of their antagonism, both meet in a foundational fact: the "humiliation of consciousness" and the decentering or dislocation of the origin of meaning. Both also, in the dialectical comprehension that Ricoeur proposes, are mutually summoned and intersect: "[T]he most prophetic significances of the Saint are always grafted and operate on the remains of some archaic myth....The eschatology of consciousness is always a creative repetition of its archaeology" (*Le conflit des interpretations* 73).

Thus, both the masters of suspicion, among whom Ricoeur includes Marx, Nietzsche, and Freud, and the phenomenologists of religion, incarnated by Van der Leeuw, Otto, and Eliade, seek to question by diverse paths the privileged place which consciousness has in modern thought; its "pretension," in the words of Ricoeur, "of knowing itself from the beginning" (*Le conflit des interpretations* 63). For the school of suspicion the sense of symbol, such as it appears in the consciousness, is the product of a sinuous path where intra- and extrapsychic mediations exist, configuring its level of real structure. The idea that symbols open by themselves an autonomous sense to consciousness is an illusion. For the school of recollection the real is that sense of symbol that is revealed from an exteriority of the subject: it is the quality of the *numen* that expresses its potential.[1]

Our intention here is to relate these distinctions with the role played by Eliade's investigations into the basic qualities of myths and rites, and their existence in the past and present from a comparative intercultural perspective.

REALITIES OF MYTH

Published in 1963, Eliade's *Aspects du Myth* (*Myth and Reality*), was written by request for the collection "World Perspectives." As Eliade states in the preface to the French edition, different observations presented in his previous works are here developed again, the specific purpose being a more systematic reading of a key point of human behavior. One of the points to be stressed about the originality of this work within the Eliadean *corpus* is its metacomparative character and its humanistic content. Here the author establishes comparisons between the different mythic systems of primitive peoples or of the large historical religious systems, searching for their bonds in a root structure supported by the concept of the "irruption of the sacred," increasing the level of comparison by adding contemporary themes. Among these he includes modern art, the "atomic fear" and its apocalyptic condition, and the "camouflage" of mythic thought in historiography and in mass-cultural products of the modern world such as comics. It is here he finds the "humanistic cause" of this work, and here Eliade ventures upon the comprehension of modern, that is, (at least apparently) desacralized, "phenomena," which confers an ethical quality on this work. This characteristic is made manifest in the analysis of other contemporary events such as Melanesian cargo cults, which in 1960, at least in public discourse and certain scientific interpretations, had "irrational" or "instinctive" content. Here the author's judgment is categorical and he exhorts us to "make the necessary effort to understand the mythical antecedents that explain and justify such excesses and give them a religious value" (*Myth and Reality* 3–4).

Myth and Reality begins with a rather theoretical chapter where Eliade works on the conceptual axis from which he will inquire into the diverse dimensions of the work. This is the axis of *mythology* and *temporality*, on which subjects six of nine chapters focus, and which we may sum up under six fundamental topics: (1) the privileged ontological status of origins, (2) the world's temporal/existential renewal, (3) congruencies and differences between originary times, and (4) end times (cyclic or linear), (5) intellectual technologies, and (6) experiences of temporal control.

A second parallel axis is that of *historical comprehension*—the metacomparative character referred to earlier—analyzed concretely in the inquiry about the vicissitudes of myth in Western civilization (its periods of greatness and decadence, of permanence and camouflaged emergence). It must also be made clear that the first of these topics, which Eliade calls the "prestige of origins," seems to act as an essential hermeneutical tool of the whole work. The approach to cosmogonies and eschatologies, shamanic and psychoanalytic therapies, the spatial symbolism of cosmic renovation, the eternal return and the passing of time, seem to be permeated by this central idea underlying all mythical thought. In the beginning is the key of all existence, hence the essential, in millennialist eschatologies and in psychoanalysis or modern art. It "is not the fact of the *End*, but the certainty of a *new beginning*" (*Myth and Reality* 75–76) (emphasis original). This concern of the author with time and temporality, which all mythical-ritual complexes seek to "dominate," either by inhibiting or recreating, is one of the major features of Eliade's thought, the analysis of which is manifest in several of his works (*Myths, Dreams and Mysteries; Cosmos and History: The Myth of the Eternal Return; The Sacred and the Profane;* among others).

Delving into a comprehensive reading of psychoanalytic epistemology, something upon which he had already ventured in *Myths, Dreams and Mysteries*, Eliade exhorts us to interpret it from his "plane of reference" (*Aspects du Mythe* xii). He thus reveals two essential characteristics that are installed as cosmological bridges between psychoanalysis and mythic thought. The metaphor of the bridge is important here since it implies a nonreductive vision of both phenomena, identifying the bonds that unite them without negating them. These two characteristics are linked, although the first is nearer to the theoretical order, and the other to the "beatitude of origins" and the "return backwards," respectively.

In *Myth and Reality* Eliade develops an analysis of myths, and of the rites associated with them, whose focus is influenced by the classic work of Bronislaw Malinowski on the social, cultural and *existential* function of myths in primitive societies. Likewise, he presents a historical scholarly analysis of the transformations in the social and cultural evaluation of myth in the Greco-Roman, Judeo-Christian, and European tradition in general. He points out the specificity of Greek and Roman traditions, and how their future formed the ways of the world belonging to Western society.

The gradual structuring of the perspective, and the resultant emotions, of modern humanity, are detailed with much precision, and the influences received from other traditions, such as the Iranian, Hindu, and Egyptian, among others, are introduced. Eliade's view is situated in the existential and ontological plane, and in the social functions that myth and rite fulfill. The great transformations operative in Western culture, from the essential importance of writing vis-à-vis orality, through the "demythification" and desacralization of myths initiated by the Greeks in the fifth century BCE, up to the contemporary existence of some structures of Christian religiousness, certain manifestations of modern art in the mass media, and the practices of consumer society, afford us a clear view of what happened within Western tradition. Eliade's is an overview that shows Western culture from within and reveals the features it shares with other traditions. It offers valuable data on how the Western spirit was formed and its particular cultural mode of connecting with the sacred.

BETWEEN OPENNESS AND SUSPICION

Within the hermeneutical field analyzed by Ricoeur we could place Eliade in the tradition that emphasizes recollection and attention to sacred symbols. It is a place nearer to the *numinous* and its effects on the life of human beings who appeal to myths and rites to recurrently replenish that tremendous and mysterious power. Eliade himself attends to the power of symbols, placing them principally in those societies where myth is "alive"—archaic or primitive societies, although not only in these. He reveals the recurrent structures of myth and feels for the tone and rhythm of the impact of the Great Time (*illud tempus*) ritually produced in social life. He observes a counterpoint throughout this work between those societies and "modern" ones, where he tries to identify practices and ideas that show the presence of myth and rite, though transformed in multiple ways. It is important to Eliade to talk of his own modern society, and his work is almost that of a native, of a religious specialist (in the words of Victor Turner), a native of a deep and peripheral part of Europe.

Eliade furnishes elements for an understanding of the social and cultural value of myths. For him it is important to identify the structures of mythical thought such as the ideas of the rupture of profane time, the archetypes of repetition that take on primordial time, initiatory processes, cosmogony, and the prestige of origins. As pointed out earlier, Eliade is interested in inquiring into the social function of myths, analyzed in specific historical and cultural contexts, although these are always comparable, since the search is oriented toward mythic structures and man's attitude vis-à-vis the sacred, from an intercultural view.

It is interesting to point out that what Ricoeur identifies as poles of tension within the hermeneutical field, recollection and suspicion, which synthesize a key tension of modernity, are somehow implicit in Eliade's work. In fact, the mode of recollection may align with an attitude of loyalty and confidence in the *numinous* message of the symbol, which brings it near to the contexts of "living myth." From within this context, it is clear that there are no "symbols," but only gods, deities, and potentials that reveal their power. The universe is a sacred cosmos, and any event may be a sign, a *hierophany*. When speaking of symbols we are already on another existential level—that of philosophy, with its various degrees of analytical distancing from those living experiences.

We believe that the pole of suspicion, which might also be instantiated by Claude Lévi-Strauss (and authors such as Roland Barthes, Michel Foucault, Jean-Paul Sartre, and Louis Althusser, among many others), may go back to its ancestors, in the words of Eliade, to those Greek scholars who began to demystify ancient mythology, introducing the suspicion regarding their true nature. This process, gradual although unique in the history of human thought (if we agree with Eliade in this) resulted not only in the upsurge of Greek systematic philosophy and its late epigones in Western science, but also inaugurated a different way of being in the world, which is a crucial mark that characterized this cultural tradition from others around the planet. In short, scholars and analysts of recollection are just as interested as were those primitive believers of myth and rite in the message of the gods and their myths, believed to be true and exemplary histories, although such analysts englobe them in the linguistic and ambiguous formula of the symbol. That is, they are placed in a position of exteriority with regard to the sacred. They nonetheless accept it as the master level of reality, self-justified, and origin of meaning.

On the other hand, the "masters" of suspicion are interested, as the old Greek critics and their successors were, in what is *behind* the message of the gods, the myths and the rites, condensed in the cryptic message of symbols. They believe there is a "backstage" and that not all the apparent must be believed as such. Eliade thus clearly shows the historical background of the suspicious attitude, which is a central posture of the burgeoning philosophical thought that later transformed the ontology of modern being. The historical religions have only partially recuperated from being part of a desacralization and global demythification of reality.

However, Eliade, when historicizing this process of gradual demythification of the world, at the same time identifies and compares elements from the modern world that seem to recreate, with different hues and, at times, different functions, those structures of myths and mythical thought. In this way (and here the links with the comprehensive dialectics that Ricoeur sustains are evident), a sort of creative and culturally informed mediation could be proposed between the poles of recollection and suspicion, and of studies of apparently irreconcilable truths. This would act, as we already suggested, as a bridge allowing a dialogue between radically different cosmologies. The experience of contact between different classes of religious and cultural alterity appears to have been a determinant in an attitude of openness. In this, Eliade's and Ricoeur's thought seems to run parallel, since both, using different conceptual languages, try to penetrate the conflictive drama of Western modernity. They delve into the roots and also into the contemporary manifestations, allowing themselves be carried away neither by the certainties of numinous recollection nor by the apparent truths revealed by suspicion. Both acknowledge the transformations that originated the modern ontology, but this acknowledgment has suggestions of creative comparison and partial synthesis: one regarding the relationship between humanity and the sacred, the other concerning the hermeneutics of the symbol.

Eliade gives a profound analysis of the future of the modern world in an illustrative intercultural dialogue on its dimensions and realities. Although he presents much ethnological evidence from primitive societies and ancient cultures in an analytical attitude combining the two hermeneutical postures pointed out by Ricoeur, he furnishes us with examples of how myth and/or mythic thought appear in different cultural practices. Sometimes masked in wonderful stories or expressed in images in mass media, fiction, the anxiety for success, the pleasures of consumerism or suburban life, mythic behaviors and structures are observed. One way or another, all these activities are related to the opening of the Great Time, the prestige of origin, and the eternal struggle between Good and Evil. It is a posture that expresses some ambiguity and an evolutionist touch, but at the same time he speaks of certain "residues" or "degraded" aspects of mythic behavior in modern man and infers mythic thought to be a constitutive part of the "human condition."

In spite of its intercultural perspective, many of the problems and questions addressed by Eliade on the sacred and the reality of myths are possible only if they are thought from Western *episteme*. We could affirm that when we find mythic behaviors vis-à-vis the sacred in indigenous groups, rural sectors, or in urban zones, with less influence from the legacy of philosophy and science, other questions arise that widen the horizon of thought, of the existent, and of the nature of criteria of truth.

Placing himself in a Western intellectual attitude, Eliade seeks for invariants in mythic structures in human societies, arriving at the identification of what we call "existential universals," which would be those structures that are a constitutive part of the human condition. On another level of the search, but equally universalist, we could place the endeavor of Claude Lévi-Strauss, who wishes to discover universal invariants of cognitive order in mythology and in so-called *pensée sauvage*. Both searches have this universality in common, and their difference lies in the localization of structures. For Eliade they are found fundamentally at the surface of social life, of existence, and of ontology. This can be observed in his notion of "living myth," where we find its principal features: "[I]t supplies models for human behavior and, by that very fact, gives meaning and value to life" (*Myth and Reality* 2). On the other hand, for Lévi-Strauss the keys of myths are found in the depth of the code and in the mental. Myth is a cognitive model, an engineering of human intellect; the "moral" (in general terms) remains subject to the operations of "mythic" mentality, the science of the concrete (*La Pensée Sauvage*).

This notwithstanding, both concur that the mythic, in its different modes of expression is part of something specifically human. Eliade suspects the concealment of the mythic in modern practices. Lévi-Strauss seeks the truth farther away from the apparent: for him the surface of phenomena would resemble the notion of consciousness of the school of suspicion, as a place of reception of perception, never as the production of sense, which must always be sought in the depths of the intelligible.

FINAL WORDS

As thinkers of modernity, both Eliade and Ricoeur belong to the Western philosophical and intellectual tradition, to which myths, rituals, and the whole sphere of the sacred is troublesome and threatening. This is so because they, in one way or another, undermine the certainties upon which Western reason was constituted, which led to the development of the scientific canon. Other classic terms, emerging from the encounter between Western reason and the rest of the world, are magic, civilization, superstition, and belief, among others. All of them are clearly relational and, in this regard, both authors worked patiently to uncover their historical nature and conceptual limits. In spite of these efforts, paradoxically, it is Eliade, with his vast intercultural erudition, who displayed a nostalgic attitude to that "forgetting of the sacred," which had occurred in the West. Yet it is Ricoeur who offers us tools to understand the work and word of the sacred in any situation, not feeling modernity as a permanent distancing from the experience of the sacred.

Without taking a definitive viewpoint in this regard, we could propose that in the Western world we have witnessed a sort of "flight of the sacred" toward heterodox areas of social practice, some of which were addressed by Eliade—avant-garde art, mass media, and the practices of consumer culture. From an anthropological viewpoint, this "escape" does not represent a profound problem. Instead of experiencing nostalgia for the lost sacred, it is necessary to find, honoring our Durkheimian legacy, the sociological conditions of possibility of that collective boundary of intense symbolic density which is the sacred. However, Eliade's contribution is formidable for our understanding of the structural and existential dimensions within which the sacred and myths are articulated. Occasionally we stand astonished by the wide range of his religious curiosity, the honesty of his analyses, and the rare philosophical skill required simultaneously to pass through both the doorways of attention to the numinous and research of its historical becoming.

To conclude, we suggest the following: before the emptying of meaning produced by the hermeneutics of suspicion and the filling of it in the plenitude of recollection that regards the universe as a sacred cosmos, it is possible to focus our analysis on a middle path. It can be characterized by a dialectical complementarity that nourishes both poles, avoiding their mutual neutralization. We believe that modernity is an unfinished project and that intercultural evidence provided by anthropology enriches Western ontological and epistemological assumptions. This evidence itself carries ways of being in the world that question the certainties of the Western ethos. Many of them, disguised under the weird dress of myths and rituals little understood by the layman, show, as Eliade has said, Western philosophy's provincialism, and the questionable universalization of its criteria of truth through history.

We consider that beyond recollection and suspicion, the very mythic nature of the human condition would be, according to our standpoint, the human poetic skills to build worlds of meaning through forests of symbols, metaphors, metonymies, and other expressive devices of the kind. For that reason, and here Ricoeur comes to our aid, we should not have nostalgia for the forgetting of the sacred, but should develop a new dialectics to acknowledge its current manifestations. To do so we need to consider what social agents do in fact recognize as the ultimate meaning, which would allow them to liberate themselves from the anguish about time (the terror of history)—a basic fact of the human condition in Eliade's thought.

A last comparison between Eliade and Ricoeur is worthy of mention. Here we give attention to the latter's analysis of symbol and metaphor. Symbols, in Ricoeur's words (*Le Conflit des Interpretations* 72), "hesitate in the frontier line between *bios* and *logos*," between experience and knowledge. Because symbols can bear the power of recollection, here the *bios* with its openness and multiplicity of experience is, for that very reason, irreducible to *logos*. Cosmic symbolism is an excellent example: the numinous experience escapes from the trapping of the word, of language; "such to speak of power is to speak of something that is not speech, even if this implies the power of speech" (*Le Conflit des Interpretations* 74). Metaphor, on the other hand, is entirely linked with logos, as a free invention of discourse and semantic innovation. In this sense, we consider that Eliade's work approximated thought and imagination to the power of sacred experience, sometimes, but not always, expressed in language. As a mysterious bridge between bios and logos, Eliadean explorations through the mythic and the sacred provide useful ideas and data to identify, now without nostalgia and through an anthropologically oriented pragmatism, those universal existential traits whose power of *poesis* may turn the brightest and darkest sides of humanness dramatically real.

NOTES

1. In his seminal work, *Le conflit des interprétations*, 1969 (*The Conflict of Interpretations*, 1970), Ricoeur works in detail on these notions. From that work this paraphrase has been extracted, particularly from the first part, "Hermeneutics and Structuralism."

II

The Interpretation of History

Mircea Eliade and the Myth of Adonis

Ulrich Berner

INTRODUCTION: THE DEBATE ON ELIADE AND THE THEORY OF ELIADE

Eliade is probably the most controversial figure in the history of religions as an academic discipline. His work has had a strong polarizing effect: on the one hand it has been criticized aggressively, as, for instance, by Edmund Leach; on the other hand it has been defended vehemently, as, for instance, by Mac Linscott Ricketts.[1] Such an extremely controversial debate in the field of religious studies is always in danger of becoming a religious controversy itself, that is, a worldview controversy between religious and nonreligious scholars of religion. Religious scholars will be more inclined to defend Eliade's approach by reconstructing a complex methodology believed to have been underlying his work—ultimately, perhaps, in order to defend their own religious worldview. Nonreligious scholars will be more inclined to attack Eliade's approach by deconstructing his methodology believed to have been insufficient—ultimately, perhaps, in order to attack religious worldviews as such. Regarding this extremely controversial debate that may be, at least to some extent, a worldview controversy, the question arises whether it will be possible to avoid joining one or the other group, that would mean neither to accept nor to condemn the Eliadean approach totally. In any event, the science of religion should not be used one-sidedly, biased towards either a defense or an attack on religion.

The first basic consideration is that it might be reasonable to distinguish between Eliade's methodology and his theory. His methodology may be insufficient while his theory of religion may still be worth considering.[2] The second basic consideration is that it might be reasonable to apply the theory of Eliade not to religion on the whole, but to a limited subject of research only (cf. Berner, "Mircea Eliade" 343–56). Eliade's theory, especially the concept of "sacred space,"[3] could be used, for instance, in the interpretation of ancient Mesopotamian hymns that were created in praise of a city.[4] Applied to such a limited subject of research Eliade's theory may prove to be useful, at least in some cases. Perhaps the basic mistake lies with the attitude of expecting Eliade to explain everything or nothing in the study of religion. So it may be basically wrong both to follow him respectfully and to neglect him totally.

Concentrating on what might be taken as the center of Eliade's theory, that, is the portrait of archaic man as *homo religiosus* transcending history and living in a mythical world of sacred time and space, the first question is whether this *homo religiosus* did exist at all.[5] This question is to be discussed here, not, however, by putting together as many examples as possible, in an Eliadean style, but by focusing on one historical example where Eliade's theory may or may not be applicable. Such an example is taken from an ancient text that has been ascribed to Lucian of Samosata: the treatise on the Syrian Goddess (*De Dea Syria*), written in the second century, describing, among other things, the myth and rites of Adonis, a phenomenon that at first sight fits well into the Eliadean portrait of *homo religiosus*: archaic man living in a mythical world of sacred time and space.

Since Lucian is known as a skeptical mind and a critic of all kinds of superstition,[6] his description of religious phenomena could be of special relevance for the debate on Eliade. The Lucianic authenticity of this text, however, has been discussed controversially.[7] In any case, the treatise on the Syrian Goddess remains relevant in this context as a reliable source on Syrian religion in the Roman period (Dirven 159–63). Eliade himself was not particularly interested in this area of the history of religions—he was apparently more interested in the related myth of Tammuz and in ancient Mesopotamian religion.[8] However, Eliade has taken up the myth of Adonis in his fictional writings, combining it with central elements of the Judaeo-Christian tradition and of Hinduism, thus giving it a prominent place in his creative-hermeneutical work.[9]

THE MYTH AND RITES OF ADONIS IN THE LAND OF BYBLOS

The treatise on the Syrian Goddess contains considerable information about sacred sites and rituals in the land of Byblos. The author reports, for instance, that he saw "a great sanctuary of Aphrodite of Byblos" in which the rites of Adonis are performed, and he claims having learned about the rites from the worshippers themselves:

> They say, at any rate, that what the boar did to Adonis occurred in their territory. As a memorial of his suffering each year they beat their breasts, mourn, and celebrate the rites. Throughout the land they perform solemn lamentations. When they cease their breastbeating and weeping, they first sacrifice to Adonis as if to a dead person, but then, on the next day, they proclaim that he lives and send him into the air. (Lucian *De Dea Syria* 6)

The periodic performance and the location of the ritual as well as the myth of the dying and reviving god—all this corresponds nicely to the Eliadean concepts of sacred time and space although it should be noticed that the rites are said to be performed "as a memorial" of the suffering of Adonis. This may indicate an awareness of the historical distance from the mythical event, based on a nonmythical conception of time as irreversible, not as cyclical. However, the author reports another interpretation of these rites giving a different account of the mythical background: according to the author, Lucian, some inhabitants of Byblos would say that the Egyptian Osiris is buried among them and that these rites are performed not for Adonis but for Osiris. The evidence given for this interpretation is the arrival of a head coming from Egypt to Byblos every year, quite miraculously, as the author remarks. The author confirms this account, declaring that he himself saw the Byblian head during his stay at Byblos (*De Dea Syria* 7).

Although the mythical background referred to in this account is different, the mythical interpretation of the ritual is essentially the same and corresponds to Eliade's theory equally well.

The author goes on to describe "another marvel in the land of Byblos," and this is perhaps the most interesting phenomenon in this context, since it seems to come even closer to the Eliadean concepts of sacred space and time:

> A river from Mount Lebanon empties into the sea. Adonis is the name given to the river. Each year the river becomes blood red and, having changed its color, flows into the sea and reddens a large part of it, giving a signal for lamentations to the inhabitants of Byblos. They tell the story that on these days Adonis is being wounded up on Mt. Lebanon and his blood, as it goes into the water, alters the river and gives the stream its name. (*De Dea Syria* 8)

At first sight, this account confirms Eliade's theory of *homo religiosus*, portraying archaic man as transcending history and constructing a cyclical conception of time. According to the story (myth) told by the local people there seems to be no historical distance from the mythical event in the past: the mythical event itself is said to take place every year in an eternal return. Therefore, it could be maintained that an essential element of Eliade's theory of religion, the portrait of archaic man as *homo religiosus*, is very well confirmed by an authentic source from antiquity that might even be said to have been based on fieldwork in a wide sense—the author of the second century, Lucian, claims to have gotten his information from the local people themselves. However, this would be only half the truth. For the author goes on to report another version he was told during his stay at Byblos:

> This is the general version, but a certain man of Byblos, who seemed to me to be telling the truth, recounted another reason for the phenomenon. This is his account: "The river Adonis, stranger, comes through the Lebanon and Mt. Lebanon has a quite ruddy soil. Then strong winds come up on these days and deposit the earth, which is quite red, in the river, and the

soil makes it blood red. The cause of this phenomenon is not the blood, as people say, but it is the land." (*De Dea Syria* 8)

This interpretation of the natural phenomenon differs significantly from the first one since it is apparently based not on a mythical but on a rational conception of nature, which may even remind the modern reader of a scientific approach to natural phenomena (cf. Berner, "Concepts of Nature in Greek Religion" 27–45). There is no indication in the text as to whether this man of Byblos did or did not participate in the rites of Adonis. He may have participated although he had a different relationship to the mythical background of these rites. In any case, it would be illegitimate to neglect the second interpretation, the rational one, as being nonreligious. It could as well be regarded as a different kind of religiosity based on a different type of worldview that does not allow the application of Eliade's concepts. Such a kind of religiosity, which looks quite strange and uninteresting from an Eliadean point of view, is well known from antiquity: skeptic philosopher Pyrrhon was elected high priest in his hometown, and obviously he did not hesitate to take over this religious role (see Diogenes Laertios IX, 64, and cf. Berner, "Religionsphänomenologie und Skeptizismus"). A comparable phenomenon is the Epicurean attitude toward religion: an Epicurean philosopher would participate in religious rituals without taking seriously the mythical background. The fact that many ancient philosophers, for example, Plutarch of Chaironeia, attacked the Epicurean attitude as hypocrisy does not entitle the modern historian of religions to exclude such a nonmythical attitude as a nonreligious phenomenon (see Plutarch, Non posse suaviter vivi secundum Epicurum 1102 BC. cf. Berner, "Plutarch und Epikur").

There is even a third interpretation of the same natural phenomenon to be discovered in this very text, that is, the interpretation given by the author, Lucian, himself. It might be called a philosophical or a theological interpretation: after indicating that he considers the second account, that is the rational one, to be true the author concludes by saying: "But even if his version is correct, I consider the chance intervention of the wind quite divine" (*De Dea Syria* 8).

Accordingly, this ancient text contains already three different interpretations, which might be called the mythical, the rational, and the theological, referring to the same natural phenomenon, and correspondingly there are also three different attitudes toward the myth and rites of Adonis. Therefore, it does not seem legitimate to identify only one of these interpretations as "the" religious worldview of archaic man and to consider only one of the corresponding attitudes as representing *homo religiosus*. Certainly, an adherent of Eliade's approach would be interested only in the mythical interpretation of the natural phenomenon and the ritual, as was James George Frazer, when he wrote, obviously referring to this very text by Lucian: "Every year, in the belief of his worshippers, Adonis was wounded to death on the mountains, and every year the face of nature itself was dyed with his sacred blood" (Frazer 30). Frazer, however, had different reasons for focusing on the mythical interpretation of nature, therefore selecting just this aspect of Lucian's text,[10] since his approach was based on a totally different attitude toward religion, as compared to Eliade's.[11]

THE DOUBLE TASK OF THE HISTORY OF RELIGIONS

Lucian may or may not be the author of the treatise on the Syrian Goddess. In any case, Lucian's work is of relevance for the study of religion, since he was so much interested in the terrestrial side of religion, that is, the social context of religious phenomena including even the material interests that may be involved in religious activities. Surprisingly perhaps, Andrew Lang, one of the founding fathers of the history of religions and a critic of Frazer's approach (see Andrew Lang, "Mr. Frazer's Theory of the Crucifixion"), seems to have appreciated Lucian's work very much when he wrote: "Ah, Lucian, we have need of you, of your sense and of your mockery!" (Lang, *Letters to Dead Authors* 49).

Lucian has given several examples of how religion can be used for nonreligious ends. The most famous example, probably, is Alexander of Abonouteichos, the "false prophet," who earned his living out of the oracle of Glykon which he had created himself and kept manipulating all the time to his advantage. According to Lucian's account, Alexander and his partner, before founding their prophetic shrine and oracle had discerned "that human life is swayed by two great tyrants, hope and fear, and that a man who could use both of these to advantage would speedily enrich himself" (Lucian, *Alexander the False Prophet* 8).

It is understandable, that this prophet, according to Lucian, showed special hostility toward the Epicurean philosophy, going as far as burning works of Epicurus publicly (*Alexander the False Prophet* 47). Another example given by Lucian is the biography of Peregrinus, cynic philosopher and for a limited period of time a Christian, whose love of glory was so strong that he burnt himself publicly, at Olympia, after the games of AD 165. Lucian's accounts are satirical and polemical, of course, and it is an open question whether they hit the truth in each case (cf. Diskin Clay, "Lucian of Samosata" 3430–45).

Such a critical perspective on religious phenomena, however, must not be neglected in the study of religion if it claims to be a historical discipline deserving its name. Doing historical studies the scholar of religion has to ask all kinds of "destabilizing and irreverent questions" such as, for instance, who wins and who, conversely, loses (see Bruce Lincoln, "Theses on Method" 225f.). On the other hand, the critical and contextual approach to the study of religion must not lead to such an extreme as to neglect and forget those questions Eliade had been concerned with throughout his work, that is, the careful interpretation of each religious perspective itself—the effort to understand and describe how religious people see the world.

Hermeneutical reflection on the religious self-understanding in all its ramifications—including nonmythical conceptions—as well as critical reflection on the terrestrial side of religion with all its implications—including nonreligious motivations: that is the double task of the history of religions as an academic discipline, being neither reductionist nor antireductionist. The target of criticism in the debate on Eliade, therefore, should not be the falsity of his approach to the study of religion but rather its one-sidedness and the limitedness of its focus—his being interested only in hermeneutical reflection and, in this field, focusing mostly on one kind of religiosity.[12]

NOTES

1. Edmund Leach, "Sermons by a Man on a Ladder"; Mac Linscott Ricketts, "In Defence of Eliade"; cf. Ivan Strenski, "Love and Anarchy in Romania" 391; Douglas Allen, *Myth and Religion in Mircea Eliade* xif.

2. German philosopher Kurt Hübner, for instance, has taken Eliade's theory very seriously: *Die Wahrheit des Mythos* 81f.

3. Cf. David Cave, "Eliade's Interpretation of Sacred Space," in Rennie, *Changing Religious Worlds*, 235–48, especially 237–39.

4. This is done by Daria Pezzoli-Olgiati: "Stadt als heiliger Raum? Drei mesopotamische Beispiele," in: Axel Michaels et al., *Noch eine Chance* 47–66.

5. This aspect of Eliade's theory has been assessed critically by Kurt Rudolph: "There has never been and never will be a *homo religiosus* who merges completely into a cosmic sacrality in order to transcend 'history' and 'time.'" "Mircea Eliade and the 'History' of Religions." Cf. also John A. Saliba, "Eliade's View of Primitive Man."

6. Concerning Lucian and Skepticism see Heinz-Günther Nesselrath, "Kaiserzeitlicher Skeptizismus in platonischem Gewand: Lukians 'Hermotimos'" 3451–82.

7. Cf. Lucinda Dirven, "The Author of *De Dea Syria*," *Numen* 44 (1997): 153–79; Tomasz Polanski, *Oriental Art in Greek Imperial Literature* 80–104. The authorship of Lucian is maintained, for instance, by Simon Swain, *Hellenism and Empire* 304–308, and by Nesselrath, "Lukian: Leben und Werk," 27.

8. See Eliade, *Cosmos and History: The Myth of the Eternal Return* 100–102. Adonis is mentioned by Eliade alongside Osiris, Tammuz, and Attis as one of the young gods who are killed and (sometimes) resurrected: *Myth and Reality* 110. Eliade seems to have followed Frazer's interpretation of the equivalence of Tammuz and Adonis: see Frazer, *The Golden Bough* Part IV: Adonis Attis Osiris 6f.

9. See Eliade, "Die Brücke" (The Bridge), in: *Phantastische Geschichten* 205–38. Cf. Berner, "Erforschung und Anwendung" and "Die Bedeutung der Religionswissenschaft."

10. Frazer does not mention the fact that the natural explanation of the phenomenon is already given as one version in the Lucianic text itself (225).

11. Frazer's *Golden Bough* is described as "a sort of counter-Bible" by Robert Fraser: *James George Frazer, The Golden Bough* XXV.

12. Discussing the one-sidedness of this approach one would have to take into account the historical context of its origin and development, particu-

larly the exile situation in the West during the cold war era. Concerning the "cultural war" Eliade was engaged in, cf. Steven Wasserstrom, *Religion after Religion* 17f. Eliade's political involvement in interwar Romania and its implications for the assessment of his scholarly work have been discussed controversially. Cf. Rennie, *Reconstructing Eliade* 143–77; McCutcheon, *Manufacturing Religion* 74–100.

In Search of a Methodology: Eliade's Hermeneutical Approach in the Study of Ancient Egyptian Texts

Brigitte Ouellet
(translated by Bryan Rennie)

> It is solely insofar as it will perform this task—particularly by making the meanings of religious documents intelligible to the mind of modern man—that the science of religions will fulfill its true cultural function.
>
> —Quest 2

Although Mircea Eliade had some interest in the religions of the Near East, very few Egyptologists today rely on his writings in order to engage or expound upon the religious aspect of this specialist area. His work might be outdated, uninteresting, misunderstood, but might it yet contain some interesting leads for a hermeneutic of Egyptian texts? This is the fundamental question posed for researchers into the methodology of the study of religious facts and ideas in ancient Egypt.

This article suggests various contributions to the elaboration of a hermeneutic of Egyptian texts implied by the application of the intentions that govern an "Eliadean" hermeneutic and, at the same time, indicates changes implied by advances in textual interpretation. Initially I will present a brief critique of Eliade's work as a historian of religions, made known to us by his publications, insofar as his acquaintance with the religious ideas and phenomena of ancient Egypt is concerned. A collation of the categories of Eliadean thought with the categories of Pharaonic thought will then be necessary to respond adequately to my initial question. Secondly, I will make my point about the state of research and the different problems involved in the establishment of a method of Egyptian textual interpretation to bring me to my conclusion on the not insignificant contributions of an Eliadean hermeneutic.

A BRIEF CRITIQUE OF ELIADE'S WORK

INADEQUATE REFERENCE TO UNTRANSLATED PRIMARY SOURCES

In general, specialists in ancient religions reproach Eliadean hermeneutics for its apparent indifference to the primary texts. Indeed, Eliade does frequently refer to religious ideas and phenomena drawn from already translated, and thus already interpreted, texts, but, as far as ancient Egypt is concerned, he is never under any delusion: he was *"a generalist"* (*Journal III* 93). Nevertheless, it must be recognized that Eliade only wrote his "generalizations" after prolonged study of his subject, that he always referred to the most recent publications in the field,[1] and that he based his opinions on the standard works of his time.[2] This kind of generalization, in the context of his definition of the history of religions, constitutes a synthesis of religious facts and ideas that in no way tries to reduce but to integrate them (*The Two and the One* 211).

Still, from the point of view of the hermeneutical process, the fact that he did not himself have access to the sources is a major handicap to the greater appreciation of this generalist's substantial contribution. It is understandable that there thus persists a certain ambiguity as to the validity of the results obtained, without even considering the multiple critiques issuing from different disciplines with their own methodological criteria.[3] However, it must be appreciated that for the historian of religions, hermeneutics regulates a tension between the historical and phenomenological dimensions and constitutes a synthesis of specialization and generalization in which the former is subordinate to the latter because of the intentionality of the structure of the religious phenomenon (*The Myth of the Eternal Return* 96–97; *Journal II* 121). Furthermore, it cannot go without mention that in literary hermeneutics research has made enormous progress with specialists such as Eco, Gadamer, Rimmon-Kenan, Ricoeur, to mention but a few, and the consequences of their research could bolster an approach to religious facts. It was with just cause that Eliade himself had, in the last years of his life, indicated on several occasions that, after phenomenology, literary criticism in the larger sense could become an important tool for the historian of religions since it focuses on "language," which, in itself, is a hierophanic phenomenon. Does not literature take on the function of myth? (*Ordeal by Labyrinth* 177). This did not go unnoticed by Bryan Rennie, who, quite recently, ventured to see this as opening a promising avenue that could lead beyond Eliade and thus contribute to an advance in research, principally in the analysis of "contemporary" religious phenomena (*Reconstructing Eliade* 248–49). Thus, it is obvious that this proposal involves the "whole" of religious facts and also that the history of religions as the study of "archaic" religious ideas and beliefs, could profit from it—all the more because the text, even if fragmentary, is more often than not our only witness to the discourse of the ancients.

THE LACK OF SYSTEMATIC METHODOLOGY AND OBSOLETE RESULTS

The second serious criticism of Eliade's position is its lack of systematization, which is sometimes seen as homologous to relativism and overgeneralism. The hermeneutics that Eliade proposes to us is "the hermeneutic of religious creations," which he describes as a "total hermeneutics."[4] The latter is essentially implicit and introduces the dynamic between the hermeneut and the text referring to these "creations" on an ontological basis. Under Paul Ricoeur's influence, and for similar reasons, Eliade has in fact assumed a priori the fact that in applying the organic and integral comparative method of George Dumézil one does not don the garb of the philologist but of the interpreter.[5] Moreover it should not be forgotten that all criticism carried out from a methodological perspective must take into account the sociocultural and political context of the author, the extent of his knowledge, and his personal stake in his intellectual milieu, and also take account of the whole of his work both academic and literary.[6] It is thus necessary to distinguish between criticism and revision of the methodological problems that Eliade's intellectual legacy poses today.[7]

Whatever may be the case, the historian of religions himself recognized his lack of systematization: "In my work I have tried to elaborate this hermeneutics, but I have illustrated it in a practical manner, based on documents. It remains now, by me or some other, to systematize this hermeneutic" (*Journal II* 313). This is the *keystone* in an understanding of his apparent lack of system. A deeper study of Eliadean hermeneutics demonstrates that the characteristics proper to its subjects lead it to renounce entirely any system that would make it into a normative method by leading inevitably to the reduction of the religious fact. The singularity of the subject rests on the implicit aspect of religion as defined by the categories of Eliadean thought (see below for these categories), a better knowledge of which elucidates the precedence of the structure of religious phenomena over the historical situation.

Here, perhaps, is the most disturbing aspect of such a hermeneutics, because the will to avoid theorizing religion that underlies this methodological nonsystematization entails the loss of the methodological security resulting from adherence to a theory. But must this result in a methodological impasse? I prefer the "keystone": Eliade's originality is apparent in his proposal, not of a research method or of a theory for analyzing religion, but in the "practical application" of a hermeneutical process in which hermeneuts enter into a dialectic between themselves and their subject. Whoever understands the dialectic and even the paradox into which hermeneuts are thrown by taking this step—despite the pressure of the critics—easily recognizes the advantage of these assertions and the avoidance of scientific "objectivity," of overspecialization, blind rationalism, and historicist and methodological reductionism.[8] Historians of religions must go beyond historico-cultural appearances. They must decipher and translate the sense and meanings of the religious patterns that they study[9] and to do this, their theories and methods must develop with their own specific research experiences.

Interpreters must inevitably work with more than one area of specialization in order to compare and validate results conforming to the characteristics of the study, while developing their own methodologies. The interpretative process is thus liberated from the yoke of its hypothetical support and becomes a useful *multidisciplinary tool* offering a kaleidoscopic comprehension of an object of study that is naturally polyvocal. The definitions of religion and its manifestations are in constant evolution and their comprehension is subject to the hermeneuts' understanding and to their ontological experience. The hermeneut becomes the catalyst in a double-dynamic: "text-hermeneut-text" and "hermeneut-text-hermeneut" that enables, at one and the same time, the adjustment of the act of interpretation and, in consequence, the choice of methodological tools and approaches (Marino, *L'herméneutique de Mircea Eliade* 25–27).

On the other hand, this "keystone" supports paradoxical arches of relativism and of universalism over the hermeneut and the result of their researches and confronts the reader with a plurality of "truths, reasons, or rationalities," not to mention the ontological assumptions that this hermeneutical dynamic entails.[10] These are certainly problematic ontological assumptions, but, considering the nature of the hermeneut and of the process of interpretation, they are inevitable! I will return elsewhere to this idea of a plurality of "truths"—no stranger to literary postmodernism (see *Reconstructing Eliade* 232–38)—and to the hermeneutics that I urge upon Egyptian thought.

Before a more thorough exploration of the compatibility between Eliadean and Egyptian categories, allow me to remark that the claims made by Eliade concerning Egyptian religious facts and ideas, in general, turn out to be correct[11] except in a single case.[12] Keenly aware of his own limitations and of the risks resulting from the hermeneutical process that he had adopted, Eliade wrote in his *Journal*—just as he completed the editing of the chapter preceding the one on ancient Egypt, which was to appear in the first volume of his *History of Religious Ideas*—to this effect:

> I have never referred to their interpretations [that is, those of specialists] except insofar as they overlapped those of the generalist that I am. I could not under any circumstances accept responsibility for the interpretation or the commentaries of an Orientalist, for example, whether he is a philologist, archeologist, or an epigraphist, who, after having read and translated a religious text, would attempt to explain it or to present it from the perspective of notions that were in style eighty years ago.... (*Journal III* 93–94)

Of course, if certain claims have become obsolete it is those that rely on the interpretation of a particular translation that has since been revised[13] or on a reference to a historical fact that has since been reconsidered.[14] Eliade goes so far as to propose his expertise as a historian of religions in the famous *Querelle des Égyptologues*, which shook French Egyptology from 1949 to 1961, at that time resistant to the symbolic thought that it associated with an unscientific current of interpretation.[15] He explains that in the horizon of the archaic mentality, symbolic thought "breaks open" the isolation of immediate realities: "Symbolism *adds*," he says, "a new value to an object or an activity without any prejudice whatever to its own immediate value" (*Images and Symbols* 178, italics original).

References to ancient Egypt remain on the whole infrequent in the Eliadean corpus, with good reason, since he admits that "despite the familiarity of its images today, Egyptian religion remains conceptually distant from us" (*The Eliade Guide to World Religions* 102). But whatever is the case, for the most part the historian of religions puts himself at the center of the aforementioned double dynamic in researching the phenomenological structure of religious facts and ideas (such as paradigm and repetition, etc.), which he subordinates to our understanding of Egyptian history.[16] It is from this perspective that one can see the merit of his work: a set of tools that encourage reflection and promote discussion of "the religious mode of being."

CATEGORIES OF ELIADEAN THOUGHT AND EGYPTIAN CATEGORIES

The implicit meaning of religion, according to Eliade, depends upon the following categories: "hierophany," "the irreducible sacred," "the dialectics of the sacred and the profane," "the *coincidentia oppositorum*," "*homo religiosus*," "symbols and symbolism," "myth and mythology," "*illud tempus*," and finally "history and historicity." Frequently analyzed (e.g., in Rennie, *Reconstructing Eliade* 1–117), these categories are here transposed with those that fashioned the religious thought of ancient Egyptian civilization to serve the role of a brief homologization. This exercise proposes a sensitization to the elementary structure of this thought; thorough investigation thus begins with the systematic interrelations between the categories that constitute Egyptian discourse as a significant network of religious meanings.[17] This move has the advantage of facilitating understanding and analysis of the relation between heterogeneous forms of hierophany, the various attitudes that they entail and also the discourse that relates them.

Neter, corresponding to the concept of hierophany, is translated as "god," and should not be related to the term *theos* whose Greek origins indicate a reality more Western and Mediterranean than Egyptian. For the Egyptian, *neter* is a cosmic reality, essentially *djeser* (sacred), *ka* (vital), *weser* (effective), and *ba*[18] (performative), which is manifested in several *kheperu* (forms). The most ancient symbol to express *neter* is a sort of baton about which are wound strips of cloth (𓊹), later the hypostatic form becomes theriomorphic (𓃩), and then anthropomorphic (𓀭) for reasons of identity and pedagogy.[19]

The irreducibility of the sacred is apprehended as such through the dynamism of "the one and the many" conveyed by the paradoxical presence of "sacred being," at once transcendent and immanent.[20] Egyptian language has several related expressions to qualify the different aspects of the sacred beyond the "good/bad" distinction. Best known among them, beyond a doubt, is *dsr*, which designates the spatialization of the thing rendered sacred by the act of power that is the "rite." There are also other terms such as: *akh* (brilliant, glorious), *netery* (divine), *wab* (pure), *sekhem* (powerful, effective), etc.[21] In truth, the qualities of the sacred conceal several levels of being so that Egyptian *homo religiosus* is in constant ontic rapport with the sacred through the intermediary of numerous self-referential hierophanic archetypes. Its existence depends not only on the balance of the vital force, *ka*,[22] but is also dependent upon the life (*ankh*) that relies on the *Grundlage* that provides Order/Harmony/Justice (Ma'at—cf. *Pyramid Texts*, Spell 586; §1582; *Coffin Texts*, 35c-g; and *Book of the Dead* §85). Moreover, it is written in the *Coffin Texts* that Ma'at is that regulatory force of life that calms the disruptive, evolutionary, complementary force, Isfet, which provokes change and brings about catastrophes on every level.[23] Hence it is of no surprise to find in column 67 of the *Prophecy of Neferty* that "Ma'at will return to its throne when Isfet has been subdued." On the other hand it must be recognized that life is possible only because of the dialectic of the sacred and the profane, manifested in this incessant oscillation between Ma'at and Isfet (*cf. Coffin Texts* §80 and 307; IV 62b-j, m-n).

In the same context, death is essential as a predetermined transition of the natural vital force to a supernatural state of being promoted by funerary rites such as the *Opening of the Mouth* (*cf.* Goyon, *Rituels funéraires de l'ancienne Égypte*). Life on earth as such is organized as one of countless episodes that progressively integrate and perfect various perspectives on being in the sacred, or, rather, on Life. This integration, furthermore, relies on the periodic regeneration of this vital force that is the sacred, the creative source of Nun,[24] passed on and evolving since the dawn of the *Sep Tepy*, that is, the First Time.[25]

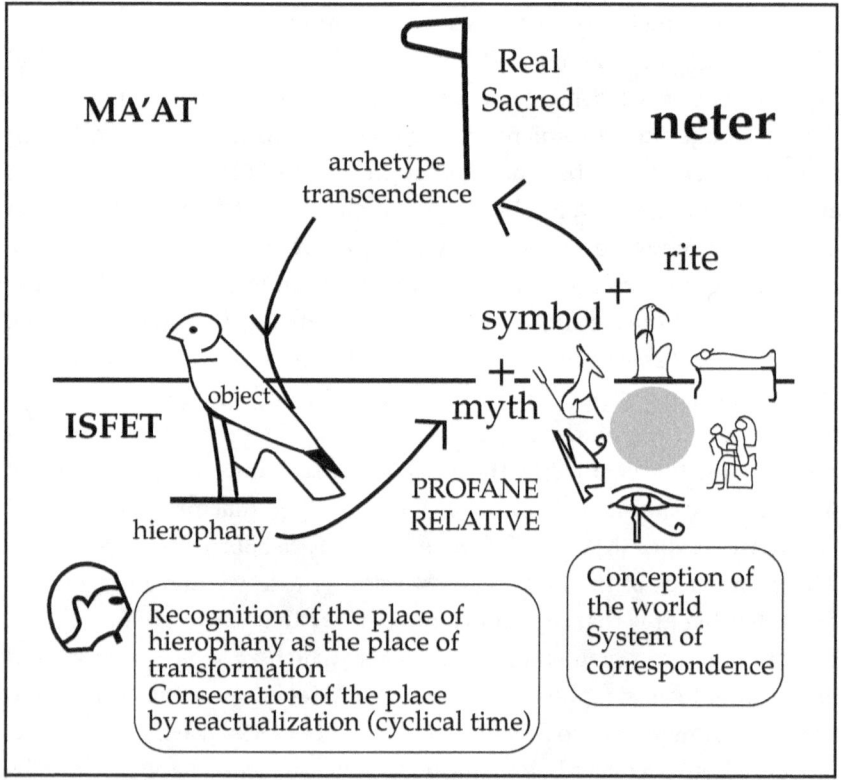

Figure 4.1. The Dialectic of the States of Being in the Sacred

Whatever may be the theological synthesis put forward by the temples and the various theological schools, everything in this universe is thus interdependent whatever its sphere of emanation (human, superhuman, natural, supernatural, etc.), whence the importance of the ontic connections with the sacred, that is, Life in motion, and the effects they have on the whole collection, vouchsafed by the Pharaoh, the ideal paradigm of the living being, *homo religious*, through the office inherited from his ancestors.[26] As the model of the superhuman, consciously integrating himself into this indispensable and vital dialectic, Pharaoh, cosmic Son of Ra and chthonic Son of Isis, assimilates himself to different divine creations and entities of all sorts.[27] The veritable *axis mundi* of Egyptian society, the Pharaoh is the regulatory authority par excellence, at once leader, father, son, priest, the righter of wrongs, and the *neter*, whose acts and the whole of ritual can be summed up in a single act: the presentation of the statuette of *Ma'at* (𓐙—Karenga, *Ma'at, the Moral Ideal in Ancient Egypt*). In this act, he proclaims the fulfillment of his duty, and thereby, he shows his people the meaning of life (*The Kouban Stela of Seti 1st* I.11, and *Pyramid Texts* §278–79, 299). In fact, his offering of *Ma'at*, which decorates thousands of temple and tomb walls, is nourished by the royal ideology and the various cosmo-theologies in order to maintain an ethic of being in respect of the sacred. In this there is a complete system of values that models the conception of the universe and from which derive orientation for Life, the justification of its raison d'être and its passage into the afterlife; that is what Jan Bergman meant by pan-ontology (*Book of the Dead* §96; Bergman, "Mysticism" 58, 67–76).

Ancient Egyptian *homo religious* is confronted by a sort of metalanguage, which synthesizes conceptual, cosmogonic, and theological models as well as others that use rhetorical images and narratives. To ensure the efficacy of these models, the Egyptian uses frames of reference drawn from the imaginary world of fiction to encourage the emergence of "possible worlds" which, without the restrictions of actual history,[28] allow him to incorporate other modes of being, even to include certain ruptures of plane characteristic of the idea of the integration of being. This relates various expressions of the dialectic of the sacred and the profane as well as their interactions and their effects on living beings. The symbolic and metaphoric languages used inspire discourses that are highly performative,[29] mythic,[30] liturgical, royal, cosmo-theological, as well as iconographic. The tradition transmits and maintains this veritable network of meanings through themes frequently connected to an ambivalent metaphysics such as the daily combat of Ra against the serpent Apophis, the struggle between Horus and Set, the union of Osiris and Ra, the lamentations of Isis and the dangers of the chthonic world, the establishment of the *axis mundi* in the raising of a pillar (*djed*), etc. Thus, the "profaning" reality of the vernacular presents that of "possible worlds" through various points of view to constitute, for example, a parallax of worlds or of discourses as other ideas are fragmented and juxtaposed, contrasted, or superimposed;[31] the one possesses the multivalence, the ambivalence, of the many.

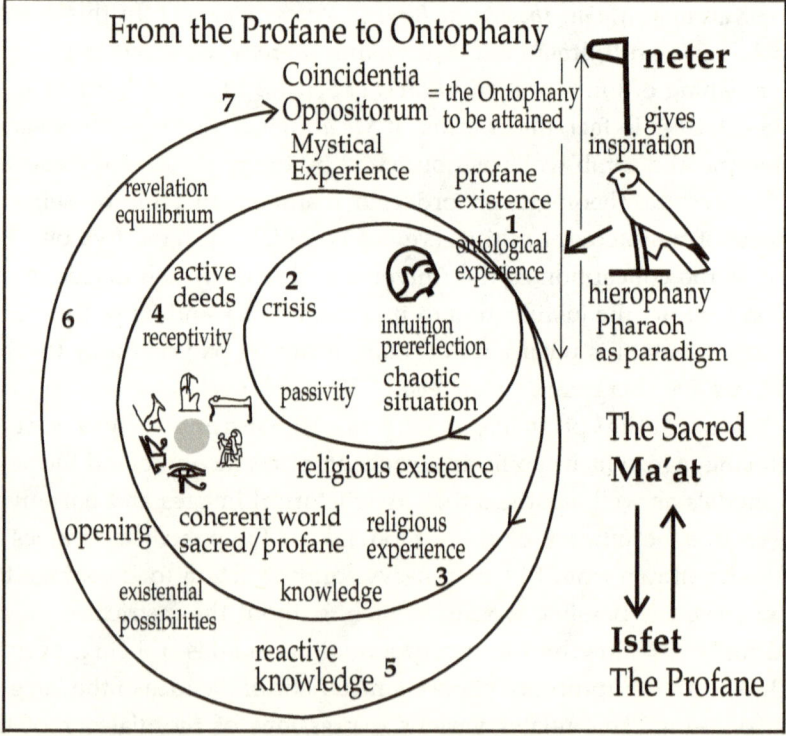

Figure 4.2. The Integration of Being in the Sacred

The diagram above depicts a schematic illustration of religious experience showing the multiple modes of being that mark the process of the sacralization of being, from the profane to the *coincidentia oppositorum*, from the existential crisis provoked by the hierophany to the ontophanic arrival of integration (Douglas Allen, *Myth and Religion in Mircea Eliade* 74–87). Egyptian scribes thus elaborate their discourse in order to exploit the wealth of meaning brought about by a plurality of approaches, of enumerations, of paradoxes, of tensions, or of conceptual juxtapositions. Here, writing is the art of constructing a "perfected utterance," an art that sets up a *"jeu philosophique"* containing a filigree of resources and rhetorical forms cunningly interwoven one with another.[32] The hermeneutical process thus promotes synthetic thought so that it may come to know the numerous potentialities of discourse in these forms. This intention of inducing an interpretive engagement in the "textual interlocutor" is not restricted to literary or artistic discourse. It appears inevitably in some fundamental concepts of Egyptian thought, especially in the categories connected with ideas of time and history.

Words relating to time frequently contain determinatives that refer to space and vice versa. The ancient Egyptians do not seem to have made distinctions between these categories in the same way as do we. Their space-time is always connected to the phenomenon of Creation in which the manifestation or division of time predominates, and for a good reason, because a good number of narratives thus made cosmogonic references referring to *illud tempus*.[33] For example, in *The Book of the Sacred Cow*, the frame of reference is relative to the moment when "it came to pass that Ra, after training the royal family . . ." (S I, 1) which, by analogy, amounts to our "once upon a time . . ." The initial moment of this type of discourse is situated in an indeterminate past and the temporal expressions that follow are determined by the function of the narrative. In fact, these "perfected utterances," just like fantasy discourse, deliberately encourage the ambiguity of the temporal frame and promote a multiplicity of interpretations, which necessarily plunges the interpreter into uncertainty.[34]

For the Egyptian who understands his universe to be a tension between Ma'at and Isfet, where the power of Ra's light guarantees continuity in the cyclical regeneration of life, terrestrial time is confined to that which is measurable (calendar, seasons, stage of life, etc.), as was the life cycle of Osiris, and as is the reign of each Pharaoh. That which is beyond the human capacity to measure is considered timeless as it is outside of terrestrial time. This time, closely connected in terms of open duration to the concept of immeasurable space, suggests, rather, a "pseudo-eternity," defined as *djet*, under its durational aspect and linear range, or *neheh*, under its regenerative aspect and cyclic development. Actual history thus never repeats without evolving, since it is entirely a creation in a dynamic of perfectibility, but, concomitantly, the menace of a frightful cataclysm that would not only disturb but destroy the divine order by wiping out the memory of time past, is always present.

The meaning accorded to historical circumstances rests on the ambiguity of time, which vacillates between paradigms of temporal fragmentation—illustrated by the cycle of Osiris and the improvement of life—and evolutionary immutability—seen in the cosmo-solar and lunar cycles. The Egyptian who desires to be self-consistent and who respects the ethical imperative of the Ma'at offering, has no interest in passing on the historical singularities of the tribulations of individual existence in a factual, journalistic retelling.

As Eliade reminded us, the religious mode of being to which the Egyptian belonged could not reduce his existence to *"the awakened consciousness of its historic moment"* (*Images and Symbols* 171 n.13, italics original). He must increasingly seek to surpass his precursors since factual event is at once a continuation of the creative impulse, so that today is similar to, but different from, yesterday, but, if he does so, it is solely in the context of the exemplary. Factual history is then reconstituted, reinterpreted, and retransmitted in the light of Pharaonic ideology and in the categories that constitute their "perfected utterance."[35] One has to await the arrival of the XVIIIth dynasty to see the appearance of a concern for the transmission of historical chronicle, and still it must be confessed that they do not in any way resemble classical written sources because they are marked in the style of Egyptian thought with a kind of royal propaganda and a desire to perfect reality.[36] The discourse here is not the fruit of historiography but of a will to historicize the tradition in order to transmit and transcend it by producing exemplars.

Research into the implicit meaning of Egyptian religion with the aide of Eliadean categories permits a reconstruction of the indispensable fundamental bases of knowledge (*Grundkenntnisse*), but moreover of the globalizing understanding of the Pharaonic religious mind. These basic schemes commit hermeneuts to placing themselves between the known and the unknown among the exogenous realities with which they are confronted so as to evaluate the distance in relation to themselves, while suggesting a delimitation of the interpretive process. From then on, it is easier to allow oneself to suggest some investigative tools more adequate to a knowledge of the characteristic limits of one's objects of study and to confront one's subsequent interpretations instead of imposing ipso facto one's methodological preferences. In the same way, the exercise allows us, from the very first, to make out the weaknesses and the compatibilities of the interpretive methods and theories to which researchers must have recourse and subsequently to adjust them.

TEXTUAL METHODOLOGICAL PROBLEMATICS AND THE CONTRIBUTION OF ELIADEAN HERMENEUTICS

In a specialization in which a great deal of research depends upon analysis, on the understanding and interpretation of thousands of texts carved into walls, inscribed on papyrus and other artifacts, the interpretive process remains practically ignored. In fact, the distinction between a "fragmentary interpretation entailed by a certain approach" and "the application of a hermeneutical process" remains, to all intents and purposes, nonexistent. Furthermore, an analysis and quick consideration of the historical situation reveals the occasional idea culled in passing from such authors as Campbell, Levinas, Eliade, or some other, often taken out of context and transplanted literally into the Egyptian context to explain some fact.

Now, the clarification of the categories of Egyptian thought has allowed me to assert that the products and the discourse that accompany it necessitate a surpassing of the ancestral, primordial tradition it transmits, in keeping with the principle of Ma'at as personifying "order/truth/justice." As a result, hermeneuts absolutely must consider that the object of their interpretation is immersed in a "maâtian" functional pluralism that reorganizes history according to its own demands. The latter exceeds my academic remit since Egyptian pragmatism does not at all seek to supply historical evidence in its discourse and its output. The act of interpretation must rely on the written or archeological "self-evident facts" as well as on the provisional understanding acquired of the distinctive characteristics of the thought of the milieu whence these "self-evident facts" came. To subtract these self-evident facts from the characteristics, or vice versa, is to ignore the process of hermeneutics and to reduce it to a limited, estimated gloss.[37] Neither the historical-archeological method to which Björkman and Redford accustomed us,[38] nor the approaches of linguistics nor even of literary criticism developed by Loprieno, Foster, Baines,[39] etc. constitute in and of themselves an adequate insight into Egyptian religion to the extent that each result affirms itself as "truth" as opposed to alternative results thus shown to be "fallacious," although fragmentary by nature. Isn't it pretentious to claim the final word in an interpretation when, for the ancient Egyptian, this would turn out to be impossible since the discourse concerns "living" texts that are, like temples, performative and constantly under reinterpretation?

This rather deplorable situation results from overspecialization and from the diminution of the "religious" sphere in the training of Egyptologists. The current tendency has been clearly described by Redford who, concerning textual interpretation, wrote:

> Problems relating to interpretation of textual sources place an unusually heavy burden on historians of ancient Egypt. Not only must they be completely conversant with the language(s) in which the material is written, but they must also have epigraphic skills and knowledge of cursive.... Identifying genre, *Sitz im Leben*, an intended audience often demands introducing literacy theory, form criticism, and orality theory into the discussion. (Redford 107)

This attitude confirms the radical priority that Egyptology accords epigraphic and paleographic results, which reduce discourse to the characteristics of its writing in such a way that the structure of the expression is taken as an obvious fact of research instead of just one of the available resources by which one reveals its multiple meanings.[40] As we have seen, in order to counter the reductionism and historicism that this entails, Eliade proposes to go beyond the horizontal, linear, historical level of which Redford spoke, by adding a vertical, phenomenological level (Loprieno, *Ancient Egyptian Literature*, adopts the same perspective). We have seen that the characteristics of Egyptian thought comfortably agree with those of Eliadean thought, but do Egyptians texts then lend themselves to such a hermeneutic?

What I mean here by "text" is more than just written documents in the strict sense but designates all "rhetorical discourse" whose composition intentionally subscribes to the dialectic of the sacred and the profane as a sort of metalanguage, that is, to the Egyptian belief in the perfecting of life.[41] Although different, the decoration of a temple, the invention of a story, even a copy of *The Book of the Dead* with its vignettes, are all inspired by the same categories of thought in which poetico-religious and speculative thought inextricably entwine.[42] Writing, consisting of sacred characters, is a creative act of "shapes and outlines" (*sesh, kedu*), set forth in all their glory as *paroles parfaites* (*medut neferut*). The specific characteristics of such discourse depend on the context, support, subject, and referent, on form as well as function. It is thus not surprising that scholars have experienced difficulty in producing a satisfactory definition of Egyptian literature,[43] capable of grasping in depth the totality of its characteristics; all the more so since we inevitably restrict it to its literal meaning and that we do so according to our Western Judeo-Christian tradition.

Whatever literary theory one may endorse, it must inevitably recombine the hieroglyph, the aesthetics of form, the cultural specifics to which it refers, and the orchestration of the structure in a rationality peculiar to Egyptian poetics. Over the last thirty years the modern concern to establish a theory of Egyptian literature, with the help of other disciplines, has indeed allowed a fleeting glimpse of the complexion of

Egyptian discourse and an initial grasp of its deep realities. On the other hand, in order to improve our results, it is important to recognize that our conclusions and our critiques of the "texts" are relative, because, despite the utmost will for objectivity, they necessarily belong to a hermeneutical dynamic exemplified by the whole of the Eliadean corpus, as we have seen. Still, between intentionality and the processes initiated by the hermeneut, the text—or more accurately, the "fragment of the expressed world" or "fragmentary texts"—remains the vehicle of meaning and is indispensable to all work!

In this light, the hierophanic value of Egyptian texts would be understood as similar to that elucidated by the Eliadean hypothesis of a hierophanic relation between word and religious experience. A priori, the texts contain dynamic, interacting, underlying, homologous structures that emphasize the performative aspect of discourse ("Literary Imagination and Religious Structure"). To get at them, scholars must take into account two parallel poles of analysis; literary and religious, since it is in bringing out this double perspective that we may appraise the gap between discourse on the "manifestation of the possible" and on the presence of being "other" outside "factual history," or, rather, between sacred narrative and history (see n.30 above). For are not the literary world, and perhaps even more so the religious world, constructed on a world of possibilities?

Thus determining what is at stake in the text, different "meaningful expressions" can be analyzed from the phenomenological point of view through the constructions of the peculiarly Egyptian imagination determined by religious structures. It is here that a structural analysis understood within the "levels of penetration into the text"[44] would be desirable. Now, to this very day, there is no vocabulary for the elementary structures and constructions inherent in the texts of Egyptian religious phenomena and languages that can give an account of the integration of the multiple organic interactions that connect them.[45] For understandable reasons we persist in considering them individually in literary, artistic, grammatical, or other specificity. To the best of my knowledge, only Foster's concept of "Thought Couplets" explodes the language of methodological specialization and surpasses the constraints of particular approaches to serve as the basis for an open terminology.[46]

An in-depth investigation of Eliadean hermeneutics enables an evaluation of the intermediation of religious structures in literary structures of discourse in relation to what is known of factual history. The process encourages a combination of methodological approaches on a tripartite model (historical, literary, phenomenological) all the while requiring the self-authentication of preliminary conclusions and presuppositions.[47] Although very demanding, it also, by its aspiration to synthesis and total hermeneutics, tends partially to close the gap between the text, the hermeneut, and the Egyptian spirit with its concern for the essential interactions between its being, writing, and living context. The scholar must then be attentive to the slightest characteristics of the text in order to apply the best tools. So *The Embalming Ritual*, cannot be studied from the same perspective and with the same methodological tools as a text such as *The Tale of Two Brothers*.

One must dare to allow oneself to be led by the play of Egyptian interpretation and Eliade's tripartite hermeneutics; together they mark the passage to a better grasp of the art of combinative thought that introduces the reader into an initially disconcerting world of signifiers and signifieds. To understand the process inherent in Egyptian intentionality is hardly a simple thing since it requires on the one hand stripping bare our own thought and, on the other hand, integrating knowledge of Egyptian stylistic and rhetorical representations. The various updated approaches bring to light an intellectual process that appears commonplace since we use it every day; the association of ideas (Derchain, "Théologie et littérature"). The latter employs literary and artistic means that are neither more nor less than the "norms" rationalizing the ideas that structure Egyptian thought to create the "perfected utterances," essential to the use of a word chosen in a particular context (Empson, "Assertion in Words"). The interpretation of things, texts or walls, is thus never self-enclosed, so to speak, but functions to return the world, the experience, and the meanings for the reader, like bouncing a ball against a wall; the "interlocutor" plays back the world of the signified, that is, reactualizes the world of the text by participating in it. For the ancient Egyptian the text must constantly evolve, whence the fact that variations become adaptations, a way of renewing the "letter," the word, or the knowledge that it contains. Is this, perhaps, how we should understand the words that Ptahhotep dedicated to his son?

> Do not take a word and then bring it back.
> Do not put one thing in place of another.
> Beware of loosening the cords in you. (. . .)
>> Speak (only) after you have mastered the craft
>> (*Ptahhotep* 608–15)

For sure, the hermeneutical process to which Eliade invites us is not without its failings, and whether one be for or against it is not the question at issue here. On the contrary, it is important in our research to bring oneself into the interpretive process in order to consider its contributions in context, in its intentionality, and from our contemporary perspective. Surely we must consider ourselves before we can hope to perfect our understanding of religious facts and ideas? The question of the method of approach to Egyptian texts here becomes secondary to the "self-evident object" of a preliminary exploration, because the latter is only an instrument dependent on the convictions and considerations that make the hermeneut the active agent by which analysis and translation are carried out.

Following upon the Eliadean hermeneutical process and in order to make our histories useful, our research must bear fruit and our inquiries be intelligible and accessible to our contemporaries by actualization or by the exemplification of the ancient religious facts in other historical, modern facts ("Methodological Remarks on the Study of Religious Symbolism" 88). Contemporary rereading in the light of actual discourse puts into perspective a belief, an ancient religious fact, a problem relevant to modern *homo religious*, by promoting reflection and exchanges within the context of the academic study of the meanings thus revealed. In short, it is necessary to build a bridge between history and religion, all the more because this rereading subscribes to the same processes as the combinative play of the ancient Egyptian scribes.

In conclusion, it is imperative to correct the error created by the objectivization of the interpretive process which makes too little of our presuppositions and too much of the gulf between self and object, which removes all religious quality from the "text." The work of historians of religions, just as that of Egyptologists, must be able to expose our limitations and situate our results in the midst of the totality of the humanities. This is all the more important in an era in which the tendency toward overspecialization is augmented by the rationalization of the disciplines, entailing methodological normativity.

The study of ancient religious facts and ideas is not the fruit of some romantic nostalgia for a lost golden age, barely good for stocking the dusty shelves of university libraries, because it contains ideas and questions on which the present state of human heritage can be rethought. Isn't history an enigma, eternally misremembered, and isn't the human being a hermeneut who, from conception has been, is, and will remain in search of meaning?

NOTES

This article is a summary of the introduction to the third part of my doctoral thesis, *Le Papyrus de Berlin 3024, l'herméneutique d'une ontophanie*. I would like to take this opportunity to thank Dr. Bryan S. Rennie for his kindness and patience in its translation.

1. Especially when he could have no access to sources written in a language of which he had no mastery (Tristan, Coulianu et al., *Mircea Eliade. Dialogues avec le sacré*).

2. The Egyptian texts he mentions are translated by eminent specialists such as Gardiner, Moret, Vandier, Sethe, etc. See, for example, the chapter on ancient Egypt in his *History of Religious Ideas*, volume I 85–113, or again, in *Cosmos and History: The Myth of the Eternal Return* 30 n.54 on Egyptian royalty.

3. An interesting analysis of the scholarly criticisms put forward in this way can be seen in Rennie, *Reconstructing Eliade* 179–212.

4. *Journal II* 121; *Quest* 1–2; 29 n.7; 57–61, where he refers to some of his preliminary suggestions.

5. Ries, "Science des religions et sciences humaines" 337. On Dumézil see Ries, "Archéologie, mythologie, philologie" 14–21.

6. A work whose "organic" nature one cannot deny since Eliade writes, "[I]t is only the totality of my writings that can reveal the meaning of my work. . . . I have never managed to write a book that represents me totally." *Ordeal by Labyrinth* 187.

7. It is in this sense that one should understand the title of the symposium at the 18th International Congress of the IAHR in Durban from 5 to 12

of August 2000: *Mircea Eliade's Vision and Our Present Understanding of Religion*, as well as Rennie's chapter, "Eliade's Political Involvement," in *Reconstructing Eliade* 175–77, and also Robert Ellwood's *The Politics of Myth* 79–126.

8. Cf. Eliade's section on "The Inhibitions of the Specialist" in *The Two and the One*, 193–95.

9. Long, "The Significance for Modern Man of Mircea Eliade's Work." For the distinction between "sense" and "meanings" see Marino, *L'herméneutique de Mircea Eliade* 37 and Rastier, "Sens et signification" 8 *et passim*.

10. For Eliade multiplicity in the variety of solutions initiates critical and philosophical reflection. *Quest* 133. See also Rennie, "Relativism," in *Reconstructing Eliade* 121ff., especially the conclusion of that section on page 132, and the section on ontological assumptions, 197–204.

11. To give only a few examples: on the conflict between Osiris and Seth as well as on the intimate relation between the regeneration of historical time and primordial time (*sep tep*), see *The Myth of the Eternal Return* 29 and 56; on the microcosm as world-image see *Myth and Reality* 40 and 48, *Images and Symbols* 37–41, *A History of Religious Ideas*, vol. I 85–113. However, more caution should be taken in consulting *The Eliade Guide to World Religions* as this is a posthumous publication written with Ioan Couliano.

12. This is the case of the understandable error of Henri Frankfort on the subject of the ka (i.e., Life force, *Kingship and the gods* 64) taken up by Eliade (*A History of Religious Ideas*, vol. I 85–113), which claims that the ka, the vital energy of being, would never have been depicted. Now, hieroglyphic writing contains the representation of the ka (see signs D160–D188 of the extended library of hieroglyphs in Hannig, *Die Sprache der Pharaonen, 2800–950*).

13. One can find several extracts from Egyptian texts, collated and classified by religious topics, in *From Primitives to Zen*. Even though the translations are out of date the classification remains valuable since it relies on the dominant religious topic of the text.

14. More than half a century separates us from the historical observations he reports and these inevitably must, for the same reason as the classics of Egyptology, be updated. For example, section 30 of *A History of Religious Ideas*, vol. I and sections 13.3 and 13.6 of *The Eliade Guide to World Religions*.

15. Varille, "Il faut attaquer les problèmes essentiels de l'égyptologie. Querelle des égyptologues—nouveaux débats" 269–74; De Gandillac, "Le temple dans l'Homme et l'homme dans le monde. Symbolique du temple égyptien," 359–73. [The quarrel was between "realists" and "symbolists." See *Images and Symbols* 177, ed.]

16. *The Myth of the Eternal Return* 37, where he mentions the paradigmatic myth of the struggle between the Hero and giant serpent that he recognizes in that of the Pharaoh and the serpent mentioned in the *Book of Apophis*.

17. For more details see Ouellet, *Le Papyrus de Berlin 3024, l'herméneutique d'une ontophanie* 2004, 231–41. Hornung in his book *Idea into Image: Essays on Ancient Egyptian Thought* unfortunately reduces these fundamental concepts of the understanding to simple iconic ideas instead of understanding them as the categories sine qua non of the ancient Egyptians' system of thought.

18. The term and its derivatives are here employed in the double sense of "performative" as the result of an enunciation and of effectiveness, see Vernus, "Langue littéraire et diglossie" 557, n. 2.

19. For a good synthesis of the concept of *neter* and of the problems inherent in its comprehension, see "The Egyptian Gods" by Tobin, 35–56 and Goedicke, "God," 57–62.

20. As in African thought, cf. Cikala, "L'homme africain et le sacré." See also Hornung, *Les dieux de l'Égypte: Le Un et le multiple*.

21. For a more complete list see Erman and Grapow, *Wörterbuch der ägyptischen Sprache* VI 75 and *Pyramid Texts* §621a–c; 752a–753b; *Coffin Texts* IIB 4,7,3; VII 448a–c, etc.

22. On the subject of the inherent relations between the different elements of creation, see *Coffin Texts* 80, II, 28–43. On the *ka* as vital essence (e.g., *Book of the Dead* §15).

23. "Ma'at will return to its throne when Isfet has been subdued." (*Jw MAa.t r jjt r s.t = s Jsf.t dr.ty r rwty*), *The Prophecy of Nefertiti* 67. Isfet is frequently associated with the chaos that some have associated with the *Unordnung* of the German scholars (Jean Leclant, "Espace et temps, ordre et chaos dans l'Égypte pharaonique" 223).

24. The original source of Nun conveys the heterogeneous quantities and qualities of the demiurge Atum, whose name derives from the verb *tm*, "to complete," "to achieve," rather than "to exist." It designates not only that which is, but also that which comes to be, or, rather, that which tends toward perfection (*nefer*) and peace (*hotep*). (*Coffin Texts* §317, IV, 114i, B2L; §335, IV, 188/9a + c; §80, II, 40c and Bickel, *La cosmogonie égyptienne avant le Nouvel Empire*, 134. Nun is the dark and shadowy Creator, limitless potential. It is not surprising that life (*ankh*) should be intimately associated with the glorious light or with divine power (*akh*). (*Coffin Texts* I, 81e).

25. It is in the context of regeneration that the Royal Rites must be placed, such as the jubilant celebration of the coronation (Reeder, "Ritualized

Death and Rebirth: Running the *Heb Sed*"), or again, the use of the example of the "First Time" in the royal ideology (Vernus, "L'idéologie pharaonique").

26. Pharaoh, divine Son of Atum and of Geb, is the pillar of Egyptian civilization and his actions guarantee the permanence and stability of the universe. Cf. *Pyramid Texts, Spell* 586 §1582–83, passim; Eliade, *A History of Religious Ideas*, vol. I 86 and Ouellet, *Divinisation et culte du souverain dans le Proche-Orient ancien*, passim.

27. Cf. amongst others: *Pyramid Texts, Spell* 506, 535, 577; *Coffin Texts, Spell* 945, VII, 159–61; *Book of the Dead* §76.

28. See Eliade, *Journal I*, 12 (20 January 1946), 15 (12 March 1946), 20 (19 July 1946), 90 (3 April 1949); Ricoeur, *Time and Narrative, vol. III: Narrated Time* 241–74, especially 246 n.3; Shlomith Rimmon-Kenan, *Narrative Fiction: Contemporary Poetics* 29–42, 59–70; Ruth Ronen, "Fictional Entities, Incomplete Being."

29. On the "performance" aspect of this type of discourse, cf. Ricoeur, *Time and Narrative, volume II: The Configuration of Time in Fictional Narrative* 97–101.

30. Or, rather, I should say "mythemic" (*les mythèmes*) (Bickel 265–83).

31. It would be very interesting to go more thoroughly into the functional parity of fictional discourse in Egyptian, Eliadean, and postmodern writing. Rennie has already opened discussion of the two latter points (*Reconstructing Eliade* chapter 17).

32. Derchain also calls them "generative thought alliterations" (allitérations génératrices de pensées) in "Théologie et littérature" 354. It is thus that the texts of the wisdom tradition (*sebayt*) develop, such as the well-known "Dialogue of a Desperate Man with his Soul," (cf. Ouellet, *"Le désillusionné et son ba"* chapter 1.2.2). For the expression "perfected utterance" (*discours parfaits*) (i.e., md.wt nfr.wt) cf. Vernus, "Langue littéraire et diglossie" 556–57.

33. Leclant, "Espace et temps, ordre et chaos dans l'Égypte pharaonique" passim. For a discussion of the meaning of *illud tempus* and *in illo tempore*, see Rennie, *Reconstructing Eliade* 81 n.1.

34. "In this sense, the time of the narrative participates in eternity and contributes, paradoxically beyond any consideration of precision or chronology, to the timelessness of myth" (Guilhou, "Temps du récit et temps du mythe" 88–89).

35. Vernus, *Essai sur la conscience de l'Histoire dans l'Égypte pharaonique* is a very interesting study of the concept of history.

36. [The XVIIIth dynasty was that which included Akhenanten, proponent of the monotheistic worship of Aten—ed.]

37. It is thus not rare to see archeological digs or the results of scientific analysis come to contradict Egyptian statements. For an example of the mis-

understanding of hermeneutical process, see Van Walsem, "Interpretation of Evidence."

38. Björkman, "Egyptology and Historical Method"; Redford, "Historical Sources: Textual Evidence."

39. For example: Loprieno, "Defining Egyptian Literature: Ancient Texts and Modern Theories"; Foster, "Thought Couplets and the Standard Theory"; Baines, "Prehistories of Literature: Performance, Fiction, Myth."

40. It is to this knowledge that Eliade refers in his *Journal III* 93–94. For example, how could one explain the case of the honorific contraposition in the construction of royal names without reference to religious facts and ideas?

41. Pharaonic interior design, for example; Lurson, "Symétrie axiale et diagonale: deux principes d'organisation du décor de la salle E du temple de Gerf Hussein." For connections between text and image, see Bryan, "The Disjunction of Text and Image in Egyptian Art."

42. On this, see Ricoeur, "Poétique et symbolique"; and "From a Hermeneutics of Text to a Hermeneutics of Action" 105–266.

43. Loprieno, "Defining Egyptian Literature" and Assmann, "Cultural and Literary Texts."

44. The use of this expression, which I appropriated from the vocabulary of geology, effectively renders my point. Like stratified rock, the text is constituted by a sum of organized meanings that must be deciphered.

45. The analogy with the Internet is not without interest because each element of the Egyptian text is to be taken in its entire array, like an immense Web site or hypertext with hyperlinks, expressing themselves simultaneously on several planes through several "languages" and referring the one to the other in a myriad of significative possibilities enabled by the information superhighway. Egyptian text, its discourse, its expressions are of this same order.

46. Foster, "Thought Couplets in Khety's *Hymn to the Inundation*"; "Wordplay in *The Eloquent Peasant*: The Eighth Complaint."

47. For example, in my doctoral research on the *Lebensmüde* (*Le Papyrus de Berlin 3024*, 231–41), after a reading of earlier research and a preliminary analysis of its "textual" characteristics, I concluded that a combination of literary criticism and of structural and phenomenological analysis of the metalanguage would promote such self-authentication.

The Significance of Mircea Eliade for the Study of the New Testament

Joseph Muthuraj

INTRODUCTION

This chapter is not born out of extensive research aimed at testing and evaluating the overall contributions made by Mircea Eliade, but has grown out of a sustained reading of the works of Eliade, which led to an appreciation and appropriation of the "message" in his writings. The paper is restricted by a lack of access to Eliade's corpus as a whole. I am not working in a place where the complete works of Eliade are or can be made available.[1] Further, a huge amount of secondary literature on Eliade was not within my reach, and this has prevented me from situating my reading of him within contemporary efforts to study Eliade.[2] However, there is a proverb in the Tamil language, which says that every part of a sugar cane is sweet and no one needs to eat the entire sugar cane to testify to its sweetness.

    I formulate my experience of reading Eliade as a student engaged in the study of Christian theology, particularly that of the New Testament, with the purpose of making use of his insights in the search for developing new perspectives and paradigms to do theology. New Testament discipline is one of the fields of study within "Theology" and NT subjects are part of theological curricula. It is nourished by those scholars who have competence in philology, historical criticism, literary criticism, philosophy, sociology, and history of religions (Epp and MacRae, *The New Testament and Its Modern Interpreters xxi*). The study of the NT, however, still remains as a branch within the intellectual tradition of the Western Enlightenment era.

HISTORY OF RELIGIONS SCHOOL IN NT SCHOLARSHIP

In the past two centuries, there were serious attempts to study the NT from history of religions perspectives. Scholars of repute, Wrede, Hilgenfeld, Pfleiderer, Gunkel, Dalman, Deissman, Bousset, Reitzenstein, Weiss, and Bultmann made significant contributions.[3] Equally influential were scholars such as Wellhausen, Harnack, Jülicher, Feine, Heinrici, Deissner, who opposed the new methodological principle, namely, history of religions, for the study of the history of early Christianity.[4] Space does not permit me to evaluate the contributions made by all of them or even any one of them. The main characteristic of the history of religions school was "to interpret primitive Christianity within the framework of the religions of the time" (Boers, *What is New Testament Theology?*). It sought to explain Christianity as a product of the development of the spirit of classical antiquity. It was argued that the designation "history of primitive Christian religion" and not "New Testament theology" is more suitable to refer to the study of the New Testament (Hasel, *New Testament Theology*). Hence the task of New Testament scholarship was regarded as an attempt to depict primitive Christian religion. Its questions, therefore, were rightly concerned with the relationship between early Christianity and contemporary religious phenomena found in Judaism, Hellenism, and Orientalism.

Jewish and Hellenistic antecedents were uncovered by many studies. The significant contribution made by the history of religions was that it brought to light the role played by oriental religion and piety in the formation of NT religion (e.g., Bousset, *Kyrios Christos*). However, many scholars regard Orientalism as a bane of Christianity and describe it in a pejorative sense as being syncretistic. The term *oriental* is often used as referring to something inimical to the true nature of Christianity. Some even understand and interpret New Testament Christianity as a triumph achieved over the oriental religions.[5] As a student of history of religions within NT studies, which remains largely Occidental in its approach and conclusions, I look for further inspiration from history of religions scholars, particularly from the contributions made by Eliade to the study of the religious dimensions of NT religion. In the past half-century, Christian theology and history of religions functioned with little mutual influence (again, Cobb 5). It is hoped that my reading of this historian of religions will help to create an interest among NT students to incorporate some of his insights into the study of New Testament. The streams of both disciplines should flow close to each other so that there might take place a creative interplay of their perspectives.

AN INDIAN ATTEMPT

The second objective of my reading the works of Eliade is that India left an indelible mark on his spiritual quest, which actually received its impetus and animation from Eliade's brief stay in India. Eliade devoted himself fully to the task of learning Indian religion and philosophy. He regarded Surendranath Dasgupta as his master and guru. Eliade drank from the wells of Indian religious heritage.[6] His knowledge of Yoga, Indian philosophical systems, Indian epics, Vedas, Upanishads, Buddhism, Jainism, Indian folklore, art, alchemy, popular myths and rituals has made him one of the best Indologists that the West has ever produced. He also has showed a sympathetic attitude toward India's struggle for freedom from colonial rule. These have generated within me kindred feelings toward Eliade and hence the question I would like to ask is, "Is Eliade showing the way for an Indian student who is engaged in the study NT history and Theology?"

IS ELIADE A CHRISTIAN THEOLOGIAN?

First of all, it is to be noted that Eliade has shown a covert interest in Christian theology. Eliade spoke of the "theology" implied in the history of religions, which he attempted to decipher and interpret (Olson, *The Theology and Philosophy of Eliade* 45). But he felt that he was not accountable for the faith of his fellow men, which probably is the duty of a theologian. He was not a "theologian" in the traditional sense of the term and did not undergo any formal theological training (Olson 54). In many places, he begins a discussion or an explanation of a religious phenomenon in a theological fashion but, to the disappointment of the theologians, he does not take them farther. The following words indicate his typical reaction: "I am not speaking theologically, for which I have neither the responsibility nor the competence" (*Images and Symbols* 157–58). Yet one can catch a glimpse of theological reasoning underpinning his writings. Eliade's sources, which gave theological coating to his creative work, came largely from the writings of the early Church Fathers. Nonetheless, he felt that the polemical stance taken by the Church Fathers against other religions was not strictly necessary "in our own day" (*Images and Symbols* 157). Biblical references are very rarely found in his writings,[7] yet he deals with Biblical themes such as God, Christ, cross, baptism, and symbols and images in the Bible.

Death of God Theology—Sky and Sky Gods

Eliade wrote about "the sky and sky gods" when Christian theology was shaken at its very foundations by the "Death of God" theology. He spoke of "God up there" when theologians such as J. A. T. Robinson were busy abolishing the mythical language of a three-storied universe that underlies early Christian thought and experience. Robinson argued in favor of "the detaching of the Christian doctrine of God from any necessary dependence on a 'supernaturalistic' worldview" (Edwards, *The Honest to God Debate* 236). He understood this as a prophetic aspect of the church's ministry to the world (*Honest to God Debate* 241). At this time atheism was regarded as the Christian Gospel that should be preached to the world (Altizer, *The Gospel of Christian Atheism*). T. J. J. Altizer, for example, maintained this boldly by stating, "Throughout its history Christian theology has been thwarted from reaching its intrinsic goal by its bondage to a transcendent, a sovereign, and an impassive God" ("The Death of God and the Uniqueness of Christianity" 129). Eliade criticized the Death of God theology and argued that it was based on an understanding of God who was withdrawn from the earth and forgotten by human beings (*deus otiosus*). For Eliade, God is indefinable and the moment we attempt to define God in clear-cut language we then lose the mystery of God (Olson 105). The second chapter in *Patterns in Comparative Religion* provides a good treatment on the subject of "The Sky and Sky Gods." There is almost a universal belief in a celestial divine being that created the universe, guarantees the fecundity of the earth, and protects life. The sky is associated with a wealth of mythological and religious significance. " 'Height,' 'being on high,' infinite space—all these are hierophanies of what is transcendent, what is supremely sacred" (*Patterns* 109). The Supreme Beings associated with sky hierophanies are creators, and they give life. These sky gods phenomena were subjected to monotheistic beliefs. These motifs are reflected in the speeches made by Paul and Barnabas in Lystra (Acts 14: 15–18) and the famous proclamation by Paul before the Areopagus in the multireligious city Athens (Acts 17: 22–31).

Cosmic Christianity

The Letters to the Ephesians and Colossians make reference to a "Cosmic Christ" (Eph. 1: 17–23; Col. 2: 5–11). There are theologians in India who spoke of the "cosmic Christ." Eliade's idea of cosmic Christianity has some interesting theological features. He understood Christianity not in terms of the categories of Western Europe. He observed that the myths and symbols of pre-Christian Europe survived in Christianity in Central and Western Europe as St. Georges and St. Eliases (*Myth and Reality* 171), whereas in Southern and Southeastern Europe, the church was imbued with many cosmic symbols. The religious experience peculiar to the rural populations was nourished by what he called "cosmic Christianity." Cosmic Christianity, for Eliade, was a peasant-centered religion with its array of cosmic liturgies and religious folklores (*Myth and Reality* 172). It was not a paganization of Christianity and was not expressed by a scholastic theology. It was a popular theology that was built on the meaning and significance of seasonal festivals and religious folklore, which reflect the life of the common folk. Thus, cosmic symbols of folkloric themes such as water, tree, vine, the plough and the axe, the ship, chariot, etc., which had been already assimilated by Judaism were passed on to the church, which gave them sacramental meaning.

Christology

Christology received a new dimension in Eliade's popular theology, which has cosmic dimensions. His Christology, in one sense, was local and was bound with the social and political realities of Romania. Romania's literary creations and religious observances, according to Eliade, are entrenched in devotion to Christ. Eliade then went on to claim that the images of Christ in the Gospels stand in no contradiction to images of Christ in religious folklore. But he did not go on to demonstrate it, which a NT student would have liked him to do. For a Christian, Eliade considered the incarnation of God in Jesus Christ as a supreme hierophany, a manifestation of the sacred (*Sacred and the Profane* 11). In Christian folklore, the Cross is conceived as Cosmic Tree, a universal symbol of hierophany. The tree constitutes religious life and is seen as (1) altar, (2) image of the cosmos, (3) cosmic theophany, (4) symbol of life, (5) center of the world and support of the universe, (6) mystical bond between tree and men, and (7) symbol of resurrection of vegetation of spring and of the "rebirth" of the year (*Patterns* 266–67). Theology of the Cross is a theology of the Cosmic Tree, an ideogram in several cultures but particularly in Mesopotamian and Vedic writings. The idea of cosmic renovation symbolized by the World Tree was continued by the salvation from the Cross (*Two and the One* 210). Eliade explained the cosmic Christianity of the rural population as being dominated by "nostalgia for a Nature sanctified by the presence of Jesus" (*Symbolism, the Sacred, and the Arts* 38). This nostalgia has social and political dimensions, as it is for the restoration of Nature from wars, devastation, and conquest. It also refers to the state of liberation from the exploitation of the peasants by various classes and masters. For Eliade, liberation was "a passive revolt against the tragedy and injustice of History" (*Myth and Reality* 175).

Hence, social justice and liberation are central to the popular Christology envisioned by Eliade. He saw in Marxist communism a messianic Judeo-Christian ideology at work. According to Eliade, the great eschatological myths of the Asian-Mediterranean world and millennialist structures underlie Marxism. Thus, Marxism is embedded in Judeo-Christian eschatological hope of an absolute end to history. The content of this hope is: (1) Marx ascribes soteriological function to the proletariat, (2) the apocalyptic conflict between Good and Evil exists in society, and (3) the final victory belongs to Christ. Eliade brought sacredness to the peasant struggle in history and saw a Christological basis for achieving victory at the end (183–84).

Eliade clearly saw a role for Marxism, which, he thought, enriched the myth of the Golden Age found in many religious traditions by working toward building a classless society (*Myths, Dreams, and Mysteries* 25ff.). What is to be noted here is that Eliade saw some religious basis for Marxism but he had no hierophanic explanation for what he called, "the racist myth of 'Aryanism.'"[8] He did use the word *Aryan* in his writings but the sense in which it was used during World War II is not to be found. Eliade contended that Nazism replaced the Judeo-Christian eschatology with Nordic paganism. Christian values were abolished in order to rediscover the spiritual sources of race. When this was translated into political realities, Eliade described it as "a pessimistic vision of the end of history" (*Myths, Dreams, and Mysteries* 27).

Whatever his political affiliations were in Romania and whether his political ideology backfired or not, it should be said that Eliade probably was a nationalist who had a cosmic vision. Eliade was a nationalist to the extent that he desired freedom for the peasant communities of Eastern Europe from oppression and invasion. In his own words, "As for the rural peoples of Eastern Europe, they succeeded in bearing disasters and persecution principally by virtue of the cosmic Christianity.... The conception of a cosmos redeemed by the death and resurrection of the Savior, and sanctified by the footsteps of God, of Jesus, the Virgin, and the saints, made possible."[9] The terror of history was the time in bondage for Romanians who were in the hands of oppressive forces, which invaded Romania time and again. He summed it up thus: "There is no effective military or political defense against the 'terror of history,' simply because of the crushing inequality between the invaders and the invaded peoples.... Small political groups of peasants could not long resist the masses of the invaders" (*Zalmoxis* 254). But the folk genius gave the most effective response through folklore, which transformed these misfortunes into moments of joy and happiness. This quest and longing for freedom, according to Eliade, was sustained by their devotion to cosmic Christianity.

Cosmic Christianity transcends narrow nationalism. Eliade affirmed that cosmic Christianity existed not only in places such as rural Romania but was also to be found in rural religious life in India, Africa, and the Mediterranean region. It injects solidarity among the suffering masses whoever they are and wherever they happen to live. It is in this struggle for identity, which cuts across geographical and ethnic boundaries, Eliade found the true meaning of Christianity. In this sense, Eliade can be seen as a theologian of cosmic Christianity.

MIRCEA ELIADE AND PAUL TILLICH

It is generally accepted that Eliade's contributions have had a wide influence in other fields of study, even among theologians. What does Christian theology have to do with history of religions? There are those who advocate the meeting of the two in a manner that will benefit both. There are, on the other hand, those who think that the concerns of the two are not compatible with each other. The relationship between the two disciplines is discussed from the point of view of theology providing the normative base to the study of religions. Douglas Allen is of the view that history of religions must be "aided by and dependent upon a normative discipline such as theology" (Allen, *Structure and Creativity* 77). Joseph Kitagawa, a colleague of Eliade, admits that a theological history of religions is legitimate and admissible but should be kept distinct from the "humanistic" history of religions, which develops sufficient understanding of classical forms of religious phenomena. For Kitagawa, *Religionswissenschaft* and theology can interact but they remain separate. Eric J. Lott, one of my mentors, stresses that Christian theology should be dependent upon religious studies. He suggests, "For theology cannot function reflectively and contextually in an isolated state of independence from other religious traditions and ignorant of the findings of religious studies" (*Vision, Tradition, Interpretation* 233).

The main concern was with regard to theologians' attitude toward other religions and this was deeply challenged by history of religions research. Hendrik Kraemer, for example, took the Bible as the basis for judging the value of other religions. He argues that "theology is fully entitled to formulate the case and to say its personal word on the problem of religion and religions, on the basis of its peculiar presuppositions" (*Religion and the Christian Faith* 143). Kraemer considers Hindu spirituality to be antagonistic to biblical revelation. He maintains, "It is impossible, from the Indian standpoint, to understand and interpret true Christianity adequately. It can, in principle, only be a rock offence, 'foolishness' " (117). Certainly, one will find that Kraemer's views are at odds with Eliade. The most effective criticism against such theology comes from Kees W. Bolle. In his article "History of Religions with a Hermeneutic Oriented toward Christian Theology?" Bolle criticizes the form of theological hermeneutic that operates along the lines of certain fixed contrasts. They are, "the others" and "we"; "paganism/heathens" and "the true religion"; "natural religion" and "the revealed religion"; etc. (111). Most NT studies are based on such fallacious distinctions and premises. He points out, "An extraneous contrast between the 'pagan' and the 'Christian' does not come up in the major (theological) arguments" (117). Bolle advocates the deprovincialization of Christian theology so that theology incorporates the idea of universality. He observes,

> It is a ghastly symptom that some modern Christian theologians, paying attention to religious man, can consider the subject closed with a few lines on Buddhism and Hinduism, the only concern being to safeguard the Christian faith on an intellectual plane by comparing it to *the other*, superficially conceived religious notions. (114, emphasis added)

Bolle concludes his article rather pessimistically by pointing to the inevitability of retaining the question mark in the title of his article with the suggestion that separation of Christian theology and history of religions could be seen as strength rather than as weakness on the part of each discipline. For Bolle, it is perhaps a gain to history of religions (118).

Paul Tillich, a distinguished Systematic Theologian, who was the personal friend of Eliade, responded most positively to the challenges that history of religions posed to the theologians. He, like Bolle, criticized theologians' viewpoint of the "other." Tillich argued that the significance of history of religions for Christian theology can only be grasped if the theologian is willing to accept and work on the basis of five presuppositions. They are: (1) revelatory experiences are common to all religions, (2) revelation is received under finite human conditions, (3) the three types of criticisms, mystical, prophetic, and secular, help to address the distortions that crept into revealed religions, (4) history of religions makes "a concrete theology that has universal significance" possible, and (5) "the sacred is the creative ground and at the same time a critical judgment of the secular" ("The Significance of the History of Religions for the Systematic Theologian"). These are the fruits of the interchange between theology and history of religion. These should be pursued and possibilities of further interpenetration should be explored. Tillich still saw possibilities for interaction and collaboration between history of religions and Christian theology. The following remarks made by Paul Tillich are worth noting:

> I now want to return my thanks on this point to my friend Professor Eliade for two years of seminars and the co-operation we had in them. In these seminars I experienced that every individual doctrinal statement or ritual expression of Christianity receives *a new intensity of meaning*. And in terms of a kind of apologia, yet also a self-accusation, I must say that my own Systematic Theology was written before these seminars.... Its purpose was the discussion or the answering of questions coming from the scientific and philosophical criticism of Christianity. But perhaps we need a longer, more intensive period of *interpenetration* of systematic theological study and religious historical studies.... This is my *hope* for the future of theology. (252, emphasis added)

Every student of theology and religion should cherish this hope and work toward its realization.

ELIADE'S CRITIQUE OF THEOLOGIANS

Eliade lived and wrote at a time when theological writings urged for the separation of "religion" and "Christianity" (see particularly Cobb,

"Is Christianity a Religion?" 3–11). When Bonhoeffer called persistently for "Religionless Christianity," and when Karl Barth declared that Christianity was not a religion, Eliade was occupied with validating religious inquiries in the study of religious phenomena. He insisted that religious phenomena can be interpreted only if they are studied as something religious. "To try to grasp the essence of such phenomena by means of physiology, psychology, sociology, economics, linguistics, art or any other study is false; it misses the one unique and irreducible element in it—the element of the sacred" (*Patterns* xi). Perhaps one should understand here the two basic distinctions made by Eliade in the methodology of the study of religious phenomena. One concentrated on the characteristic structures of religious phenomena, that is, the essence of religion and the other in their historical contexts, in order to discover and communicate their history (*The Sacred and the Profane* 232). Eliade interpreted Christian experience on the basis of cross-cultural parallels irrespective of their historical contexts, which divide humanity on the basis of language, geography, and religion.

Eliade saw differences in the roles of historian of religions and theologian. He maintained that the very procedures of the historian of religions are dissimilar from those of a theologian. A theologian aims to see in the content of a religious experience the clearer and deeper understanding of the relationship between God-Creator and man-creature, whereas a historian of religions concentrates primarily on religious symbols and completes his/her analysis of religious phenomena as a phenomenologist or philosopher of religion ("Methodological Remarks on the Study of Religious Symbolism" 88–90). Eliade's challenge to the theologians should be taken seriously (*Quest* 66–68). He criticized theologians for two reasons. He commented that theologians are "suspicious of historico-religious hermeneutics that might encourage syncretism or religious dilettantism or worse yet, raise doubts about the uniqueness of the Judeo-Christian revelation" (*Quest* 67). He recognized the importance of Judaism, from which many of the antecedents of early Christian myth and understanding of history came. Unlike an anti-Semitic theologian, Eliade stressed the firm historical connection between Judaism and Christianity. He acknowledged that "Christianity is a historic religion, deeply rooted in another historic religion, that of the Jews" (*Images and Symbols* 157). Judaism, for him, had a long religious history and prehistory and was resplendent with myths and symbols, which were acquired by Christianity. This did not leave Judaism exhausted of its meaning and significance. However, Eliade hesitated to assign a privileged position to the Judeo-Christian tradition, as he argued that there are images and symbols in Christianity, which are common properties of the entire religious history of humanity (*Rites and Symbols* 1).

His second criticism was that "many contemporary theologians have already accepted the presuppositions of the sociology of religion and are ready to accept the inevitability of technology" (*Quest* 67–68). Science and technology treat religions and religious behavior as something other than superstition and ignorance. Sociologists Weber and Durkheim made religion central to their theory of society. They drew their definition of religion from the point of view of its impact on society. This sociological definition restricts and at times eliminates other dimensions of meaning in religion.

Thirdly, Eliade observed that theological study seeks to study selected data from monotheistic religions rather than from the so-called primitive materials and, moreover, that secondary importance is accorded to religions of the Mediterranean world ("Methodological Remarks" 89). This is very much the case with NT studies, which deals with the description of early Christianity. An accurate knowledge of the broader and heterogeneous Mediterranean cultures is fundamental to that description. NT scholarship ignores the Afro-Asiatic landscape of the Eastern Mediterranean in favor of the Western Mediterranean world, which is regarded as the seedbed of European civilization. Alice Bach argues that the biblical scholar assumes a divinity that is congenial to and arises out of the myths of Greece and Rome, the Mediterranean roots of European culture ("Whatever Happened to Dionysus" 91). The discarded aspects of Rome and Greece, Egypt and Ethiopia had oriental elements derived from the religious and cultural traditions of the Indo-Iranian landscape. As a result we have an account of early Christianity that is Occidental in nature and is opposed to the other, the Orient. This created the Christian/pagan distinction in the reading of the NT.[10]

One of the contributions of Eliade that would have great significance for the study of NT history, is that he saw cultural contacts and reciprocal influences between the Indo-Iranian, Mesopotamian, and Mediterranean worlds (*Shamanism* 500ff.). Once this cultural bond is recognized then the NT world need not be narrowly defined. Quite rightly, in his second volume of *A History of Religious Ideas* Eliade considered Vedas, Upanishads, Yoga, Buddhism, Jainism, Mahabharata, Bhagavad Gita, Greco-Oriental Mysteries, and Iranian religious synthesis as forerunners of Christianity. The fact that they are a prolegomena to NT religion should be applied as one of the most important criteria for historical interpretation in NT studies. Eastern civilization can be proud of the contribution it has made to the makeup of the world of thought that saw the birth of NT Christianity. It will enable an Indian student of the NT to find his/her rightful place in NT scholarship. Eliade understood syncretism not in a pejorative sense but as something inherent in culture and religion that encouraged them to influence each other. It is not a sign of weakness but strength. We need to reexamine the methods of history and categories of theological interpretation in the light of the criticisms made by Eliade.

THE CREATIVE HERMENEUTICS OF ELIADE

History of religions has found some of its most powerful formulation in the writings of Eliade. We shall now identify some of its key principles, procedures, and methods, which can be assimilated into the methodological framework of the study of the NT. History of religions should be governed by what Eliade called a "creative hermeneutics." There are two important aspects to it.

1. Eliade urged that Western thought should be open to new perspectives by breaking the confinements of provincialism. He wrote, "Western philosophy cannot contain itself indefinitely within its own tradition without the risk of becoming provincial" (*Quest* 63). Western consciousness recognizes "only one history, the Universal history, and that the ethnocentric history is surpassed as being provincial" (52). The works of historians of religion in the nineteenth century failed to be creative and to achieve "interpretive cultural syntheses in favor of fragmented, analytical research" (58).

This suggestion by Eliade is vital for NT hermeneutics, too, as we seek to intermingle Western and Eastern modes of inquiries to acquire a holistic vision.

2. Eliade's creative hermeneutics changes man (28—I make no attempt to correct gender exclusive language in Eliade). Man and method cannot remain separate. It prepares man to encounter "foreign" worlds, their myths and rituals. Worlds hitherto unknown to Western consciousness are making inroads into history. Eliade acknowledged the value of freedom from Western rule attained by countries such as India and stressed the need for incorporating a wider world, Oriental, Australian, African, and Oceanian, into the scope of history of religions. Europe has had dialogue and exchange with extra-European spiritualities, but mainly in the field of arts. A creative encounter must happen between scholars—not just among artists. This was not merely an attempt on the part of Eliade to create a new methodological principle but a demand for a change in the attitude and approach of historians of religions toward "foreign" religious forms. Douglas Allen is right when he observes that Eliade derived "much of his methodological framework from religious phenomena of the more 'inclusivistic' Eastern traditions" (*Structure and Creativity* 200).

There are attempts in NT studies to devise methods that will introduce new forms of exegesis, informed by social scientific input. Theological education is involved in an effort to try out, practice, and establish necessary norms of hermeneutics. A theological student in India cannot ask, consciously or unconsciously, Western questions and undertake research that will be meaningful only to Westerners. The elements of creative hermeneutics as proposed by Eliade can pave the way for dialogue to create a wider cultural base for the study of the NT, which has hitherto been dominated by European and North American worldviews.

ELIADE AND RUDOLPH BULTMANN

Another important aspect of Eliade's contribution is found in his critical response to twentieth-century existentialism. Existentialism has been one of the preferred dialogue partners for NT theologians. Martin Heidegger's existentialism had a strong impact on Rudolf Bultmann's thinking, and it played a formative role in modern NT theology (Johnson, *Rudolf Bultmann: Interpreting Faith for the Modern Era* 22). The disciplines represented by Eliade and Bultmann, though different, found their hermeneutical contexts the same. Both wrote in the context of existential philosophy, which gripped Western thinking. Bultmann began writing in the early decades of the twentieth century, that is, the time between the two world wars. To both men, philosophical concerns, particularly existential philosophical issues, posed important challenges.[11] Eliade and Bultmann chose to walk by two divergent paths and arrived naturally at two different conclusions.

DEMYTHOLOGIZATION

Bultmann argued that existential language provides a frame of reference that will help us to understand myths and symbols. Many have embraced Bultmann's demythologization method. Yet the word *demythologization* is seen as bearing a negative connotation, to the extent that it became a nightmarish word to his critics. Karl Barth wrote, "If the wicked (Christian) world fails to understand him (Bultmann), much of the blame is due to his invention of this word (demythologization), so uninspiring and negative" ("Rudolf Bultmann—An Attempt to Understand Him" 102). The following remarks will help as a minimum characterization of what Bultmann meant by "myth."

First, NT cosmology is mythical in character. It views the world as a three-storied universe of heaven above, hell below, and earth in between when there is no scientific evidence for such an assumption. Secondly, heaven can neither be conceived as a dwelling place for God, nor hell as the place for Satan and his demons. Thirdly, miracles are inconceivable because "it is impossible to use electric light and the wireless and to avail ourselves of modern medical and surgical discoveries, and at the same time to believe in the New Testament world of spirits and miracles" (5). Further, according to Bultmann, the events of redemption are presented in the NT in a mythological way. God sends His son, who was the preexistent being; he becomes a man; he dies the death of a sinner; he resurrects; he abolishes Adam's sin; he overcomes demonic forces; the risen Christ is exalted to the right hand of God in heaven; he will come again on the clouds and the resurrection and judgment of men will follow. All these themes are expressed in mythical terms in the NT. The myths, moreover, represent a prescientific age, Bultmann argued (*Jesus Christ and Mythology* 35). Man has mastered the world through science and technology. The mythical worldview is no longer intelligible to him. Modern Science and modern conceptions of human nature do not allow the view that supernatural powers interfere with man and the world in which he lives. To the biologist, resurrection is completely meaningless. The myth concerning the return of Christ is untenable. In case of ailments, modern man has physicians to heal him, and in the case of political affairs he has guidance from experts in the social, economic, and political sciences, and so on. Therefore, the conclusion Bultmann reached is that *"the kerygma is incredible to modern man, for he is convinced that the mythical view of the world is obsolete"* (italics original). It is impossible to revive this obsolete view but more so with the mythical view. He concludes, "The contrast between the ancient world-view of the Bible and the modern world-view is the contrast between two ways of thinking, the mythological and scientific" (vol. 1, 3). Thus, Bultmann made the NT devoid of myth and mythical thinking.

Literary criticism and existential philosophy were the tools applied by Bultmann to study the myths. They damaged the nature and the essence of myths and showed them to be primitive errors, which need to be adapted to suit modern thinking. The result was that a large portion of the NT was consigned to mute existence, that myths have lost capacity to say anything meaningful. "Too much of the New Testament is thus condemned to silence; and this is precisely what happens to the New Testament when Bultmann's principle of interpretation is applied to it" (Throckmorton, *The New Testament and Mythology* 108–109).

Eliade, on the other hand, took the diametrically opposite view. Eliade emphasized the myths and mythical thought in religion. He held that images, symbols, and myths cannot be translated into concepts. They have many frames of reference and multivalent meanings, and hence any attempt to limit them to one meaning or one frame of reference ought to be discouraged. In a quite un-Bultmannian way, Eliade stated, "[T]o translate an image into a concrete terminology by restricting it to any one of its frames of reference is to do worse than mutilate it—it is to annihilate, to annul it as an instrument of cognition" (*Images and Symbols* 15). Eliade summed it up thus:

> These few cursory observations have shown us in what sense Christianity is prolonging a "mythical" conduct of life into the modern world. If we take account of the true nature and function of the myth, Christianity does not appear to have surpassed the mode of being of archaic man; but then it could not.... It remains, however, to enquire what has taken the place of the myth among those of the moderns who have preserved nothing of Christianity but the dead letter. (*Myths, Dreams and Mysteries* 31)

This forms a fitting reply to those who pursue demythologization as one of the ways to make the NT intelligible. Bultmann's demythologization is found congenial to the current antipathy to religious questions, which has crushed the mythical aspects of Christian spirituality.

THE UNDERSTANDING OF "MAN"

The other most important difference between Bultmann and Eliade is to be found in their understandings of "Man." To understand Man, for Bultmann and for Eliade, is to ascertain the meaning of "human existence." But Bultmann viewed man as a historic being and history stands under transitoriness. Man implies finitude, "our being toward death" (*Existence and Faith* 120). Death stands as a threat to man's life. "Man rebels against death and knows that as one who is fallen under it he is not in his authenticity" (83). For Eliade, Man was not purely a historical being. Man was not an entity bound to situation and time. Man could not be explained by his hereditary and social conditioning (*Patanjali and Yoga* 5). This understanding of man separates an existentialist historian from a historian of religions. A historian of religions takes into account authentic factors of human life other than historicity experienced at a given point of time in history (*Images and Symbols* 32ff.). Bultmann emphasized the latter. Mere historic awareness in man does not make him fully human, Eliade asserted the unconscious sector of his humanity. Eliade's humanism provided a new scenario for understanding human beings. His contention was that man cannot be reduced to his historical dimension. Man cannot be regarded as being imprisoned by historical conditionings (*Quest* 53). Religious structures, for Eliade, are nontemporal and nonhistorical (Allen, 1978 176). The Bultmannian idea of personal history that defines human existence and its authenticity were criticized by Eliade.

> His [man's] authentic existence is realizing itself in history, in time, in his time—which is not that of his father. Neither is it the time of his contemporaries in another continent, or even in another country. That being so, what business have we to be talking about the behavior of man in general? *This* man in general is no more than an abstraction: he exists only on the strength of a misunderstanding due to the imperfection of language. (*Images and Symbols* 32)

There is a nonhistorical portion of every human being, according to Eliade. Man attains to primordial humanity through images and symbols. "Dreams, waking dreams, the images of his nostalgias and of his enthusiasms, etc., are so many forces that may project the historically-conditioned human being into a spiritual world that is infinitely richer than the closed world of his own 'historical moment' " (*Images and Symbols* 13). True History and the history of human condition belong to the primordial myth and "it is in this," affirmed Eliade, "that one must seek and find again the principles and the paradigms for all the conduct of life" (*Myths, Dreams, and Mysteries* 46).

Eliade contrasted between the existence of archaic man and existence as "modern man." He understood "modern man" thus: " '[M]odern man' is such in his insistence upon being exclusively historical; i.e., he is, above all, the 'man' of historicism, of Marxism, and of existentialism" (*Myth of the Eternal Return* 156 n.12). Eliade did not recognize himself in such a man. A historicist view denies the existence of archaic man. The "archaic man" and the "historical man" (modern man) represent two types of humanity. The former, Eliade called "man of the archaic cultures," "man of traditional civilizations," "primitive man," "man of premodern societies," etc. In *The Myth of the Eternal Return* Eliade dealt with the major concern of the "valorization" of human existence, the problem of the position of "historical man" in relation to "archaic man" (141). Eliade argued that historicism, Marxism, and existentialism taught men to cope with history, to tolerate it. But archaic men defended themselves against history "either by periodically abolishing it through repetition of the cosmogony and a periodic regeneration of time or by giving historical events a metahistorical meaning" (142). The profound insight is that Eliade placed the problem of human existence and history within the horizon of archaic spirituality and not within the modern existential framework (5). It was a spirituality in which myth and archaic man belonged to each other. Primitive man did not think in terms of history. Myths were reactualized continuously through rituals and ceremonies. He felt the need for returning to that mythical moment, which was ahistorical. In this, archaic man experienced regeneration and renewal as if he entered into a newly built house for the first time (77). This unique experience enacted a primordial unity, the joy of existence that existed in creation.[12] NT theology can find valorization, and one can hear the message of the NT afresh, when a new way of reading the NT is made possible that will preserve the ancient myths and symbols and redeem one from the modern myths of science and technology.

ELIADE'S ORIENTALISM AND NEW HUMANISM: THE HOMOLOGIZATION OF WESTERN AND EASTERN RELIGIOUS THOUGHT

In *Orientalism*, Edward Said presented a powerful critique of Western orientalism. Among the attacks he made against nineteenth-century orientalists and their influence in the twentieth century, he observed that Western orientalists could be regarded as special agents of Western powers as they pursued a colonial policy vis-à-vis the Orient. He observed that in the West, the Orient was located in a comparative framework with the Occident, as if it remained beyond the Occident, which interpreted the Orient from a distance (*Orientalism* 149). He also observed that the Orient was overvalued for its pantheism, its spirituality, its stability, its longevity, its primitivity, and so forth (150), which was matched by an undervaluation of the Orient as socially backward and barbaric. So unequal are Oriental and European achievements in the stereotypical portrayal of the East: the Orient in itself was subordinated intellectually to the West (152). Western orientalists created a the model of the Orient suitable for the dominant culture, in which the general picture emphasized the escapism of sexual fantasy and familiar clichés such as harems, slaves, dancing girls and boys, ointments, and so on. Said decried the unequal partnership between East and West. A Western orientalist did not live like an ordinary citizen in the Orient. For him, to live in the Orient was to live the privileged live of "a representative European whose empire (French or British) contains the Orient in its military, economic, and above all, cultural arms" (156).

The above criticisms do not match Eliade's experience of the East, particularly in that he had a close and positive encounter with Indian spirituality, not for the purpose of ruling, subduing, and exploiting, but to discover its true humanity. Eliade stressed the need for developing a scholarly interest in the cultures of non-Western peoples, which is different from studies conducted in the nineteenth century. Eliade criticized the work of nineteenth-century Indologists as detached and reductionistic. First and foremost, Eliade did not subscribe to locating the origin of Aryan Race theory in the study of Oriental religion and culture. Based on his knowledge of Indian religion and culture, he did not submit himself to my racial theory that would have fit into the scheme of "human origin" advocated by the *Naturswissenschaft* school. Max Müller, a renowned Indologist from Germany, is credited with the popularization of the Aryan racial theory in the middle of nineteenth century.[13] Though he argued that Aryan meant only a linguistic family and never applied to race, the damage had already been done. Eliade neither agreed with the view that Hinduism belongs to the family of Aryan religions nor did he define the relationship between Christianity and other religious traditions on the basis of what was known as a "progressive history of religion." According to the latter, each religion is placed in a sequence according to some qualitative differences between them arbitrarily established. In this line, which constantly moves upward, Christianity occupies the highest and last point and is called "revealed religion."[14] Eliade argued that in Hinduism one finds a synthesis of two spiritual traditions, the tradition of Aryan language, Indo-Europeans, and Dravidian with Harappan elements. Indo-Europeans contributed to the pre-Aryan Indus civilization its patriarchal structure, pastoral economy, and the worship of sky gods (*A History of Religious Ideas*, volume I 196). Indo-European culture was thoroughly Asianized, and Hinduism represents the resultant victory of the Indian soil (*Yoga, Immortality, and Freedom* 360–61). This estimation by Eliade is in complete contrast to what other Indologists thought about the role of Indo-European tradition within Hinduism.

The nineteenth-century research in Indology reflected a different spirit of man, which failed to see the cultural heritage of the non-Western peoples as "an integral part of the history of human spirit." Their estimation of others as "inferior societies" was largely

> derived from the positivistic, antireligious, and ametaphysical attitude entertained by a number of worthy explorers and ethnologists who had approached the "savages" with a ideology of Comte, Darwin, or Spencer. Among the "primitives" they everywhere discovered "fetishism" and "religious infantilism"—simply because they could *see* nothing else. (*Yoga, Immortality, and Freedom* xiii–xiv, italics in the original)

Eliade called for widening Western consciousness with a new understanding of Asiatic societies and cultures. They were all considered as "outsiders" but there was no need any longer to see them as "foreign" to Western spirituality. He urged,

> We shall have to consider the cultures of non-Western peoples in their own right, and try to understand them with the same intellectual passion that we devote to understanding the Homeric world, the prophets of Israel, or the mystical philosophy of Meister Eckhardt. In other words, we must approach—

and fortunately a beginning has already been made—Oceanic or African myths, symbols and rites with the same respect and the same desire to learn that hitherto we have devoted to the cultural creations of the West. (*Two and the One* 13)

For an Indian student, Eliade forms a mediating ground between Western and Eastern schools of thought because of his unique understanding of Orientalism. According to Eliade, the historian of religions must include the entire religious history of humanity, from Paleolithic to the modern period, in his/her field of investigation without any prejudgment. A true dialogue cannot be limited to discussing superficial elements of religions but must address the central values in each culture. This is vital as it will help the participants in dialogue to hear, see, and touch "the rich religious soil" that nourishes each culture. In this context, a historian of religions plays an important role in bringing cultures together to interact, to speak to each other. The religious renaissance experienced by the West at the beginning of the twentieth century enabled the West to understand the spiritual horizon of the primitives, namely, "the structure of their symbols, the function of their myths, the maturity of their mysticisms" (*Yoga, Immortality, and Freedom* xiv). Eliade called this new state of affairs a New Humanism.

For Eliade, this new awakening not only represented the strength of the West but also corresponded to the problems natural to European culture. Eliade's Western Indianism is not based on Western superiority and knowledge over a weak and backward India. It denotes a confluence of West and East in which the West touches upon the strength of Indian philosophy. For Eliade, this process culminated in India beginning to assert its place in the consciousness of the West (*Yoga, Immortality, and Freedom* xiv). Amidst the problems that confronted the West an interaction with Indian spirituality took place. "We may, however, remark that the problems that today absorb the Western mind also prepare it for a better understanding of Indian spirituality; indeed, they incite it to employ, for its own philosophical effort, *the millennial experience of India*" (*Yoga, Immortality, and Freedom* xiv). The learning is not one-sided. Eliade did not propose that both cultures learn from each other. It is not philosophical syncretism. He, rather, called upon both Westerners and non-Westerners "to think in terms of universal history and to forge universal spiritual values" (*Yoga, Immortality, and Freedom* xix).

Eliade proposed a comparative method, a new way for any culture or civilization to compare itself with any other. "We propose to reverse the terms of comparison, to place ourselves outside our civilization and our own moment of history, and to consider these from the standpoint of other cultures and other religions" (*Myths, Dreams, and Mysteries* 232). He urged the European reader to acquire a vision of an extra-European civilization.

> If we can homologize the two philosophical horizons—Indian and Western—Hinduism constitutes the traditions of Aryan speaking Indo-European and that of the aborigines including Dravidians and Harappan cultural elements. It is a synthesis between the two in which the Indo-European elements merged with those of the mysticism that was germane to the Indian soil.[15]

Eliade did not see many contradictions or incompatible elements between Indian and Western philosophy. Long before depth psychology the sages and the ascetics of India were led "to explore the obscure zones of the unconscious" (*Yoga, Immortality, and Freedom* xvii). The problems of temporality and the historicity of the human being, which lie at the center of European thought, have preoccupied Indian philosophy from its beginnings (*Yoga, Immortality, and Freedom* xviiff).

Eliade, the champion of new humanity and a prophet to the West, writes,

> A number of Western investigators and philosophers may find the Indian analyses rather oversimplified and the proposed solutions ineffectual.... Western philosophers may perhaps find the jargon of Indian philosophy outmoded, lacking in precision, unserviceable.... The great discoveries of Indian thought will in the end be recognized, under and despite the philosophic jargon. It is impossible, for example, to disregard one of India's greatest discoveries: that of consciousness as witness,

of consciousness freed from its psychophysiological structures and their temporal conditioning, the consciousness of the "liberated" man, of him, that is, who has succeeded in emancipating himself from temporality and thereafter knows the true, inexpressible freedom. (*Yoga, Immortality, and Freedom* xx)

The following quotation from Eliade's novel is also worth noting:

But there is here [in India] a certain atmosphere of renunciation, . . . of control of the consciousness, of love, which is favorable for me. Neither theosophy, nor brahmanic practices, nor rituals—nothing barbarous, nothing created by history. But an extraordinary belief in the reality of the verities, in the power of man [sic] to know them and to live them by an interior realization, by purity, and above all by meditation. (*Bengal Nights*, quoted in Ierunca 344)

A welcome change is taking place in NT studies in that there is a new awareness to anti-Semitism both within the NT and in NT scholarship. A similar awareness toward the thought and practice of anti-Hamitism (anti-Orient) needs to be brought about by postcolonial readings of the NT. But I am optimistic that the new humanism propounded by Eliade has the positive edge over any postcolonial attempt to deconstruct Western Orientalism.

CONCLUSION

NT studies are immersed in a hermeneutical tradition nourished by Western thinking. The historical methodology, which provides the concepts and tools for the study of the NT, has largely ignored questions concerning the "Sacred." Eliade's achievements will help to redress the deficiency created by historical positivism, which pervades NT scholarship. There are several significant methodological contributions by Eliade to the hermeneutics of the NT, which we have outlined above. Generally speaking, the NT student has to march backward into the OT and forward into the creeds and confessions of the Christian church. Eliade, as a fine historian of religions, has shown us the wider spectrum of religious experience within which and against which the NT can be read. The worldview of the NT is far wider and broader when it includes the East and its multidimensional religious history and thought. Eliade's deep interest in myths and symbols, and in archaic and Indian (Oriental) religions will have paramount significance, first of all, for opening up the religious dimension of NT Christianity. Secondly, it offers a firm foundation on which an Indian student can build with a view to restoring some of the NT religious phenomena, which are closer to Oriental instincts and experience.

The field of Christian theology should not be defined in a way that it can exclude the other. We ought to rethink our purpose and recast our basic concepts. Significant NT scholarship can develop beyond and beside the Eliadean ideas and perspectives. A student of the NT in India will find helpful directives in Eliade. He/she should be grateful to Eliade for maintaining that myths and symbols communicate their messages even though modern (European) man can claim not to have understood them. The NT student is now free to conduct his/her hermeneutical work on myths without having to ask the question whether myths are intelligible to a particular society lived or living at a given historical moment. One can discern potential openings for more fruitful study of religious phenomena in the NT. This inspires new perspectives that will help an Indian NT student preserve the spiritual aspects of NT Christianity. In this respect, I find Eliade a most trustworthy companion. He has shown the way that an Indian can walk in his footsteps. He is a true dialogue partner for a student of religion from the Indian subcontinent. In Eliade, an Indian Christian finds a guru who opens the eyes to the wealth of Indian traditions and who has forced Indian/Oriental religious philosophy into dialogue with Western/Occidental philosophical thought. Eliade asks the modern (European) man to enlarge his "self" to discover that human aspect within him which will help him understand the myths in religion. He deplores the wrong image of India developed in the Western perception that Indian metaphysics and philosophy devalue life. The provincial modes of thought and expression have to be acknowledged as not universal in themselves. The method and function of history of religions can assist NT theologians to understand its universal claim.

Finally, Eliade venerated his Christian heritage but assumed a shy attitude toward Christian theology. It will be very difficult to judge him as someone who "stands in the periphery of every religion, by profession as well as by conviction" (Cioran, "Beginnings of a Friendship" 413), but it is unfair to call him "a religious mind without religion."

NOTES

1. It is a disappointment not to have been able to consult works such as Eliade's *Journals* and the *Autobiography, vol.1: Journey East, Journey West, 1907–1937* (to know particularly about his encounter with India and Hinduism), many of his articles and, above all, his novels and fictions.

2. I am grateful to Dr. Bryan Rennie for providing me three of Eliade's key works for my reading. My thanks are also due to Dr. David Cave who sent me his work *Mircea Eliade's Vision for a New Humanism*. I am thankful for their encouraging words!

3. For details, see Werner G. Kümmel, *The New Testament: The History of the Investigation of Its Problems* 245–80; 342–62.

4. Otto Pfleiderer (in Kümmel 210) remarks that "it is still customary to take up a shy and suspicious attitude towards the application of the scholarly discipline of comparative religion within the field of biblical theology. The few who venture to make use of it draw on themselves . . . the reproach of 'paganizing.' "

5. E.g., Frank F. Ellinwood, *Oriental Religions and Christianity*. John Cobb rightly comments, "To insist on Christian distinctiveness is one thing. For Christian theologians to be ignorant of the great traditions of the East is quite another! Second, Barth's condemnation led theologians to false views of Eastern traditions" ("Is Christianity a Religion?" 5).

6. Virgil Ierunca, "The Literary Work of Mircea Eliade" 345, rightly observes, "India did not overwhelm his [Eliade's] work and his thought; it only nourished them, opening them to myths, to symbols, to a language to which the West no longer hold the key."

7. Even in the second volume of *History of Religious Ideas* only twenty-three pages have been devoted to the birth of Christianity citing verses from NT.

8. *Myth and Reality* 183; *Zalmoxis* 20 understands the origin of the Romanians (Daco-Romans) on the basis of a mythical view of their history that

the Romanian people was "predestined to wars, invasions, and emigrations." There is no trace of Aryan racism here!

9. *Zalmoxis* 255; *Sacred and the Profane* 32 do not seem to take any moral stand against Crusaders and their conquests.

10. J. G. Muthuraj, "The Meaning of εθνος and εθνη," examines particularly the use of τα εθνη in NT and NT scholarship and questions the translations of τα εθνη as "pagans," "heathens" and "Gentiles" in the NT. I suggest the neutral meaning of "peoples" for τα εθνη.

11. Eliade perceived a resemblance between Heidegger's thought and Hindu philosophy. See, Adriana Berger, "Cultural Hermeneutics" 150. Also see n.25. Berger mentions the early formative period of his thinking in Romania where Eliade published his provocative philosophical essays and where he also participated in the first group in Romania to deal with Heidegger and Kierkegaard.

12. David Cave (*Mircea Eliade's Vision for a New Humanism* 52) has an interesting quotation from Eliade, who wrote these words as a reaction against the existentialism of Kirkegaard, Heidegger, and Sartre. Eliade says, "I believe that joy is the true structure of the new humanity which we are waiting for. I believe that the greatest sin against humanity is the despairing sadness erected as the supreme value of spirituality."

13. According to this theory, northern India was invaded and conquered by nomadic, light-skinned race of a people called "aryans" who supposedly descended from central Asia (or some unknown land?) around 1500 BC, and destroyed an earlier more advanced civilization of the people resident in the Indus Valley, and then imposed upon them their culture and language. These Indus Valley people were supposed to be either Dravidian, or Austrics, or nowadays' Shudra class, etc.

14. For an account of the impact of the Aryan doctrine among missionaries, see M. Maw, *Visions of India*.

15. Eliade considered yoga as belonging to the Indian soil and not to the Indo-European tradition, which is often praised for what it did to the Indus civilization.

III

The Interpretation of India and Eliade's "Traditionalism"

The Secret of Dr. Eliade

Liviu Bordaş
(translated by Mac Linscott Ricketts)

IN SEARCH OF INDIAN "TRADITION"

> The relations of Eliade with Indian tradition have been analyzed, although without a first-hand knowledge of the question. It must be said that from Honigberger and the Moldavian saint (*rishi*) Alecu Ghica... the attraction exercised by India on Romanians has been continued through several isolated personalities (among whom Eminescu must be mentioned), Eliade being one of the last and most famous representatives. Others have concerned themselves competently with this problem, but the fundamental chapter about Eliade has not yet been written. Concerning this part of his life, especially his months spent at Rishikesh, at the hermitage (*ashram*) of Shrī Shivananada, Eliade's memoirs are nearly silent.
>
> —Ioan P. Culianu, "L'anthropologie philosophique"

Although Eliade's relations with the works and thought of the "traditionalists" have been much discussed by various authors in the past two decades,[1] his belief in some of the ideas held by them was not proved irrefutably, in black and white, by the author's own hand, until the publication of the journal of the novel *Viaţă Nouă* (1940–1941).

In this unfinished novel Eliade introduces an "occultist," Tuliu, whose name can only make one think of the first name of Baron Evola.[2] This character is an *hombre segreto*, a bachelor of philosophy, who attends the opening of Nae Ionescu's course, lives a free life financed by mysterious sources, rarely confesses his occult interests and his esoteric faith, which he calls "traditional metaphysics" (*philosophia perennis*); he lives alone on the top floor of an apartment house in two rooms that contain a small library whose content is the key element of his characterization:

> a little bookcase on casters which held the books he valued the most: the complete works of René Guénon and J. Evola, complete collections of *Ur, Krur,* and *Études Traditionelles*, several volumes of [Arthur E.] Waite and John Woodroffe, *Notebook Nr. 6* of Gustav Meyrinck—of which Tuliu was very proud, because he knew he was the only person in Southeastern Europe who possessed a copy of this work of limited circulation—a *Faust* with commentary, and *The Melancholia of Dürer* by Saxl and Panofsky. Finally, in a corner of the study, piled on top of one another as if he wished to show a lack of interest for them, were miscellaneous volumes of Blavatsky, Allan Kardek, Annie Besant, Papus, Rudolf Steiner, and other, more obscure authors, all in French translations. Tuliu's entire library did not exceed two or three hundred volumes, but they were not books found in the house of an ordinary reader.[3]

Tuliu recommends Guénon, Evola, and Waite to his friends, and he believes in a near end of the world, precisely like Guénon and Petrache Lupu.[4]

The key to the autobiographical reading of the character is given by a notation Eliade made, for 27 July 1941, in the journal of the novel:

> I absolutely must return to Tuliu in a special chapter in which I explain his philosophy, lest the reader believe that he is a case of a simple scatter-brained "occultist." Actually, his theories are not completely foreign to mine. Tuliu will say, for various reasons about which there is not room to dwell here, things I have never had the courage to confess publicly. Only occasionally have I admitted to a few friends my "traditionalist" beliefs (to use René Guénon's term).[5]

Eliade's very early interest in psychic phenomena, magic, and occultism is manifest in articles that he began to publish in high school. From 1926 he started, gradually, to "discover" the writings of Evola and Guénon. These, however, did not have any special influence on him in those years, being rather just some among the many authors he was discovering continually. What brought him closest to the "traditional" ideas were his studies and experiences in the Indian period. After his first experiences of India, Eliade seemed to recognize the affinities of the "traditionalists" with the traditional Indian, and he ordered their writings from Paris, Rome, and Bucharest.[6] Nevertheless, it is still not possible to speak of an adherence of his thought to "traditionalism" (or "perennialism," as Antoine Faivre calls this current). The change that betrays an influence of the themes of adepts of "tradition"—which Eliade interpreted in his own way, blending them in his broad personal synthesis—gradually began to become visible only after his return to his own country, especially in 1936–1937. The systematic study of his *Jugendschriften* (1921–1928) shows that he was attracted to those authors precisely because of the fact that he had anticipated some of their ideas or problematics. After his return from India, he induced, it seems, the conversion of his friend, Marcel Avramescu, to Guénonianism. He made "camouflaged" contributions to Avramescu's review of traditional studies *Memra* and, in his signed articles made various references to the theorists of "tradition."[7] This interest is not necessarily proof of an influence exercised upon him by "traditionalism." Circumstantial evidence shows, rather, that it is a matter of a convergence of ideas and interests; and this only partially, leaving room for many divergences. After the harsh trials of the prewar and war period and especially with his becoming established in the Western academic world, Eliade's "secret" sympathy for "tradition" became even more divergent. This change of attitude seems to have happened gradually at Paris, in a period between the latter 1940s and the early 1950s.[8] It is probable that a determinative role would have been his entrance into "Eranos" (along with his participation in the conference at Ascona in August 1950) because, indeed, the "labyrinthine itinerary" of which he spoke then is more nearly the Jungian "process of individuation" than the "metaphysical realization" of Guénon. But already, in a note of 26 August 1949, not published in *Fragments d'un journal*, he wrote about the "poverty, the *'primarism'* " of René Guénon's work. Also, of the "insufferable presumption with which he so often hides his ignorance."[9] Likewise significant is the fact that in 1952 he refused to contribute to the issue of the review *France-Asie* honoring René Guénon, to which he had been invited rather insistently by René de Berval (although he did contribute to a following issue dedicated to René Grousset—cf. *Mircea Eliade și corespondenții săi* vol. 1 (A-E), 88, 89).

Nevertheless, the alternative—savant versus esotericist—which determined the Eliadean ambiguities and camouflages is not an exclusive one, because, undoubtedly, it is possible to be a savant without being necessarily a *homo academicus*, and one can have access to "the hidden" without being a champion of the esoteric. If the examples of Woodroffe and Corbin are not sufficient to illustrate this success, they show, at least, its possibility. One, it seems, not so difficult to attain as to choose, because Eliade on the one hand and Guénon on the other, both of whom had the qualities and opportunities to realize this difficult "middle way" and establish its "respectability," took extreme options. The former won a victory for the history of religions as an academic discipline and the latter for "tradition" as the authentic esotericism.

Besides the theorists of "tradition" who were active in the West in the interwar period, the young Eliade, back from India, announced to the Romanian public the existence of one active in the East: Aurobindo Ghose. Under the pseudonym Krm,[10] Eliade contributed to both of the issues of the review *Memra*, published by Marcel Avramescu. His contributions are a translation of the *Katha Upanishad* (first *valli*) and the article "A Representative of the Hindu Tradition, Sri Aurabindo" (*sic*). In the latter, he calls the Bengalese philosopher and yogi "the most 'realized' man in modern India" ("Un reprezentant al tradiţiei hinduse: Sri Aurabindo," 19–20). On another occasion, in an article published two years later, Eliade referred to Aurobindo as being, alongside Ananda K. Coomaraswamy, "the other great traditionalist thinker of modern India."[11] While later, in his Journal for 17

February 1943, following a discussion about Guénon, he noted that he considered Aurobindo as being "more perfected."[12] In 1949, together with many others including René Guénon, Ananda K. Coomaraswamy, and Aurobindo Ghose, he contributed an article to the collective volume dedicated to India and published by *Les Cahiers du Sud*, under the direction of Jacques Masui ("Introduction au tantrisme," in *Approches de l'Inde* 132–44).

The fact that the pseudonym "Krm" was Eliade's was attested by Marcel Avramescu (see Ungureanu, "Despre căile literaturii"). Recently it has been stated that the irrefutable proof of Eliade's paternity of the two articles is the fact that the author gives the reader to understand that he has been to Pondicherry himself "where no Romanian before Eliade had been."[13] There exist, however, serious doubts that Eliade had ever set foot in Pondicherry. Not only because in the articles collected in the volume *India* he travels directly from Madura to Madras, but in the article under discussion devoted to Aurobindo ("Aurabindo"), he writes twice about the ashram the latter has created "outside the city" and "is found in the vicinity of the French colonial city, Pondicherry." Now, anyone who has been there, even only in passing, knows that the ashram is located in the heart of the *comptoir* [a French commercial colony in India, ed.].

It is interesting to note here that Aurobindo and Pondicherry remained in Eliade's long-term memory. Even in one of his last novellas, *Nineteen Roses* (in *Youth without Youth*, 1979), a reference is made to Pondicherry, which is mentioned, together with Haridwar and Rishikesh, in the context of some journeys in mystical and spiritual India. Speaking about Tagore in his well-known interview with Claude-Henri Rocquet, he regrets at that time (1978) that the great poet is neglected in India "because of the great stature of Aurobindo, or of Radhakrishnan" (52).

However, I believe that the memory of the French *comptoir* is not connected with a possible visit but rather with the fact that Jenny Isaacson, his former "tantric" companion at Rishikesh (the prototype of Jenia Isaac in *Maitreyi*), withdrew into Aurobindo's ashram at Pondicherry, an episode that Eliade recalled at the beginning of the 1960s, when he was writing his memoirs:

Mrs. Perris telephoned me one morning at the Imperial Library that someone wanted to speak to me. It was Jenny. She had abandoned the ascetic life at *Svarga-ashram* and had come to see me. Even worse, she had taken residence in the boarding house on Ripon Street. She stayed about two weeks, in which time I worked only sporadically. I told her quite frankly that all that had happened between us belonged to the past. But Jenny still had hope. One day she declared that since she had failed to find "the Absolute," she was going to become a prostitute. She put on her most elegant dress, made up her face, and went to drink a cocktail in the most fashionable bar in Calcutta. An hour later she returned, discouraged and dejected. She consoled herself by going out every evening—to movies, China Town, bars. Finally, she decided to try monastic life again. She went to Pondicherry, to the *ashram* of Aurobindo Gosh. A week later she wrote me that she was happy, that "the Mother" had restored her courage to seek "the Absolute," that she had given what little she had to this *ashram* in which she had decided to remain for the rest of her life. After that I heard nothing else from her.[14]

This last statement is in fact incorrect, because Eliade sent to Pondicherry at least two letters and a postcard (on which he complained that she had not responded to his letters) to the one who had now become Chidanadini.[15] From the register of the *ashram*, which I have consulted at Pondicherry, it is revealed that Jenny Isaacson (born 2 April 1905 at Kimberly, South Africa)[16] entered the *ashram* on 16 February 1931 and left on 12 November 1933. As the writer K. D. Sethna, one of the oldest residents of the *ashram*, recalls, she had to leave due to an "amorous affair" with a young Gujarati who was "overwhelmed" by the experience and later became insane (although, it seems, not on account of this). For a time, nevertheless, she remained in the city, in a hotel.

I owe this information to Peter Heehs, historian and editor of the works of Sri Aurobindo, at the Sri Aurobindo Archives and Research Library, who, in November 1998, at my request, undertook researches in the archives and among elder members of the *ashram*. Later, in August 2000, I verified personally this information. Here is the resumé of the conversations Peter Heehs had with K. D. Sethna (Amal Kiran) and with Nirodbaran, as they were transmitted to us in two letters (in English) in November 1998:

> I spoke to K. D. Sethna (born in 1903 or so) about Jenny. He said she was a somewhat plump, red-faced, not bad-looking young girl. She played the cello like an angel. She played before the Mother too. K. D. Sethna used to chat with her while she was "in" the *ashram*. He is not sure if she was an ashramite. She had an affair with a Gujarati young man who was floored by the experience. Later Jenny left the *ashram* but remained in a Pondy hotel. K. D. Sethna saw her there too.
>
> I happened to talk with Nirodbaran this morning and brought up the topic of Jenny. He could not remember the name, but he recalled that there was a young South African woman here for a short time. She played the cello, etc. The Mother gave her "complete freedom." So far as he could recall, she was never a full ashramite—she lived outside. Then, he recalled, she went away. What happened, I asked. Oh, you know, he said. I said I had heard there was a scandal involving a young Gujarati. He remembered it. Nirod was sort of looking after the fellow while he was here. The Mother saw some possibility in him, etc. He could not remember the dramatic story Amal recounted—just that he went away and later lost his mind (no connection with Jenny implied).
>
> In the discussion I had with K. D. Sethna he admitted chastely that Jenny "was inclined toward friendship with young people of the opposite sex" and seemed to remember about a Frenchman also. The hotel where she stayed after leaving the *ashram* may be the *Hôtel d'Europe*, which she recommended also to Eliade and which has survived to the present day, being, after an interruption, returned to its original function.

One cannot help remarking the resemblance of events with the Maitreyi episode, which Eliade revealed—to her first—and which moved her so much that she wanted to be loved like the nubile Bengali. In Eliade's archive in Romania there have been preserved letters sent by Jenny after he had left Svarga Ashram and had returned to Calcutta; these begin in January from Rishikesh and resume, starting in March, from Pondicherry, continuing thereafter for several months.[17]

In March, comparing life in the new *ashram* with that at Rishikesh, Jenny wrote that "no longer do I live in a confined space 'far from the unbridled world,' but in the midst of a city" (*Opere* 2, 191). Eliade was not, therefore, uninformed about the location of Aurobindo's *ashram*. Jenny's responses suggest that he had spoken to her already at Rishikesh about the *ashram*, which, quite probably, he had heard being discussed often at Calcutta. Referring to the book of Aurobindo, *Essays on the Gītā*, Jenny writes to him: "You were right in your criticisms, including the demolishing of Vivekananda's works, after you read the book of Ghose" (189). Indeed, the article in *Memra* is based on this work, which he considers "his principal book of doctrine." He asserts that "[o]ther than *Introduction à l'étude des doctrines hindoues* by René Guénon, the book of Aurabindo Ghose is the only authorized work on Indian traditional truths which can be recommended to the European reader without fear of his being mystified," and that "[t]he reading of these books is obligatory for all who wish to know from the source an esoteric tradition" (*Memra* 19). It is probable, therefore, that Eliade himself introduced Jenny to Aurobindo's thought, and that he urged her to go to his *ashram*. He must have heard about this man in Calcutta, because his fame had not yet spread to the West (with the exception of some small groups in France), but in Bengal, where he was considered a hero, his name was well known and mentioned with respect.

In the first interview he gave after returning to Romania, distinguishing philosophers "in the European sense" such as Dasgupta and Radhakrishnan from "simple thinkers, wise in the full sense of the word," Eliade declared,

> The most representative among these is Aurobindo Ghose, who has been withdrawn in a monastic cell for thirty years.

From his little room he issues forth two or three times a year. This is the explanation for why he is unknown by us, in Europe. There [in India], however, his authority is second only to that of Gandhi.[18]

He even considered him a "true Indian," in contrast to Krishnamurti and Vivekananda.[19] Eliade had read his principal book published up to that time, *Essays on the Gītā*, but he knew also about other writings of his that had appeared in the review *Arya* and in pamphlets. In an article about the Upanishads (written at Rishikesh, but published after his return home), he makes reference to Aurobindo's studies on the language of the Vedas.[20] In a notebook of fragmentary notations, the young Indianist recorded—only a short time before leaving Dasgupta's house and going to Rishikesh—his opinion of "Aurobindo Ghosh, who is one of the few minds of modern India who has dared to assimilate and perfect Sanskrit wisdom" about the meaning of the word *swaraj*.[21] This proves that he was conversant also with his political and nationalistic thought. In an article about the Upanishads, from the same series composed at Rishikesh, Aurobindo is given as an example of a contemporary *rishi*.[22] The article in *Memra* was written, in all probability, in that period, and only "recycled" later, as had happened with the translation of the *Katha Upanishad*, the manuscript of which was found in his archive at Bucharest among other papers dated "Calcutta, 1929-Rishikesh, 1930."[23]

In her first letter from Pondicherry, Jenny wrote with enthusiasm,

> If you are in search of a true, authentic *rishi*, superior to any you could find in India or the whole world, then you could find him in the person of Sri Aurobindo, a perfected and completed being, with a great power, vigor, and experience. If you are in search of the most exalted philosophy and at the same time of a practical method for living and realizing something, here you will find them. If you are looking for an ideal *ashram*, where everything is intended to reveal magnificently the most valuable qualities of each individual, and where nevertheless everything is subordinated to the love and service of the Divine,

where the practical and spiritual parts of life are perfectly harmonized, and the practical side serves as the most efficient way of realizing the spiritual, then here you will find what you are seeking. (*Opere* 2, 189)

This letter seems to have had a powerful effect on Eliade, since, in his response, he expressed his intention to visit the *ashram* in the near future and even to stay there for a while (190). In fact, when he left Rishikesh, he had said to himself, "I would have to start all over, from the beginning, later, in another *ashram*" (*Autobiography* I, 199). Was he thinking of Pondicherry, of Almora,[24] or of Kashmir, where, likewise, he had planned to withdraw for five or six months? (*Autobiography* I, 208). Writing him again, Jenny assured him, "I'm sure that you will find in Aurobindo what you seek, and that you will be satisfied from all points of view, even the intellectual, a fact which can say much" (*Opere* 2, 190). "You must judge, of course, and I will let you make your own discoveries when you come" (191). In the article published in *Memra*, Eliade speaks in the superlative about the *ashram*, considering that "it is, perhaps, the only place where traditional science and technique are preserved unaltered by Theosophical stupidities and positivistic irrelevance." The article concludes, significantly, with the sentence, "A good share of the effective knowledge about India comes from there, through France."[25]

Since Eliade never reached Pondicherry, it is hard to say if the intention expressed to Jenny was a sincere wish, which, for various reasons, he could not fulfill or if it was only a noble but momentary thought, after the reading of an enthusiastic description. It could be that the answer is found in the fact that he met, in a suburb of Calcutta, a new *guru*, who was said to be "superior even to Aurobindo Ghose," (*Şantier* 1935, 161) and owing to whom, Eliade claims in his autobiography, he postponed his plan to go to Almora and Kashmir.

Eventually, this plan had to be cancelled, according to Eliade, due to his being obliged to return home to fulfill his military service (*Autobiography* I, 208). But this seems to be only a later justification for having left India prematurely. The correspondence with his family shows that he had decided long before this time to return to Romania at the end of 1931.[26] In a letter of 18 June 1931, when he planned to leave India at the end of September or the beginning of October, he wrote: "I could not leave for Kashmir in the light of the news I received, since the scholarship is for ten months only. At the same time, knowing that I cannot prolong my stay in India at least another year more, I must work enormously at the Library" and "there is no need now to file deferment papers with the army, because I will present myself personally for deferral immediately upon my return" (249–50). It is interesting to note that, even a little while after his arrival at Calcutta, Eliade proposed to go into Kashmir, to Shrinagar, to spend the hot months that began in April. It is not known for what reasons he ultimately preferred Darjeeling and Sikkhim, but probably they were of a financial nature, as is shown by the correspondence with his family. In July of that same year he proposed that in October he would make a long excursion to Benares, Agra, Lucknow, and Shrinagar, in March 1930 to go to Shrinagar in May, and even to stay there until the beginning of the Bengalese monsoon; while in January 1931, again, to go to Kashmir as soon as the heat began in Calcutta. Not one of these plans was carried out.[27]

Eliade had very little knowledge of the southern part of the Indian peninsula anyway, a region he accused of mystical degeneracy, and he did not seem attracted to it. Probably he wouldn't have visited it, had he not had to take part (as the Romanian representative of the YMCA) in the international Congress of Christian Students held at Poonamalee (near Madras), as a way of obtaining a British visa for India (the scholarship from the Maharajah of Kassimbazar not being yet officially confirmed). He came through Colombo, Rameshwaram, and Madras, avoiding Pondicherry, for which he would have needed another visa. Later, in Lisbon, when he was interested in the work of Camoës, Eliade regretted that he had not traveled in the south, thinking melancholically of Malabar.[28]

Unfortunately, we do not have the letters Eliade sent to Jenny.[29] Until someone discovers what happened to her after she left Pondicherry and where she ended her life, we will not know if any exist or not. It may be that she returned to South Africa or went somewhere in Western Europe or North America. It is not impossible that she disappeared during World War II, sharing the fate of so many of her people, because, had she lived until the sixties, when the name of Eliade became known throughout the world, she probably would have tried to contact him or to visit him, as did Maitreyi.

THE HIMALAYAN "MYTH"

> Many of Honigberger's statements, accepted by his contemporary biographers, are based on false data or on documents later falsified. What interest did Honigberger have to mystify an existence that had been truly fabulous, displayed under the sign of mystery and adventure? "The Secret of Dr. Honigberger."
>
> —*Two Strange Tales*

Eliade's "India," as he himself always represented it from the moment he returned to Bucharest until his death, camouflages several personal myths: the "myth" of the Himalayan episode, the "myth" of his forced departure from India after only three years in order to satisfy his service at Bucharest, and the "myth" of an eventual return to a "cave in Himalaya." The Himalayan "myth" refers to his leading the life of an ascetic for six months at Rishikesh in the Himalayas where he supposedly was initiated into yoga by Swami Shivananda, and "self-initiated" into *tantra* together with Jenny. This myth has contributed gradually to the creation of his image as initiate and wise man.[30] In this way, his claim that the phenomena described in the journal of Dr. Zerlendi in the novella *The Secret of Dr. Honigberger* come from his "personal experiences" in the Himalayas, was simply assumed, and his death was considered nothing less than a *mahāparinirvāna*. However, examining closely his articles about India, his journal, his "remembrances," and his correspondence, one can see many discrepancies among his assertions about the Indian period and especially about the months spent at Rishikesh. They cast a shadow of doubt upon the sincerity and truth of his testimonies and leave the impression that he wanted to falsify certain aspects of his life and personality.

Studies about Eliade delimit his residence at Svarga Ashram, variously, as between September and March, October and March, or

October and April. These variations reflect the disagreements among the various references he himself made to the six or seven months spent in an *ashram* in Himalaya—actually, at the foot of the Himalayas, for Rishikesh is situated at the modest altitude of about one thousand feet. The first time he mentions the "six months in Himalaya to gather information about techniques of meditation" is in the *Curriculum vitae* that accompanied his doctoral thesis, defended in 1932 (*Psihologia meditației indiene* 14). He maintained the same thing in various interviews, from the first, right after his return to Romania until the last, given at Chicago a little while before his death.[31] In the second edition of *India* (1935, 11), he writes about the "Himalayan monasteries in which I lived from September 1930 until March 1931."[32] In the preface to the last, revised edition of *Yoga, Immortality and Freedom* (1967), the six months at Rishikesh and the three years in India are mentioned—under the aegis of his professor, master, and guru, Surendranath Dasgupta, although in reality he worked with him just a little more than a year and a half.[33] In *Ordeal by Labyrinth* he asserts: "I stayed there, at Rishikesh, for six or seven months—until April, more or less" (*Ordeal by Labyrinth* 40), and in his autobiography: "I left in March, just as abruptly as I had come, after having lived the life of a hermit for nearly six months" (*Autobiography I*, 188; see also 200). It is, however, surprising to discover, that the time was not six months nor was it a life of a hermit.

Eliade arrived at Haridwar on the morning of 29 September, and for four days he visited temples, a library, and the Gurukul College (*India* 100–108, and *Autobiography* I, 187–88). Then he spent the night in a *dak-bungalow* in the town of Rishikesh, and discovering Svarga Ashram a few kilometers upstream, he moved there the next day. His residence at Svarga Ashram begins, therefore, on approximately the fifth of October. In some studies it is stated that Eliade stayed at Rishikesh in the *ashram* of Swami Shivananda.[34] At that time, however, Shivananda did not have an *ashram*, but resided in the old Svarga Ashram, thus being a guest like Eliade, who also received a *kutiar*. He would construct his own *ashram*, on the opposite bank of the Ganges, several years later, little by little, as his fame grew. In the period when Eliade met him, he was known in only a few circles in India (Eliade had heard about him in Delhi). Shivananda's *kutiar* is preserved today as a memorial. I tried several times, during my stays at Rishikesh, to identify the *kutiar* in which Eliade lived "at about 100 meters from his" (cf. the *Journal* entry for 2 September 1957), but the *ashram* officials told me each time that no document exists in the archive about the various residents and visitors over the course of time. However, I was able to identify it from the correspondence received by Eliade at Rishikesh as being *kutiar* #6. He left the *ashram* at the beginning of the month of January, as is proved by his published correspondence,[35] probably on the seventh.[36] Thus, he spent just three months at Rishikesh, but even these were punctuated by journeys and visits in the region: to Peshawar with Arthur Young, to Kapurthala and Amritsar to visit palaces and temples, to the Oriental College in Lahore to see collections of manuscripts, and to Rurki, where he was invited by an Indian Christian family to celebrate Christmas. On the other hand, at Rishikesh he met many people, not only hermits, but also visitors, like that "Miss" (Banerjee) whom he accompanied to Brahmapuri or the one with whom he had a whole evening's literary discussion (*India* 120, 122)—while a good part of the time that he spent in his *kutiar* was dedicated to his doctoral thesis, articles for *Cuvântul*, and his novel, *Lumina ce se stinge*.

Nor can it be said of Swami Shivananda that he was his *guru* in a traditional sense, as he would be called later by Eliade, and then by some commentators on Eliade's life. Their relationship, even limited to the three months spent at Rishikesh (less than that, in fact, since the Swami was absent during a good part of this period), does not seem to have been that of *guru-shishya*. Eliade excuses himself mysteriously, in several places, for having to maintain discretion about his "initiation at Rishikesh." This "initiation," however, does not seem to have been anything more than an introduction into the techniques of *pranayama* and meditation. Swami Shivananda was, rather, a temporary instructor in *hatha-yoga*—one, it is true, viewed with much respect by Eliade, but still, only an instructor: "He guided me a little in the practices of respiration, meditation, and contemplation" (*Ordeal by Labyrinth* 41).

In his memoirs, Eliade gives the impression that his relationship with Jenny lasted several months: that she arrived "around Christmas," that the fateful night occurred sometime in February, and that their "tantric self-initiation" lasted into March, when Eliade claims he returned to Calcutta.[37] The third notebook of his journal published in *Șantier*, comprising the period March-November 1931, begins, anachronistically, with a note about Jenny: "A brief settling of accounts with Jenny. I prove to her how ridiculous it would be for her to follow me to Calcutta. We met, we were intoxicated, we collaborated with fury in the most mediocre fall. What sense would there be in prolonging this spiritual lunacy?"[38] But farther on, there is another note from January which, together with many journal pages about Jenny, were used for the unfinished novel *Victorii*, later being carried over into *Întoarcerea din rai*: "I regret the loss of my chastity and my isolation, lost for nothing, for a simple sensual struggle, after which we are both dejected and feel stupid."[39] And again, the diary gives a different version from the *Autobiography* of the beginning of their relations, a version closer to that in *Maitreyi*:

> When I told her down to the last detail the story of M. and me, Jenny began to cry and gave herself to me. What I believed then, or what I wrote in my notebook, I don't know. But yesterday's letter discloses an interesting fact: Jenny thought I loved her, and that that was why I had confessed the episode with M. Stupid. I didn't love her at all. I loved M. like a madman, and in order to verify that passion, to know its limits, I had attempted the confession. Strangely, the confession and the carnal knowledge that followed, indirectly undermined the memory of my love for M. As much pleasure as I had rolling on the rug with Jenny, *both hystericized and unconscious* [emphasis added], in the end I could only state: if I can do this, I'm beginning to lose M.[40]

If Jenny came indeed sometime before Christmas, while Eliade—as we know for certain—returned to Calcutta in the first week of January, their relationship was consummated in a period of two or three weeks, and was nothing more, it seems, than a brief amorous episode, perhaps resembling that described in the novel *Maitreyi*.[41]

All these things show that Eliade tried to manufacture, for his Romanian and Western public, the image of a man who—even if he had not brought back a "Himalayan message"[42]—had had, in India, essential experiences. The attempt springs from the same inner impulses that he recognized in the occult stories of his friend Van Manen, in

> his craving to justify somehow the thirty years spent in India, a land without miracles and without fakirs, a monotonous, flat, depressing land—if you don't succeed in breaking away one day from all the charms of the city and setting out resolutely on the road: to *find*, or else to not return. (Șantier, 156–57)

Already in the preface to the second edition of *India*, comparing his experience with those of Alexandra David-Neel, Nikolai Rörich, and Giuseppe Tucci, he wrote: "To my knowledge, no [other] European has ever stayed six months in a Himalayan hermitage; or if he has stayed, he has written nothing about the life and the people there."[43] It seems, however, that in this boasting he was prompted in advance by colleagues of his generation who, in the pages of Bucharestian reviews, even before the "Himalayan" episode, had written about his Indian "adventures" in exaggerated sentences such as the following: "He has roamed the country of inner mysteries, he has penetrated the secret of Tibetan monasteries, and he has been initiated into the practice of those who have gone beyond earthly life through contemplation" (Jianu, "Ecouri din depărtări" 1). Among his disciples and admirers later on, the historian of religions came to be considered not only an initiate but even a *mahatma* and a *bodhisattva*. One of the most popular representations of the young Eliade became his photograph at Rishikesh, clad in the saffron robe of an anchorite. In "traditional" circles, however, his activity was viewed as just intellectual research—useful and fascinating, to be sure, but limited to preliminaries and the surface of the phenomena that he studied.[44] Even among those who have not exaggerated his mystical Indian experiences, the impression was cultivated that what the young Eliade sought was initiation and spiritual realization—and they have lamented his abandonment of this quest in favor of academic recognition and literary success. However, all the writings and activities of the young seeker show that he was not as contemplative as might seem from the problematics that preoccupied him, but an ambitious man who believed in the primacy of the spiritual, who was driven by the impulse to *do*, to *create* in a direct way, was determined to change his life, to create for himself an exemplary destiny and to change the lives of others as well.[45] He opposed the terror of history not by transcending it, but by creating history.

India gave depth and clarity to Eliade's vision. It cannot be disputed that his experiences were essential for him, for his generation, and, to an extent, for the Western twentieth century, but they are still far from being the great lesson India could have taught him. Perhaps this is why Eliade tried to give them dimensions they did not have, or touched on them only in passing. About this aspect of his Indian life, which Eliade bathed in legend and mystery, there were other more lucid consciousnesses among the colleagues of his generation, such as Constantin Noica who describes him as an "adventurer who perfects his interior legend" ("Notații" 2), or Pompiliu Constantinescu who calls him "the little prophet gone to India to load himself with provisions of mystery" (5).

Moreover, Claude-Henri Rocquet, listening to his testimonies, said to him directly: "As for me, I no longer know what to think. I feel I'm in the situation of the 'old man' in your last novel [*The Old Man and the Bureaucrats*]. You have an almost devilish gift for throwing your listeners off the scent, for twisting and turning your plots so that one becomes unable to tell true from false, left from right" (*Ordeal by Labyrinth* 48). Indeed, in narrating his life, Eliade becomes his own character and the old man Fărâmă passes on this side of the mirror in order to recover the past reality together with all its unfulfilled possibilities. Traversing time in a reverse order, at some crossroads he prefers other roads than the ones he has taken, and he now "corrects" the course of his life by reintegrating into a symbolic plane that which he has failed in the concrete plane of experience.

EXPERIENTIALISM AND INTIATION

> But I want the results of my experiences to modify the lives of others. I want to have sons, that is. And anyone can be my son, since no one can be himself.
>
> —*Isabel și apele diavolului* (1929)

All these observations, perhaps pedantic but necessary, lead to the question that justifies our interest: Was Eliade truly initiated in one of the spiritual traditions of India? Initiation is an idea linked inextricably to that of tradition, being considered the operative part of it, the process through which traditional knowledge is transmitted to the disciple by the master (the depositor of the tradition received through initiation and realized through personal work), and through which he obtains spiritual realization. In the various Indian religious traditions, initiation is, without exception, the superior and complete form of knowledge. However, when Eliade speaks about his initiation, the word as such is used either in its common, profane sense, or else (although not made explicit) the content to which he refers is revealed to be a profane one.

In an interview given after his return to Romania, he described his stay in India in terms destined to envelop him in a mystical aura.

> My activity consisted of extraordinary studies of the Sanskrit language and research on Indian mystics. I made various acquaintances, I established relations with wandering monks, ascetics, and religious beggars. All these were my professors. They recommended to me hermitages where I met the authentic source of philosophy and knowledge. I would leave Calcutta and for whole months no one knew anything about me. They were the intervals in which I, too, wandered, visiting the monasteries of India. (Robot, "Cu Mircea Eliade" 38–39)

If the perspective in which these testimonies are put is destined to create a certain image, they are based, none the less, on true data. Leaving aside his attraction for personalities such as Gandhi and Tagore, Eliade showed a special interest, going to the point of contact, with four living currents of spiritual traditions in northeast India: Bengalese Vaishnavism (as reformed by Chaitanya), the Neo-Vedantism of Vivekananda and the Ramakrishna Mission, the "Integral Yoga" of Aurobindo Ghose, and Lamaistic Buddhism. With the exception of the last, for which his interest at that time was limited to superficial visits to a few Sikkhim monasteries, the other currents were modernized reforms. Moreover, in the case of Aurobindo Ghose, the reinterpretation of tradition was accompanied by harsh antitraditionalist critiques and by an opening toward Western culture (visible in their true extent only after the posthumous publication of the writings dating from the days of his reclusion) which make his thought to be, in the present day, viewed with suspicion by traditional Brahmans.

In September 1929, eight months after his arrival in Calcutta, when they were en route to Shantiniketan, Dasgupta promised to initiate Eliade into yoga practice. From the fragments of the journal published in *Şantier*, we do not learn if that initiation took place, but a little while later, after returning from Tagore's university, we find him noting a certain "very complicated mental practice" which has produced a state of "goodness," peace, and "light," after which silence spreads definitively (*Şantier*, 65, 73–74).

While he was staying at Calcutta, Eliade frequented the monks at the Neo-Vedantin monastery Belur Math, at the edge of the city (especially his friend, Swami Nilakananda), and even accompanied them to the *kumbha mela* at Allahabad in January 1930. In his visits around Calcutta, at Puri, at Benares, or at the Buddhist monasteries around Darjeeling, he sought to know more closely the life of the Indian yogis and mystics. When his father asked him to find a fakir to make demonstrations in Romania, he replied, "I know at Puri an extraordinary tantric yogi, but he would not agree to show off anything."[46] True yogis and tantrics do not betray their secrets to anyone who visit them out of curiosity, even savants. How much could the young orientalist learn from his visits? And how could he hope to receive initiation without giving elementary proof of his aspiration for it? Because, the fact is, he did not remain, nor take seriously the invitation to remain for twelve years alongside "the first yogi" he met in a Bengalese *basti* ("Cel dintâi yoghin . . ."), or fifteen years in a lamaistic monastery in Sikkhim (*India* 94).

After his banishment from the house of Professor Dasgupta, Eliade wrote to him about his leaving for Rishikesh "to take the Hindu initiation": "I will be a brahmacarin for life."[47] It seems he was still thinking of the Vaishnavite tradition, as it had been reformed by

Chaitanya, into which he had hope to be accepted—at Puri—in order to become Maitreyi's husband.[48] However, not in Rishikesh and Uttar Khand, which was the country of yogis and tantrics of Shaivite or Shakta sects, could he find this tradition. After arriving in Rishikesh, Eliade wrote to Khokha Dasgupta, "I am a Hindu now" (*Europa, Asia, America* 162). But we have already seen how he understood this, and how he spent the three months at the base of the Himalayas, ending with the breach of his *brahmacarin* commitment.

Finally, having returned to Calcutta, Eliade believed he had found his guru in the person of a rishi, the head of a family, in a suburb of the city, somewhat as did his friend of a later date, C. G. Jung, who, in the three weeks he spent in India, refused to visit Ramana Maharishi in his refuge at Arunachala, but, profoundly impressed, spent much time in the company of a disciple of his, a man with a family in Bombay.[49]

The yoga techniques he had learned from Dasgupta and from Swami Shivananda—which demand rigor, self-mastery, constancy, a pure life, and the renunciation of most "worldly" things—he followed only episodically. In the first interview he gave after his return to Bucharest, being asked if he still practiced the system of yogic postures and breathing techniques, he replied, "No. It is bound up with a way of life, food, and a very severe psychic and physical discipline" (Preda 24).

Thus, all these things remained just "experiences," like many others—some exactly their opposite—which the young Eliade ventured in those years, because they were intended to "assure him immortality" through literature, that is, through "passing into the consciousness of others."[50] To this Eliade, we believe, is applicable the messianic aphorism from the first novel written in India, which we have used as an epigraph to this section. And from these experiences—also initiatory in their way—there was begotten the one who, a decade later, spoke through the mouth of Tuliu in the novel *Viața nouă* : "I am not a practitioner. I am content with principles, that is, more precisely, with the clear and coherent understanding of them. . . . I have more faith in Guénon, because he, like me, works with principles" (*Viața nouă* , 157, 161).

NOTES

1. See bibliography for details, especially Fiore; Monastra; Baillet; de Turris; Montanari; Mutti; Pisi; Hansen; Quinn; Wasserstrom; Spineto, "Mircea Eliade and Traditionalism" (adapted in this volume); Rennie, "Religion after Religion" and "M.E.: A Secular Mystic." Although the subject began to be discussed widely only in the 1980s, it was known and mentioned long before. See, for example, the observation of Al. Piru: "Taking as its model the ethnographic and folkloric studies of René Guénon, J. Evola, Ananda Coomaraswamy, etc. who tried to establish the unity of traditions and symbols that lie at the base of the ancient oriental, American, and occidental civilizations ..." etc., in *Panorama deceniului literar românesc 1940–1950*, 521–22. In what follows, I will emphasize only some facts and data not previously taken into consideration.

2. Other instances in which Julius Evola is used by Eliade in literature are found in "The Secret of Dr. Honigberger" (*Secretul doctorului Honigberger*): his disciple from Iași, J. E., who "attempted, under the direct influence of Honigberger, an initiation of the yogic type, and failed miserably," and in "Nineteen Roses" (*Nouăsprezece trandafiri*): Ieronim Thanase.

3. Eliade, *Viață Nouă* 155. Among the Romanian books should be mentioned also *Dacia preistorică* by Nicolae Densușianu, whose role in stimulating the creativity of both the Romanian Guénonians and occultists is well known. Pages 153–66 of *Viață Nouă* constitute a whole "Tuliu chapter" in which the name of Guénon is mentioned six times.

4. Petre Lupu (1908–1994), Romanian shepherd who supposedly received a revelation in 1935 (the first of many) at a place called Maglavit, site of an ancient shrine, which then became a center of pilgrimage.

5. Eliade, "Jurnalul romanului *Viață Nouă*," in *Viață Nouă* 212. From this point one can begin the best archeology of the multiple strata—of a contextual-historical nature, but also, and primarily, of a cultural-spiritual one—which represents the engagement in history of the Eliadean idea of the "primacy of the spiritual" and in which the "traditionalist" sympathy meets with the Legionary. The novel is planned to reflect the entire drama of modern Romania and "of course, the Legionary tragedy will play the essential role" ("Jurnalul *Viață Nouă*" 203). He writes it with "the sentiment and certitude that I have begun the most important book in Romanian literature, the novel through which I attempt a regeneration of my people ... which is the greatest act of

Romanianism" (206–207, 213). The simultaneous opening toward "traditionalism" and Legionary mysticism, but also the "occult" presuppositions of other Eliadean motifs is developed in Bordaş, "Istoria doctorului Honigberger."

6. In June 1929, at Calcutta, he read the books of Guénon, *La crise du monde moderne* and *L'homme et son devenire selon le Vedanta*, which are some of those he ordered specially from Paris. Cf. Eliade, *Europa, Asia, America . . . , Corespondenţă* I, A–H, 265. Then he asked that Evola's reviews, *Bilychinis* and *Krur* be sent from home (272). In May of the same year, Evola also sent him, on request, his last publications: the 1929 issues of *Krur* and *La Torre*, the books *L'uomo come potenza* (1926), *Imperialismo pagano* (1928), *Teoria dell'individuo assoluto* (1927), and *Fenomenologia dell'Individuo assoluto* (1930). Cf. *Mircea Eliade şi corespondenţii săi*, vol 1 (A–E), 276.

7. See §2 of my study, "Secretul doctorului Eliade" 73–76. In the same period, more precisely in the fall of 1933, there occurred what was publicly recognized as Eliade's "conversion" to the current of Romanian traditionalism, initiated by Eminescu and continued through Iorga, Pârvan, and the *Gândirea* generation, down to Nae Ionescu.

8. The period 1945–1955 was one of transition and reestablishment in the life of Eliade. Concerning his verbal declarations about Guénon in this period, see the letter of Mihail Vâlsan to Vasile Lovinescu of 1957, cited in Claudio Mutti, *Eliade, Vâlsan, Geticus e gli altri* 39–40. See also Eliade's late references to Guénon, Evola, the "primordial tradition" in which he cannot believe, and to the illusion of its adepts who believe that they are possessors of "secret teachings" in *Ordeal by Labyrinth* and the *Autobiography*. In one of the versions of "L'anthropologie philosophique" (dated July–August 1974) destined for the L'Herne volume, Cahiers 33, *Mircea Eliade* (1978), Ioan Petru Culianu wrote: "Could Eliade be considered, together with a Guénon or an Evola, a champion of 'traditionalism'? Perhaps so, but it must be said that his influence has surpassed by far that of Guénon as well as Evola, because Eliade knew how to preserve the magical label of academic 'science,' while being at the same time more open to the message of diverse cultural currents of his epoch (to the psychoanalysis of Jung, for example, criticized by Guénon). The fact that he assimilated completely the 'tools of the doomed West' assured him a wide audience in circles which, although not being 'traditionalist,' felt the same 'nostalgia for origins,' " (Culianu, "Experienţă, cunoaştere, iniţiere" 241).

9. Unpublished excerpt from the Journal manuscript in the Regenstein Library at the University of Chicago. Supplied by Mac Linscott Ricketts, whom the author thanks.

10. As to the origin and significance of this curious and rare pseudonym, I have not found any statement or indication. Claudio Mutti opines that it could be the consonants of the Sanskrit *karma* or the Arabic root *karîm* (1999, 104). I add, as being more probable, *kṛm* or *krīm*, the Kālī-mantra in the tantric cult.

11. "Ananda K. Coomaraswamy," *Revista fundațiilor regale* IV:7 (July 1937): 183–89; republished in *Insula lui Euthanasius* 222.

12. Cf. Eliade, *Diario Portugués* 85. Original Romanian supplied by Ricketts.

13. Tolcea, *Eliade, ezotericul* 52, n.43. Even if he had visited the capital of French India, he certainly was not the first Romanian to do so. It is true that the Romanian public knew almost nothing about the Romanian travelers in India who had preceded Eliade. They were numerous enough by the second half of the nineteenth century, even if none of them compared to him in stature.

14. *Autobiography vol. 1*, 202. The episode at Rishikesh is found on 196–200. In an Epilogue to the novel *Maitreyi*, attributed to a friend of the author, which Eliade later suppressed, the following passage is included: "He [Allen] saw Jenia Isaac again, and the story became complicated. I myself met this young Jewish woman when she came to Calcutta to look for Allen and, being refused, she tried to become a prostitute. I remember that she went to Firpos, dressed elegantly and strikingly, in order to attract the attention of the European public. Jenia seemed more sincere and more intelligent than she had appeared in my friend's letter. Moreover, she was accustomed to say, 'All or nothing!' and since she had not succeeded in becoming an ascetic, she preferred to try prostitution rather than fail at mediocrity. I and, indirectly, Allen had stopped her from carrying out such a decision, made in an hour of despair. Jenia Isaac is now living in an *ashram* in South India, where she has bound herself to an oath of silence for five years." Eliade, *Opere* 2. *Maitreyi* 390–92. Eliade refers to Jenny and this vow of silence in an interview of 1948 where he speaks about his experiences at Rishikesh: "a young Finnish woman, of Jewish descent, who came from South Africa where she had made a name for herself as a musician in a Johannesburg orchestra. She went on to Pondicherry near Shri Aurobindo and, following her spiritual experiences, I learned that she had taken a vow of silence for five years." Aimé Patri, "Mircea Eliade nous parle des méthodes de l'ascétisme indou" 51 (thanks to M. L. Ricketts for supplying this interview).

15. Her name as an initiate, as it appears in the register of the *ashram*. See also Roman Palit, "The Grace," in Pandit, ed., *Breath of Grace* 94.

16. Eliade says Johannesburg in his memoirs, and Capetown in *Maitreyi*. In the latter he adds that she belonged to a family of Finnish Jews, established

since the end of the nineteenth century in South Africa. He describes her in this way: "rather young, expressionless, a round face, blue eyes, a girlish voice, contrasting with a sturdy frame, tall, strong, with sinewy arms and a broad chest." Formerly a cellist in the Capetown municipal orchestra, but performing also in Johannesburg, she had renounced everything to seek "the Absolute" in India, which had been revealed to her by the books of Ramacharaka (William Walker Atkinson and Baba Bharata) (*Opere* 2, 138–40).

17. Five letters from Jenny are reproduced in a weak Romanian translation in Eliade, *Opere* 2, 184–91. The first three letters are sent from Rishikesh-Haridwar, in January, and the last two from Pondicherry, in March. From their content, it is evident that they are not the only exchanges of correspondence between the two in the period January–March 1931. Moreover, the editors mention that Jenny continued sending letters until the summer of that year, and that they have reproduced "only a few of them, the ones that have the most visible contingency with the problematics of the novel" (184). In the volume, *Mircea Eliade și corespondenții săi* vol. 2, 292–302, in the section on Jenny, only the first three letters from Rishikesh, in the original English and in Romanian translation, are reproduced.

18. Preda, "Viața indiană. De vorbă cu Mircea Eliade." The statement that Aurobindo had lived "withdrawn in a cell" for thirty years is incorrect; he had taken refuge at Pondicherry in 1910 where he had gradually built an *ashram* around him, but only in 1926 did he begin his withdrawal into a cell.

19. "Spiritualitate și mister feminin" 153. Also incorrect is the statement made here that "Sri Aurobindo shut himself away for seventeen years at Pondicherry."

20. "Let us take an example tiresomely common in the *Vedas* to which Sri Aurobindo Ghosh draws attention: cattle (*go*)." Eliade, "Upanișade," 1932, reprinted in *Erotica mistică în Bengal* 65.

21. "*Swaraj* is a Vedantic idea, inasmuch as it entails independence through one's own means, not "good-government," but "self-government." Because, for an Indian, liberation, independence, *swaraj* (in metaphysics and morals, *mukti*) cannot be given, either by the neighbor or by a foreigner. It is a personal matter, conditioned by the karmic equation of the individual or the race. It must be gained by its own means. I doubt that the Mahatma is conscious of the Indian nature of his campaign; he is interested, rather, in its universal, human, Christian aspect. But Aurobindo Ghosh, who is one of the few Indian minds of modern India who has dared to assimilate and perfect Sanskrit wisdom—inclines toward this Vedantin Indian sense of the word *swaraj*." *Erotica mistică în Bengal* 176. The note is not dated, but it follows

another that carries the date of 5 September. Internal evidence as well as the fact that the cycle (begun on 2 June 1930) is concluded after a few other notations shows that it is prior to his departure for Rishikesh.

22. "In the experience of a rishi (men who have not disappeared from India, even today, for example, the philosopher Aurobindo Gosh [sic]) ... ," Eliade, "Metafizica Upaniṣadelor," III, 1933; reprinted in *Erotica mistică în Bengal* 80.

23. "Note, extrase, bibliografie," in *Erotica mistică în Bengal* 93–102. In a letter from Rishikesh to Khokha (Sukumar Dasgupta) dated 5 December 1930, Eliade wrote, "I have translated *Katha Upanishad* into our language and have completed a long article on the philosophy of the Upanishads ... I can say about the Upanishad: 'It has been the solace of my life and it will be the solace of my death.'" See Maitreyi Devi, *It Does Not Die* 253, 241. (In the original Bengali edition, the subject and verbs of the last sentence were plural. The statement comes from Schopenhauer who wrote: "It [i.e., the reading of the Upanishads] has been the solace of my life; it will be the solace of my death." *Parerga* 2, 185 [*Werke* 6, 427].)

24. In a letter to Petru Comarnescu, as early as 19 February 1929, Eliade had written, "Perhaps I will be accepted into the Mayavati Monastery, Almora (Himalaya), where the yoga is authentic." Eliade, *Corespondenţă* I, A–H, 173. On other occasions he expressed his distance from the Vedantin philosophy and the thought of Swami Vivekananda, both of which lie—undogmatically, however—at the basis of the Advaita Ashram in Mayavati.

25. "Un reprezentant al tradiţiei hinduse: Sri Aurabindo" 20. Pondicherry was, at that time, the capital of the scattered French colonial enclaves in India, which today form a Union territory under the Indian central government.

26. See the letters to his family of 15 October 1930 and 22 January 1931, reproduced in *Erotica mistică în Bengal* 241 and 244.

27. See the letters of 23 January, 17 April, 24 July 1929; 10 April, 1 May 1930; 22 January, 2 April, 11 June 1931; in *Erotica mistică în Bengal* 193, 201, 203, 210, 234–35, 236, 244, 246, 247. All these letters are published also in *Europa, Asia, America* I.

28. An Indian theologian from Kerala, living in the United States, who met Eliade on the campus of the University of Chicago, told us that the professor had declared that he had traveled in Malabar, and even had passed through this man's home town. My attempt to raise arguments against this statement was insistently resisted.

29. In the Shri Aurobindo Ashram Archives and Research Library only three letters related to Jenny are preserved: in the first, sent in October 1931

from a hotel in Durban, her sister asks for news of Jenny and asks her to write; the second is the reply written by Nolini Kanta Gupta at the request of Aurobindo Ghose, saying that Jenny is well and will write soon (dated 10 December 1931); the third is a letter of thanks from Jenny's sister to Nolini Kanta Gupta (January 1932). I owe the discovery of these letters to Peter Heehs.

30. Even the taking in jest of this image created in his Indian period, seen in pamphlets, sarcastic journalistic caricatures, and cartoons appearing in the era (in which Eliade is portrayed as a fakir, a Gandhist *satyagrahi*, and a turbaned mystic) constitutes proof of the seriousness with which his Indian "myth" was received.

31. Preda, "Viața indiană. De vorbă cu D-nul Mircea Eliade" 23 and O'Hara, "Mircea Eliade."

32. In the third edition, edited with a preface by Mircea Handoca, Bucharest: Editura pentru turism, 1991, 28. In the novel *Maitreyi*, the hero withdraws "into a bungalow between Almora and Raniket," between the months of October and March. Cf. Eliade, *Opere* 2, 133.

33. Cf. *Yoga, Immortality, and Freedom* xxii. Also the period of three years will be enlarged to four. In a letter to Ananda K. Coomaraswamy (Paris, 26 August 1947) he told the Anglo-Sinhalese scholar that he spent "more than three years in the Indies." (The letter, from the archives of the Princeton University Library, was communicated to me by Mac Linscott Ricketts.) In the second letter sent after the war to Papini (Paris, 12 May 1952), he writes that he spent four years in India (see the original French correspondence in Bordaș, "Une 'correspondance' spirituelle"). The same statement will be made later in writing and in interviews. Cf. for example, "Mircea Eliade: Chicago's humanistic historian of religion," *The Grey City Journal* (18 May 1979): 14–15 and Vittorio Vettori, *A Colloquio con Mircea Eliade. Rivalutazione della categoria del sacro per un nuovo rinascimento mondiale*, L'Osservatore Romano, Roma, 28–29 November 1983, 3, where it is made in the presentations that precede the interviews. (Thanks to M. L. Ricketts and Corneliu Horia Cicortaș for copies of these.)

34. See, for example, "the Swargashram of Shiwananda," in Culianu, *Mircea Eliade* 16, 37, and "the hermitage (*ashram*) of Shri Shivananda," ("Experiență, cunoaștere, inițiere," 254, see also 273).

35. In a letter to Valeriu Bologa, dated at Calcutta on 3 February 1931—although speaking approximately—he wrote: "I left Calcutta in September and returned only on 15 January." Cf. *Europa, Asia, America* 81. (What is interesting is that this letter was first published in December 1969, in *Steaua*, Cluj,

long before the appearance of *Ordeal by Labyrinth* and the *Autobiography*, vol. I, in both of which the "six-months version" is reaffirmed.) The second letter of Jenny sent after his departure bears the postmark 15 January, and on 22 January Eliade himself wrote to his parents from Calcutta. Cf. *Europa, Asia, America* 314–15. On 20 January Professor Dasgupta sent him the second "warning letter" at Calcutta. Reproduced in Romanian in Eliade, *Opere* 2, 166–67. In a letter of 11 February Khokha wrote him: "I heard recently that you arrived a month ago," 175. The letter of Jenny postmarked 15 January was written the day before, in the evening. From it we learn that it is the second sent from Rishikesh, and that it follows Eliade's answer to the first ("I wrote you a long letter, but you replied with such a short, cold, standoffish one, and nothing about yourself," 185). Since it took at least three days for a letter to travel between Rishikesh and Calcutta, Eliade must have left Rishikesh before 7 January. Moreover, on the day he left Dasgupta's house, he had sent a letter to his parents informing them of his plan to make a visit to Romania and asking them to send him a ticket from the S.M.R. (Romanian Maritime Society) from Alexandria to Constanța for the period 1 January to 1 March 1931. Even if he later decided against the visit to Romania, we have here yet another proof that his sojourn in Himalaya was foreseen as for a period of approximately three months only. In another letter of 15 October in which he announces that he has given up making the trip home, he writes nevertheless that he intends to remain in Himalaya another two months ("in order to build a physical constitution of iron and at the same time to study close-up the technique of the Yogis") and in January to settle in Benares. Cf. letters from 11 September and 15 October, reproduced in *Erotica mistică în Bengal* 241–42, and in *Europa, Asia, America* 310–12.

36. The last article in the Himalayan series, published in *Cuvântul* under the title, "Din 'necunoscuta Indie,' Leproșii" ("From 'Unknown India,' Lepers"), is postmarked and dated, Munikhereti, Himalaya, 7 January 1931. Since this is in downtown Rishikesh, it means that Eliade had left Svarga-Așram and was on his way to Calcutta.

37. *Autobiography I*, 196–200. In *Maitreyi*, Jenia Isaac is made to arrive "at the beginning of February" (*Opere* 2, 138).

38. *Șantier* 117. Other places where Jenny is mentioned: 120 ("I have humiliated Jenny"), 131, 147–48, 149, 174, 175.

39. *Șantier*, 147–48. In the novel the phrase is slightly different: "my violated virginity and pride...." *Întoarcerea din rai* 74–75.

40. *Șantier* 149. Cf. *Maitreyi*, in *Opere* 2, 143–44. In one of Jenny's letters, her jealousy betrays a second feminine presence in Eliade's life at Rishikesh:

"your dear Miss Bannerjee." She writes of the "flower-like face and dainty form of your dearly beloved," and accuses him of having arranged to see her after leaving the ashram. *Mircea Eliade și corespondenții săi* vol. 2, 292.

41. In the period of his stay at Rishikesh, Eliade was preoccupied with the problem of tantrism, not only for his doctoral thesis, but also for the novel *Lumina ce se stinge*, at the center of which is a sexual act performed coolly, lucidly, detached from any voluptuousness, like a tantric sexual ritual. See *Lumina ce se stinge* vol. II, 72–73, where Manoil, the one who committed it, explains the metaphysics underlying the act. In an interview of 1933, Eliade declared that he intended to write the sequel to *Maitreyi* when he reached forty. Robot, "Mircea Eliade scrie romanul generației lui: foame, sex și moarte."

42. "For me, an understanding of traditional religious values is the first step toward a spiritual awakening. Whereas [Allan] Watts, and others like him, believed—and maybe they were right—that one can speak directly to the masses with something resembling a 'message' and awaken them that way. I myself believe that we are 'condemned'—products of the modern world that we are—to receive any revelation through culture." *Ordeal by Labyrinth* 62.

43. *India* 28. Nevertheless, he himself tells about two Englishmen, independently of each other, who withdrew into Himalaya and had become *saddhus*. One, a doctor of law from London, had renounced the world, becoming Swami Advaitananda; the other, a soldier, Arthur Young, donned the clothing of an anchorite under the name of Swami Jnanananda. They, indeed, and others like them, seem not to have written anything about their experiences. *India*, 114–15, 127, 131–38, and *Autobiography* I, 195–96.

44. From a Guénonian position, Florin Mihăescu, for example, writes that Eliade returned from India "not with an initiation—as was expected—but with a wealth of documentary material from which the first version of his study about yoga would take shape." Commenting on Eliade's remarks about the illusory "initiations" of contemporary esotericists made to C.-H. Rocquet, the same author asks, "How is it possible for a non-initiate to know that the real initiation of Guénon is an illusion?" Mihăescu, "Mircea Eliade e René Guénon" 15, 17.

45. Eugéne Ionesco states that Eliade, "instead of being an initiate, limited himself, and became resigned to being only a scholar, a great scholar, but nothing but a scholar." See Tacou et al., *Cahiers de l'Herne, Mircea Eliade* 272–73. Florin Mihăescu speaks of "the evolution of the Romanian writer's thought, from a believer and seeker of an initiatory realization, to an agnostic historian of religions preoccupied with academic research and international recognition," 18. This explanation—advanced in one form or another by other authors

too—which would have the advantage of making immediately comprehensible the complex cerebral and spiritual life of Eliade—is based, in both of its assumptions, on myths and rumors created around his personality. While Eliade did not become an agnostic, he was always primarily concerned with his affirmation in the world as an exceptional creator. That this was a powerful and constant preoccupation even throughout his sojourn in India is proved emphatically by his whole correspondence with his family in that period.

46. Letter of 10 April 1930, in *Erotica mistică în Bengal* 235; *Europa, Asia, America* 303–304.

47. Written by Eliade in English, September 1930. In *Europa, Asia, America* 216.

48. In the second threatening letter, which he sent Eliade after his return to Calcutta, Professor Dasgupta spoke about Eliade's decision to become a Vaishnava saint, and it seems that the family had made fun of him over the name Sri Chaitanya. See the letters of Dasgupta and Khokha reproduced in Romanian translation in *Opere* 2, 166 and 171. See, also, the passage in the novel *Maitreyi*, where he speaks enthusiastically about his discovery of the Vaishnava cult, of Chaitanya's life, and of his mystical love. *Opere* 2, ed. cit., 62–63, 77.

49. "My life is a tragi-comedy. To have to spend three years in India, to wander far and wide—in order to find my man a few kilometers from my house in Howrah . . ." *Șantier* 161. The rest of the note referring to this guru was omitted from the published version. The episode could be explained by the publication of the entire Indian journal.

50. *Șantier* 51. This "desire for power" colored intellectually and spiritually, had been remarked already by commentators of the time. Its fulfillment through his success in the West and his worldwide academic recognition will provoke in him gradually, however, the nostalgia for "the unfinished road" and "failed encounters." Toward the end of his life he returns meditatively, more and more, to the essential experiences of his Indian period. This inclinatin is most manifest in *Nouăsprezece trandafiri* ("Nineteen Roses," in *Youth without Youth* 153–285), and, perhaps, in the very writing of this novella. Observe, in a literary camouflage, the public impression left by his Indian episode: "[A]ll kinds of rumors were going around town—that you weren't coming back, that the Maestru had persuaded you to stay there, in India, if not permanently, then at least several years, until he should come himself" (233), and its truth, revealed in what the Maestru says to the assistant: "I'm glad you've returned home on time!" he exclaimed. "I was afraid you might stay several more days at Pondicherry. And that would have been a pity"

(228). And likewise, the attempt to reply to the key question, *"Why did my interest in drama cease so abruptly and definitively after my return from Sibiu? . . . Something intervened, something I can't succeed in remembering, that had a traumatic effect. . . . How is it possible to have forgotten everything?"* (199–200) (if one reads "drama" as "yoga"—the dramatic art being understood in the novella as a soteriological therapeutics, a technique of salvation—and "Sibiu" as "Rishikesh"). "At that moment, therefore, you had a shocking revelation, which so frightened you that, without any effort on your part, *you forgot it.* . . . What was revealed to you—that is, what simple and yet terrible truth did you learn, when you sensed that *you could never quench your thirst*—that it resists all our efforts at anamnesis?" "Perhaps it was purely and simply," said A.D.P., pronouncing the words slowly, "that if I were to continue seeing Eurydice, and thus dedicate my life to the theater, I would soon die.". . . . "Who has not been afraid on the threshold of his salvation?" [said Niculina]. "Even Jesus was afraid . . ." (250).

Mircea Eliade and "Traditional Thought"

Natale Spineto

Recent studies have laid increasing stress on the importance that the reading of exponents of what is commonly termed "traditional thought" had on the development of Eliade's ideas.[1] These studies have moved in two directions: on the one hand, they have tried to clarify, on the biographical level, the circumstances in which Eliade came to know the works of René Guénon, Julius Evola, and Ananda Coomaraswamy and used their conclusions in his writings; on the other, they have investigated the implicit or explicit presence of some key notions of traditional thought in Eliadean "philosophy" and methodology. Clearly, these are two interconnected problems, which can only be solved by the adoption of a historiographical method. The present essay aims to clarify, in a historiographical perspective, the importance and the limitations of the influence exerted by the traditionalists on the Eliadean approach, both during the period of its evolution and in its mature expressions, on the basis of an analysis of Eliade's writings and an assessment of the most recent critical studies.

THE TRADITIONALISTS IN ELIADE'S PREWAR WRITINGS

The first reference to Guénon—whom Eliade never met in person—probably dates from 1927: in a critique of the theosophical movement, Eliade cites *Le Théosophisme, histoire d'une pseudo-religion* (1921—"Itinerariu spiritual VIII (Teosofie?)" 48); and he returns to the same subject in 1932 (Ricketts, *Romanian Roots* 848). Ieronim Serbu writes that he once possessed a copy of *L'homme et son devenir selon le Védânta*, signed by Eliade and dated Calcutta, 18 June 1929 (Mihaescu 15). Eliade also read *L'Esotérisme de Dante* (1925) and *Le roi du monde* (1927), which he lent to Marcel Avramescu in the early 1930s (Mutti 36). In 1937 he expresses his regret that *Orient et Occident* and *La crise du monde moderne* have not been more widely read,[2] and he makes the same comment in another article in which he groups Guénon together with Evola and Coomaraswamy ("Ananda Coomaraswamy" and "Note și fragmente").[3] According to Mihaescu, the history of relations between the two scholars may be divided into three phases: in the first, the period of his youth, Eliade reads Guénon, admires his work, and refers to it; in the second, which extends down to the 1970s, Eliade, now integrated into Western intellectual circles, makes no mention of the writings of the French traditionalist. In the last phase, when Eliade's international reputation is assured, he starts to mention Guénon again and acknowledges his importance, though with some reservations (Mihaescu 17–18).

As far as Evola is concerned, Eliade was familiar with his work as early as 1927, when he commented on an article of his on occultism, praising the competence, the command of the evidence, and the understanding of the problem that the author shows, and accepting the idea that occultism is based on concrete experience; he criticizes him, however, for not taking account of Christianity.[4] Grottanelli (see note 1) comments that

> for Eliade, in this respect closer to Julius Evola [than to Guénon], the occult mentality with its secret traditions ... where the receptacle of a sacred power in their function of redeeming the "new man" and the Romanian nation, even though this power and redemption was meant, unlike in Evola, to be based on a "Christian approach."

In 1935 Eliade wrote a review of *Rivolta contro il mondo moderno* ("Revolta contra lumii moderne"). He considers Evola "one of the most interesting minds of the war generation" and juxtaposes him with Gobineau, Chamberlain, Spengler, and Rosenberg, while apparently considering him more "serious" than all of them; he says that he has published an essay on him divided into several parts and that he has written a study of his philosophy, though he has not published it.

As Paola Pisi points out, the review does not correspond exactly to the content of the book: Eliade writes that Evola is "anti-Christian and antipolitical . . . against both communists and fascists" (6), "an opinion about Evola which is hard to share" (Pisi 45); moreover, he misunderstands—as we will see later—the Evolian concept of "Tradition." The two men met in 1937 at the home of Nae Ionescu.[5] Writing in 1937, Eliade describes both Guénon and Evola as "dilettantes" (the quotation marks are his own), probably meaning that they have no specialized competence, unlike Coomaraswamy, Walter Andrae, Paul Mus, and Alfred Jeremias, who are cited in the same context ("Folklorul ca instrument de cunoaştere").

Later he met Coomaraswamy, a Guénonian scholar who, however, differed from Guénon in not leaving the academic world. Eliade was familiar with his work as early as 1926, before Coomaraswamy came under the influence of the French traditionalist (Ricketts, *Romanian Roots* 851), and he began corresponding with him in the 1930s.[6] In 1937 he expresses admiration for the way in which Coomaraswamy, like Guénon and Evola, shows that oriental religion and philosophy are in harmony with Western "traditionalism." For Coomaraswamy emphasized the primordial, metaphysical Tradition ("Ananda Coomaraswamy," cf. Ricketts, *Romanian Roots* 851), as is shown by the example of the sacred tree.

These biographical facts and these—albeit scanty—references to the texts certainly indicate that Eliade paid particular attention to Guénon, Evola, and Coomaraswamy, but beyond the personal contacts, encomiums, and analogies, the extent to which the reading of the traditionalists influenced Eliade's writings can only be assessed on the basis of a thorough examination of the content of the writings themselves.

Paola Pisi has carried out such an analysis, looking for actual correspondences between certain writings by Eliade and the works of the three authors in question. The results of her research make it possible to clarify some key elements in the Romanian scholar's development. In the first place, they concern his researches into alchemy. Alchemy was a subject that had already been discussed by Nae Ionescu, who, however, had merely offered a few hints; but in Evola's writings on the subject—which had been published much earlier than Eliade's, and were known to him—we find that they have some central themes in common. The cosmological and at the same time spiritual nature of alchemical techniques, and the idea of nature as an organic whole whose different levels are linked by correspondences, are features that are present both in Eliade's interpretation and in that of Evola, who in turn derives them from Guénon (Pisi 49–50), though it should be pointed out that these are standard topics in occultist studies. The multiplicity of meanings of the symbol is also characteristic of Guénon's thought (51). Eliade might also have found in Guénon the two themes of the "center of the world" and the celestial models of human constructions, which he discusses in particular in *Cosmologie și alchimie babiloniana* (published in 1937). For the symbolism of the center, however, we should not overlook the influence of Uno Holmberg and Paul Mus. According to Ricketts, the symbolism of the *axis mundi* comes from Coomaraswamy and Mus, but, as Pisi points out, Ricketts acknowledges that both scholars had borrowed it from Guénon (97, 60). As far as the *Myth of Reintegration* is concerned, Pisi notes how the notions of "reintegration" and "androgyny" are typical of modern occultism and esotericism: so there are bound to be passages in the book that recall writings of the traditionalists; we find, in the two most important chapters of the *Myth of Reintegration*, a series of concepts and arguments from the works of Coomaraswamy (54). The theme of sacrifice—and ritual—as reintegration is also characteristic of Coomaraswamy (58). The expression "rupture of plane" (*rupture de niveau*), on the other hand, is taken from Paul Mus (103, n.81). In the *Comentarii la legenda Masterului Manole* Pisi finds a concept of folklore (also present in *Fragmentarium*) similar to that of Evola and Coomaraswamy, who in turn drew it from Guénon (61). In the same work we come across the notion of archetype, linked with the ideas of participation and ritual repetition; Pisi connects the origin of the concept of archetype with Eliade's studies on the celestial models of constructions and on human sacrifice as a repetition of the cosmogonic sacrifice, and notes that these motifs are present in Coomaraswamy, linked with the word *archetype*: "This is not just a question of terminology: Coomaraswamy had used the concept of 'archetype' in the sense of 'exemplary model' long before Eliade" (68). Moreover, Eliade could also have found the term *archetype* in Andrae and Guénon.[7]

The works considered are only a small part of Eliade's voluminous production, but it is probable that an extension of the analysis would confirm these conclusions, especially as his thesis and his articles on yoga deal with subjects to which some exponents of traditionalist thought had devoted particular attention. It must therefore be concluded that some central and characteristic concepts of Eliade's thought derive some of their features—in some cases fundamental ones—directly from his reading and his use of the works of the traditionalists. This is true in particular of the concepts of anthropocosmic correspondence, of the symbol, of the sacred center, of the "cyclical" quality of traditional time, of human construction as a repetition of cosmogony, of sacrifice as reintegration, of androgyny, and of the archetype. Since these are all terms and notions that form an integral part of the theoretical framework of Eliade's postwar work, it may be said that his encounter with the traditionalists brought about a transformation. The study of Eliade's *oeuvre* leads Mac Linscott Ricketts to date this transformation approximately to the years 1936–1937 (Ricketts, *Romanian Roots* 800ff.).

The transformation may, however, be interpreted in two ways: as an adherence to traditionalist thought or as a change of perspective that is stimulated by the reading of the traditionalists, but which gives rise to a new result. The alternative may be formulated in the words that Eliade uses in his review of Evola:

> [W]orks of this kind can be read in many ways: as people who are ready to accept everything at our own risk or reject everything in the same manner; but also as people who are ready to welcome suggestions wherever they come from and who are happy to verify them in every circumstance. (*Revolta contra lumii moderne*)

To which of the two groups does Eliade belong?

A thorough analysis reveals that traditionalist concepts and terms are integrated by Eliade within a different conceptual framework. In the first place, the central notion of traditionalism, the very idea of a primordial Tradition, is lacking in Eliade. In a book on *Symbole, mythe, culture,* which he was planning at this time, he intended to demonstrate the universality of the metaphysical traditions and the unity of symbolism, but he never speaks of "primordial Tradition." He states that by "traditional culture," "we mean ... any culture ... dominated in its totality by norms whose religious or cosmological (metaphysical) validity is not called into question by any member of the community" ("Barabadur, tempul simbolic" n.1); elsewhere, he writes that "in traditional cultures (India, China, etc.) there is a certain 'fidelity' to doctrines, to norms. They show no interest in 'novelty,' 'change,' 'adventure' " (*Fragmentarium* 130). In short, the adjective "traditional" here has a descriptive significance, not a normative one (the formulation is that of Paola Pisi 99, n.69): it serves to indicate a certain type of culture, in the definition of which there is nothing that implies an adherence to traditionalism. It is significant, moreover, that in the review of Evola quoted above he defines the notion of "traditional values" as follows: "every value that does not make life an end in itself, but considers that human existence is only a means of arriving at a spiritual, transcendent reality" (6). Pisi points out that Eliade misunderstands Evola and that here traditional values become "a generic 'opening to the transcendent' " (45). Eliade, then, does not adhere to traditionalist thought, but uses a concept of "tradition" that he has reinterpreted and stripped of those very features that were most distinctive in the traditionalists.

Reinterpreted in this manner, tradition loses its metaphysical connotation: the "Platonic" nature that Eliade acknowledges as characteristic of archaic societies does not in itself imply a Platonic view of reality. This difference is also reflected in the notion of "reintegration," which is stripped of the ontological nature which Coomaraswamy gave it, and in the notion of "archetype," which in the traditionalists has an exclusively metaphysical value, whereas in Eliade it preserves a variety of meanings, which I have attempted to analyze elsewhere.[8]

Devoid of metaphysical value, tradition is not unchanging, either, but is enriched and modified by man's discoveries. Already in 1937, in *Cosmologie şi alchimie babiloniana,* Eliade emphasizes that technical progress (the discovery of metallurgy or agriculture) has the effect of changing the religious heritage of the archaic cultures (12); so he acknowledges that this heritage is dependent on historical processes.

Nor does Eliade seem to accept the thesis propounded by Evola and Guénon, according to which history has a cyclical development and we are at present in a descending phase. In *Cosmologie*, history is presented as a series of "fundamental intuitions" or "mental syntheses," which manifest themselves, degenerate, or die without any progression from one to the other (10 and see Pisi 53). Consequent on this is also a different way of judging modernity. At the end of the *Comentarii*, Eliade writes:

> Is the archaic world, which we have continually evoked in the pages of this book, so very remote from us? And does the act of "degradation" of the original metaphysical meaning, which we have also identified many times, entitle us to depreciate fundamentally all that is "modern," imposing on ourselves at all costs a pessimistic vision of history? (*Comentarii la Legenda Mesterului Manole* 136)

These are of course rhetorical questions, which Pisi suggests "constitute a dialogue at a distance from those 'masters of the Tradition' (Guénon, Evola, Coomaraswamy) whom Eliade had mentioned in the preface as emblematic examples of an antipositivistic reaction" (70–71). On the pages that follow, Eliade stresses that the archetypes continue to act on modern man—though in a nostalgic sense—guaranteeing continuity, as against the total opposition that the traditionalists found between archaic and modern.[9]

Eliade, then, adopts some traditionalist themes in order to insert them in a different context. But what sort of context is it?

In an article published in 1937 he contrasts two ways of analyzing ethnographical and folkloristic documents: the first is that of Lucian Blaga, who searches for the "style" of a culture; the second aims to "determine the unity of the traditions and symbols that are the foundation of the early oriental, Amerindian, and occidental civilizations, as well as of the "ethnographic" cultures" (*Folklorul* 28). Among the representatives of the latter school, Eliade cites Guénon, Evola, Coomaraswamy, Andrae, Mus, and Jeremias; later he also mentions Carl Hentze. The first three figures have already been discussed in detail above; as far as the others are concerned, it should be noted that Mus refers back to Coomaraswamy; Hentze, Andrae, and Jeremias have no direct connection with them. Jeremias spoke of a spiritual language common to the various cultures; Andrae was an anthroposophist—and therefore remote from Guénon's perspective—and had insisted that symbols have a metaphysical meaning, which becomes more obscure with the passing of time, as the symbols become more elaborate (Ricketts, *Romanian Roots* 853). Both authors are used by Coomaraswamy. It is not correct to describe all these perspectives as "traditionalist"; what unites them is the importance they attach to the symbol. In the same year, 1937, Eliade speaks of the rediscovery of the symbol, seeing in this rediscovery the presence of a wider cultural phenomenon than traditionalist thought (*Fragmentarium* 36–37; Ricketts 854). The notion of the symbol, in fact, must be taken as a starting point for an explanation of Eliade's interest in the traditionalists. In the passage quoted above, Eliade searches for "the unity of traditions" in the plural, that is, the element common to the various religious traditions, which, qua traditions, as we saw earlier, possess an openness toward the transcendental. And he finds this unity in the intercultural notion of the symbol. The anthropologists, too, had tried to justify the similarities between the various religious phenomena, but had done so by means of evolutionist principles. In the preface to the *Comentarii la Legenda Masterului Manole* (1943), Eliade sets against the positivist methods of Edward Tylor, Karl Mannhardt, and James George Frazer those of Olivier Leroy, Guénon, Evola, and Coomaraswamy (7). Therefore, although he does not consider them above criticism—he writes that they sometimes have gone so far as to deny "the evidence of history and completely ignored the factual data gathered by researchers"—he attributes to them the fundamental role of having supplied an alternative model to the positivist one.[10]

It is in his search for the constants of humanity, then, that Eliade appropriates traditionalist thought. But at this point, if he is himself to adhere to the traditionalist positions, he would have to define the symbol in a metaphysical sense. This, however, is a step that he does not take, because the basis of the unity of feeling of humankind lies, for him, elsewhere—in existential experience. The universality of the concept of the *coincidentia oppositorum* derives, according to Eliade, from the fact that it "answers, undoubtedly, to a fundamental human need, from the moment he becomes aware of his position in the Cosmos" (*Mitul reintegrarii* 62). As Pisi stresses, such a concept turns Coomaraswamy's and Guénon's ideas on their head, because it puts "at the origin of the ecumenicity of the *coincidentia oppositorum* a natural foundation ('the universal human need') in place of the superhuman (the *philosophia perennis*)" (Pisi 60).

ELIADE'S POSTWAR WRITINGS

After the war Eliade's references to Guénon and Evola become very rare and we might well apply to both of them what Enrico Montanari writes of Guénon, that he becomes "rather an object of interpretation than an interpreter" (134). For a formulation of the greatest differences between the perspectives of the two scholars, we may resort to Montanari. First, according to the traditionalist—and not only the Guénonian—orientation, present-day civilization is in the last phase of a temporal cycle (*Kali-yuga*): but Eliade, whose position even in his youth did not seem compatible with these ideas, writes in 1957 that the doctrine of Kali-yuga derives from a learned reworking by the Indian priestly caste. He uses the doctrine of cosmic cycles as an example to show what happens "when the sense of the religiousness of the cosmos becomes lost" (*The Sacred and the Profane* 107); in other words, he cites a doctrine that Guénon considered genuinely traditional and objectively valid as an example of what happens when one departs from the tradition.[11] Secondly, Eliade praises the value of the "primitive" cultures and considers the shaman as an archetype of the *homo religiosus*: therefore on this question, too, he adopts a position exactly opposite to that of Guénon, for whom shamanism is the degeneration of the primordial.[12] Thirdly, the different treatment of the theme of initiation should be noted: in Eliade, unlike in Guénon, there is no incompatibility between initiation and mysticism (indeed, the

Romanian scholar's main work on initiation is entitled *Naissances mystiques*); there is no technical distinction between great and small mysteries; there is no trace of the theory that the reference to Tradition serves to distinguish true initiations from pseudo-initiations; Eliade does not acknowledge the need to undergo a regular initiatory rite to start on a process of spiritual reintegration; indeed, he thinks that the possibility of oral—as opposed to written—transmission is barred to modern man; and he takes the opposite view from Guénon in attaching importance to "profane instruction" and considering the events of human life as "initiatory ordeal or trials."[13] No comparably thorough analysis has been applied to the influence of Evolian thought on Eliade's postwar writings. Eliade refers to Evola several times without ever speaking of an affinity of views with him. On the contrary, he insists on the divergences that were noted above: "[L]ike René Guénon, Evola presumed a 'primordial tradition' in the existence of which I could not believe; I was suspicious of its artificial, ahistorical character" (*Autobiography II* 152). Modern Western culture, according to Evola, is in a state of decadence or "putrefaction": a diagnosis that in Eliade's view is accurate, but only for someone who believes in the existence of Tradition. "To the extent that I believe in the creativity of the human spirit, I cannot despair; culture, even in a crepuscular era, is the only means of conveying certain values and of transmitting a certain spiritual message."[14] In particular, Eliade is confident about the consequences of the "reentry of Asia into history and the discovery of the spirituality of archaic societies," and believes that the sacred disguised in the profane may be reached through hermeneutics.

Eliade felt closer, in his postwar writings, to Coomaraswamy, who "contrary to René Guénon and other contemporary 'esotericists' . . . developed his exegesis without surrendering the tools and methods of philology, archaeology, art history, ethnology, folklore, and history of religions" ("Some notes on *Theosophia Perennis*" 169). The aspect of his thought that Eliade does not accept is his attitude toward religion, an attitude deriving from "the growing influence of Guénon's rigid rationalism": "the historian of religions is, on the contrary, fascinated by the multiplicity and variety of the ideas about God's unique mode of being, elaborated in the course of the millennia, for every theological structure represents a new spiritual creation, a fresh insight and a more adequate grasp of the ultimate reality" (170). In short, against the unity of the Tradition, Eliade asserts the multiplicity of human spiritual creations; against its primordiality, he holds that a new "theological structure" is "a more adequate grasp of the ultimate reality."

During his American period Eliade only had one student who worked on traditionalist thought: William W. Quinn Jr., who wrote a doctoral dissertation on Coomaraswamy (published under the title *The Only Tradition*). Quinn is the author of a recent article in which he presents Eliade as a traditionalist scholar. His argument is based on three main pieces of evidence: first, the 1937 study mentioned above, in which Eliade speaks of Coomaraswamy in very complimentary terms, contrasting with him the philologists and specialists who are ignorant of the most important aspect of cultures, the "metaphysical tradition"; second, an unpublished letter in which the expressions of respect and gratitude are repeated and the Indian scholar is called "master"; third, the essay "Some notes on *Theosophia Perennis*" (1979), which has been mentioned above. To this evidence must be added the personal experience of the author, who was introduced by Eliade to the study of Coomaraswamy, supported by him in his decision (opposed by the Chicago Divinity School) to write a doctoral dissertation on traditionalist philosophy, and, finally, supervised by him in his research, during the course of which he frequently had occasion to debate with him questions concerning the Tradition. So "I can affirm—and confirm," he writes, "the primacy of the sacred Tradition in Eliade's perspective on religions" ("Mircea Eliade and the Sacred Tradition" 152). Quinn's impressions derive in part from personal discussions to which only the American scholar can be privy and on which, therefore, nothing more can be said. What is possible is to examine the evidence that, in his view, attests to Eliade's traditionalism. In this connection it should be remembered that the 1937 article is part of that process of assimilation of some traditionalist conceptual categories whose importance—and limitations—have been discussed above; the letter published by Quinn merely confirms the respect for Coomaraswamy of which Eliade gave numerous other signs: the fact that the Indian scholar is called "cher Maître" is not, as Quinn seems to suggest, proof of the existence of a spiritual discipleship—in the traditionalist sense of the expression—because the French term *maître* is not particularly strong, especially not for Eliade, who uses it of many other people besides Coomaraswamy—for example, Raffaele Pettazzoni, Vittorio Macchioro, and Giuseppe Tucci, to mention only those cases I have been able to verify. As far as the 1979 article is concerned, it should be pointed out that Quinn only quotes the parts that eulogize Coomaraswamy, and that he avoids mentioning the criticisms, cited above, of some of the key concepts of traditionalist thought. Lastly, his support for Quinn's work can of course be explained by the interest that Eliade always showed in esotericism as an entirely legitimate object of study for a historian of religions.

Noting Eliade's fondness for Guénon and Evola, Daniel Dubuisson has suggested that his characteristic form of thought is esoteric. And he tries to demonstrate that this work matches the four characteristics that Antoine Faivre believes necessary and sufficient for a definition of a work as esoteric: (1) "Belief in the existence of hidden correspondences connecting many different components of the universe, which are themselves connected to the great scriptures"; (2) Nature considered as "a text waiting to be deciphered"; (3) The presence "of intermediaries—images, symbols, rituals, spirits—which the imagination can use . . . finally to penetrate the mysteries dividing the sacred world from Creation"; (4) A second birth, a metamorphosis of the individual caused by knowledge. Two other elements are optional: belief in a primordial Tradition[15] and initiatory transmission from master to pupil. Now, all these aspects—except for the penultimate one—are, in Dubuisson's view, found in Eliade, and this he takes as proof that "the Eliadean understanding of religion and the religious, is nothing more than a huge and artificial construction inspired by an attitude and by themes belonging to the contemporary esoteric tradition," in particular the tradition that nourished the fascist regimes (Dubuisson 1995, 47).

However, an analysis of Eliade's works does not confirm Dubuisson's conclusion. In the first place, Antoine Faivre, the author of the definition of esotericism that Dubuisson takes as his basis, notes that

> one might expect that [Eliade] would take an interest in the philosophies of Nature, which are part of religious history.

Eliade does not explicitly state what he means by Nature, and the small glimpse that he allows us evokes above all certain forms of rural imagination, especially that of Central Europe.

It is significant, in Faivre's view, that in the "rare texts" in which Eliade discusses modern Western esoteric schools, "he does not seem to pay much attention to an idea-force which has a place in a history of religions, that is, the idea of living Nature, considered both as a network of correspondences or 'signatures' that have to be deciphered and as a main character, *dramatis persona*, in the cosmic drama" ("L'ambiguità della nozione di sacro" 369). Nor does the second birth of the person who acquires knowledge exist as such in Eliade: he describes as initiatory trials the various experiences, spiritual and nonspiritual, that one faces during one's life, and thus uses a concept of initiation that is not only remote from the esoteric perspective but quite unacceptable with respect to it, as is shown by Guénon's harsh criticism of those who consider the difficulties of life as initiatory "trials." Just as this element does not exist, so its consequence, the elitist view of religion, does not exist either: Faivre notes that among the factors that distinguish Eliade from the school he terms "pérennialiste" is the Romanian's "disinclination to assert the spiritual superiority of an elite as against the popular masses" (370). Sometimes, says Eliade in a passage already quoted in part above, "the sense of the religiousness of the cosmos becomes lost. This is what occurs when, in certain more highly evolved societies, the intellectual elites progressively detach themselves from the patterns of the traditional religion" (*The Sacred and the Profane* 107). The elites, in other words, far from being the guardians of traditional religion, are its destroyers. Moreover, Eliade's "Romanianism" involved an exaltation of the worth of the Romanian peasants, who certainly cannot be described as elites.

More recently, Steven Wasserstrom has seen in Eliade an "inspirational if not initiatic descent from Martines de Pasqually through Louis-Claude de Saint-Martin," deriving from René Guénon (38). His theory is supported by various pieces of evidence: the first is the use of the term *reintegration*, which Wasserstrom says is characteristic of the Christian Kabbalists, central to Guénon and later Evola, and reminiscent of Martines de Pasqually's *Traité de la réintégration des Êtres créés dans leurs primitives propriétés, vertus et puissance spirituelle divines*;[16] the second is Eliade's reference to the term *tradition*, which allegedly derives from Guénon and, through him, from the Martinists (40); thirdly, Wasserstrom mentions a lecture given by Eliade to an audience of Masons, and later published in a Masonic journal, on initiation rites in the Jewish and Judaeo-Christian traditions,[17] and Eliade's participation in Henry Corbin's project of "Spiritual Chivalry," which found expression in the foundation of the Université de Saint-Jean de Jérusalem and whose organ was a series of *Cahiers* published from 1975 onward;[18] furthermore, he claims that Eliade's enthusiasm for the themes of the Christian Kabbalah was manifested in his undergraduate thesis on Italian Renaissance philosophy (403) and that his interest in Evola and Guénon, which he documents by reference to some of the texts mentioned above, show that, since Eliade never repudiated their ideas, he did not disagree with them (46). Wasserstrom's whole book sets out to demonstrate the links between the positions of Eliade, Corbin, and Scholem, the most important common element between them being their reference to the Christian Kabbalah; and this he takes to be an element that inspires the whole history of religions. It is clear that Eliade's relations with Scholem and Corbin cannot be considered decisive evidence of the esoteric nature of his work. So all that remains are the other arguments outlined above, and these seem weak: the use of the term *reintegration* is probably a reference to the traditionalists, as we have seen, but it is not evidence of a link between Eliade and the Christian Kabbalah;[19] the same is true of the term *tradition*, which the Romanian scholar uses in a different sense from Guénon; his lecture on initiation to an audience of masons and his participation—which was actually only nominal—in Corbin's project of spiritual chivalry are, of course, not decisive proof; and his degree thesis—as far as we know, for only part of it is extant—discusses the esoteric elements of the Italian Renaissance without devoting particular attention to the Christian Kabbalah or expressing any predilection for it. Finally, it is not true that Eliade does not explicitly distance himself from the positions of Guénon and Evola. In short, on a close inspection of the evidence Wasserstrom's construction does not seem convincing.

CONCLUSION

In conclusion, it does not seem to me possible to maintain an "esoteric" interpretation of Eliade's work. What we can affirm is that the reading of the traditionalists was crucial in the evolution of the categories on which Eliade based his idea of the history of religions. However, it seems clear that the traditionalist notions were reinterpreted and integrated into a different conceptual framework. The studies on Eliade's intellectual development are throwing more and more light on the characteristics of this approach, for the reconstruction of which it is necessary to take into consideration the Romanian cultural climate of the period, but also, more generally, the European intellectual debate (in Germany, France, and Italy—see Spineto, "Mircea Eliade. Materiali per un bilancio storiografico"). Only by taking account of the multiplicity of the cultural stimuli to which Eliade responds—and of which traditionalist thought is a crucial part, but only a part—is it possible to understand, in all its richness and complexity, the intellectual biography of this scholar.

NOTES

1. Ricketts, *Romanian Roots*; Montanari, "Eliade e Guénon"; Dubuisson, "L'ésotérisme fascisant de Mircea Eliade"; de Turris, "L'"iniziato' e il Professore"; Mihaescu, "Mircea Eliade e René Guénon"; Mutti, *Eliade, Vâlsan, Geticus e gli altri*; Pisi, "I 'tradizionalisti' e la formazione del pensiero di Eliade" and *Evola, Eliade e l'alchimia*; Hansen, "Mircea Eliade, Julius Evola und die Integrale Tradition"; Grottanelli, "Mircea Eliade, Carl Schmitt, René Guénon 1942." Another version of present study, *Mircea Eliade and Traditionalism*, was published in *Aries* 1:1 (2001): 62–87.

2. "Ananda Coomaraswamy." *Revista fundaţiilor regale* 4:7 (1937): 183–89.

3. Cf. Ricketts, *Romanian Roots* 848. Other references may be found in Pisi 46, where all Eliade's most important allusions to Guénon's writings are recorded.

4. "Ocultismul in cultura contemporana" 3. Scagno, *Mircea Eliade: un Ulisse romeno* 19, in Arcella et al., 9–26. For a complete survey of relations between Eliade and Evola—including the secondary literature—see Hans Hansen and Paola Pisi.

5. For Eliade's judgments on Evola's work, see Pisi 82, n.12; 88–90, n.27. Eliade's references to Evola, mainly in his postwar writings, are reproduced in full and analyzed, with an account of relations between the two scholars, in de Turris, 219–49; on relations between Eliade and Evola see also Mutti 14–28. Steven Wasserstrom mentions, in a note to *Religion after Religion. Gershom Scholem, Mircea Eliade, and Henry Corbin at Eranos* (261, n.65), a study that he has written on Eliade and Evola, but he gives no details and I have not found any record of it having been published.

6. Nineteen letters from Coomaraswamy to Eliade, written between November 1936 and March 1940, were published by Mircea Handoca, *Mircea Eliade și corespondenții sai* vol. 1, 215–37.

7. 116, n.135. For a reconstruction of the meanings of the term *archetype* in Eliade's writings and an analysis of the perspectives that influenced his works after the traditionalists, see Spineto, "Mircea Eliade e gli archetipi."

8. See Pisi 52; 59; 70. On the meanings of the term *archetype,* see Spineto, *Mircea Eliade e gli archetipi.*

9. Pisi 71. Reviewing *Le mythe de l'éternel retour,* Guénon considers "unclear" the notion of the "regeneration of time" advanced by Eliade and criticizes the idea that the cyclical conceptions of time are opposed to history (*Forme tradizionali e cicli cosmici* 21ff.).

10. In his postwar works, however, Eliade attributes this role to the phenomenologists: Pisi 43.

11. Montanari 143 (Wasserstrom 46) sees an adherence by Eliade to the Guénonian concept of time in the affirmation: "the 'post-historic era' is unfolding under the sign of pessimism" ("Some notes on *Theosophia Perennis*" 171). But the phrase comes after a passage where Eliade, after saying that he hesitates to regard Coomaraswamy (Guénonian) as a pessimist, asserts that pessimism seems to him to have become generalized in the last few decades, so much so that "one can almost say that, with the exception of Marxism and Teilhard's theology, the 'post-historic era' is unfolding under the sign of pessimism." This certainly does not seem to indicate an adherence to Guénon on Eliade's part.

12. Montanari 144. The French scholar does not, however, condemn shamanism as such, but only its most recent manifestations: Pisi 116, n.134.

13. Montanari 144–45. For the notion of human experiences as of "initiatory ordeals or trials," see, for example, *Ordeal by Labyrinth* 27.

14. 152. This, according to Hansen (40), is the main difference between Eliade, who is optimistic with respect to contemporary man, and Evolian traditionalism.

15. In fact, the first of the two nonintrinsic components of esotericism, according to Faivre, is the practice of concordances, of which the belief in the primordial Tradition is a particular case (Faivre, *Theosophy, Imagination, Tradition* xxi–xxv).

16. The concept of the "new man" on which Eliade often insists also occurs in Louis-Claude de Saint-Martin: Wasserstrom 132.

17. 41. Wasserstrom quotes the passage from Eliade: "I feel that, in initiatory doctrine and rituals, I have discovered the only possibility of defending myself against the terror of history and collective distress" (not "desires," as Wasserstrom writes: *Journal II* 86), as evidence of his personal adherence to an initiatory system. In fact the passage has a quite different meaning, as becomes clear from the rest of the passage: "I mean that if we succeed in experiencing, taking upon ourselves, or imposing a value on the terror, the despair, the depression, the apparent absence of meaning in history, as so many initiatory trials—then all these crises and tortures will take on a meaning" (86): in other words, the notion of initiation is a generic one, according to which the trials and sufferings of life become endurable if they are regarded as opportunities of improving oneself. It is a conception that, as has already been mentioned, seems unacceptable in the Guénonian perspective.

18. In an article published in 1979, Eliade discusses the *Université* without mentioning that he was one of its founding members. The omission is interpreted by Wasserstrom as evidence of his desire to conceal his links with an esoteric movement (42). But in fact Eliade clearly states that he belonged to the association two years later, in the diary published by Gallimard (probably far more widely read than the article published in *History of Religions*): it is, indeed, from Eliade's own words that Wasserstrom derives the evidence (*Fragments d'un journal II* 241).

19. Much less does it indicate a political program. Wasserstrom quotes a passage where Evola speaks of "reintegration" within a political project opposed to democracy and socialism; then he mentions a passage, surprisingly considering it political in nature, where Eliade merely states that the religious images of the peasants, with Christianization, were reevaluated and reintegrated, and acquired new names; he concludes by quoting the expression "every reintegration is a 'totalization' " (*Journal I* 26), on which he comments: "[T]his totalization, by definition 'total,' patently does not exclude the political dimension of social existence" (47): an obvious statement but one that adds nothing to our knowledge. In any case, by "totalization" Eliade here means "totality of life" (*Journal I* 26).

IV

History and Historicism

Eliade, "History," and "Historicism"

Philip Vanhaelemeersch

Eliade has been called an "antihistoricist." But what kind of "history" does Eliade reject? Clearly, he does not reject the idea of history as such. In the first lines of his *Myth of the Eternal Return* he set himself the ambitious task of developing a "philosophy of history." Is Eliade's attitude toward history really as negative as some tend to believe? It is impossible to settle this discussion if we use vocabulary that is too concrete. An example of this is the confusion between such categories as "time" and "history." That we abolish the present time does not necessarily mean that we abolish history. A yogin or shaman transcends time, inasmuch as this time is tied to duration, and attains a nonprofane, eternal form of time, but this does not mean that the yogin henceforth would no longer have a history. That the yogin has transcended time for himself does not release us from our task of understanding him. The experience of the yogin has not ceased to be a historical problem when the historian of religion realizes that the yogin transcends categories of time and history.

The best way to bring some clarity to Eliade's idea of history is by conceptualizing the term that has created and still creates so much confusion. To use the seemingly obvious *term* "history" to establish the presence or absence of the *idea* of "history" is wrong. Instead, I would suggest that we address the issue in terms of "historicism."

First, Eliade the historian of religion does not reject history as do yogins or shamans. What he rejects is a specific way of conceiving the historical character of religion: "historicism." What is this historicism?

Second, Eliade has been seriously criticized for his alleged antihistoricism. Strong criticism has come from Benedetto Croce (1866–

1952). Later scholars have continued this tradition and have criticized Eliade in the name of what they believed to be the "most mature form of historicism" (see de Martino in bibliography). To avoid confusion with the Eliadean idea of historicism, I will use the original Italian *storicismo* to refer to Italian historicism.

To summarize very briefly: There is a historicism that Eliade rejects and there is a historicism that has been used to reject Eliade (which is mainly Italian, *storicismo*). This chapter is a first attempt to disentangle these two kinds of historicism, equal in name but totally different in contents.

THE "HISTORICISM" REJECTED BY ELIADE

First, what is the "historicism" that Eliade rejects? Historicism has a wide range of meanings. None of the more commonly accepted definitions of historicism is applicable in Eliade's case. We find Eliade's ideas on "historicism" articulated mainly in his *Myth of the Eternal Return*, published in 1949. In October 1948, while working on the last chapter of *The Myth of the Eternal Return*, Eliade writes in his diary: "I've taken up *Le Mythe de l'Éternel Retour* again. I understand with greater clarity than ever the meaning of the last chapter, but I hesitate to open here, in a few pages, the 'problem of history.' And yet I must"— and he gives one good reason why he feels forced to write this last chapter: "All around me everyone is asking *how much time* do we have left, when will 'they' come?" (*Journal I* 86–87, emphasis original).

It is clear that by "they" Eliade was referring to the totalitarian communist regimes in Eastern Europe and that he was thinking of the fate that awaited the rest of the world. In spite of this gloomy outlook, Eliade could not accept the thought that history developed as it must. The desire, witnessed in archaic religions, to regularly abolish the present time and reinstate a pristine eternal time beyond history, was highly significant to Eliade. This archaic desire for an "eternal return" proved persistent, even in Eliade's own day. This indicated, Eliade believed, that the events that followed each other so quickly in the world of those days (deportation, torture, oppression) were not self-justifying. Man did not need to be the victim of history; he did not need to accept the events as they were; he could revolt against them; he could step beyond them.

For Eliade, "historicism" covers nearly every twentiety-century current of thought, from Marxism to Heidegger. It will be our task to find out which historicism he rejects and how it differs from all common forms of historicism. Eliade situates the roots of the kind of historicism he refutes in Hegel. With Hegel, history has become an irreversible flow of events. The term *irreversible* corresponds to the same word in French and is used without distinguishing the double meaning it has in Eliade. Eliade relates "irreversibility" to both the course of history and to the single events of which it is made up. Composed as it is of a series of successive moments, history is by nature irreversible. But events themselves, too, are irreversible. In this meaning the irreversibility of events refers to the fact that they are irrevocable and hence irrecoverable. To say that an event is irreversible means that the event means only what it means at the time it occurs. There is no way in which past events (or persons) could be rendered present afterward. "Irrecoverable" would be a good alternative for the term "irreversible." But since this latter term has been adopted throughout the English translations of Eliade, I shall maintain it in what follows.

Up to Hegel, historical events, and those of the past in particular, to people who had knowledge of them meant more than that they had arisen at a certain time and a certain place and disappeared at some other time. In the "archaic religious consciousness," described by Eliade, the meaning of historical events and persons was not determined once and for all in the time between their arising and disappearing. Some events or persons have no meaning for us anymore as concrete events or persons that we can precisely date and situate. They have remained in our collective consciousness only because they lost their historical character and have become archetypes. The distinguishing feature of the religious mind lies in its ability to transcend the limitations of time and to see in any event or person incarnations of older archetypes. Archetypes arise out of particular historical events or persons. But the meaning of past events and persons to later generations lies in their inherent capacity and freedom to become categories or archetypes—

any event or person can become such an category or archetype—and—corresponding with this—in our freedom to see in other historical events or persons reactualizations of these archetypes. In this understanding, the history of religions is a process of freedom.

With Hegel, this notion of freedom had to give place to the idea of an autonomous history. History unwinds itself independent of the individual. Hegel believes that historical events are what they are, not because of arbitrariness or chance, but because of "occurrence" (*Begebenheit*) or necessity. The right attitude to history, according to Hegel is that of the person who

> does not surrender to what happens, but who acknowledges the *occurrence* and its *necessity* and, because of this insight, distinguishes himself from those who see only *arbitrariness* [*Willkür*] and *chance* [*Zufall*]. . . . If we realize that it is as it *has to* be, that is, not because of *arbitrariness* and *chance*, then we also realize that it *ought* to be thus.[1]

For Hegel, history does not yet entirely determine itself as it would do later on: Each of the discrete moments that, taken together, constitute history are taken up into a dialectic which is open. The Spirit sets the horizon within which history unfolds. This openness will gradually disappear after Hegel. In Marxism, Hegel's "occurrence" and necessity turn into determinism. Marxist and other historicist approaches to history ascribe value to the historical event "as" event. The meaning of an event does not surpass the event itself. Single events have no transcendental dimension. Heidegger, though no Marxist, commits the same error as the Marxists when he singles out *Geworfenheit* as profoundly characterizing human existence. Heidegger believes that all meaning our existence may have to us derives from the mere fact that our existence is always historical. The mere fact that man is thrown into history suffices to characterize the *condition humaine*, in Eliade's reading of Heidegger:

> [I]n the various historicist and existentialist currents of thought, "history" and "historic" seem to imply that human existence

is authentic only insofar as it is reduced to the *awakened consciousness of its historic moment* [*prise de conscience de son moment historique*]. It is to the latter, the "totalitarian" meaning of history that I am referring when I take issue against "historicisms." (*Images and Symbols* 171 n.13)

Eliade's rejection of historicism is not simply the rejection of some authors and their works. This seemingly negative approach can be restated in a more positive sense if we see how Eliade himself considers "events" and what they mean to us. Let us take as an example a more or less "tangible" event (that is, an event on which there can arise no discussion whether or not it "really happened"). It is interesting to read Eliade's notes on the great trials that were held in Moscow around the end of the fifties (*Journal II, 1957–1969* 88). These are real "events" of which no one would deny that they have really happened. But what is their status? To us, who are willy-nilly subject to the historicist way of thinking, these are events that form part of a historical process. This is all the more clear nowadays when—four decades later—these events seem to have lost all meaning to us. They happened at some time in history, they determined certain later developments in Russian history and once they had done this they were only good for the archives. The events do no touch us anymore. Does this mean that they have no significance anymore either?

Eliade avoids thinking of the Moscow trials as a historicist from the very moment he reports them in his diary. "I have extracted, somewhat haphazardly, from the vocabulary of Communist trials: Titoist, Trotskyite, assassin, agent of imperialism" (*Journal II, 1957–1969* 88). These are "categories,"[2] Eliade further writes; they do not correspond to historical events or persons. Of course, Eliade did not deny that something was actually happening in Moscow (the very fact that he writes on it proves this). The meaning of these events, however, is not the fact "that they happened." The Moscow trials have no value out of themselves, as events qua events. More important is that there are certain archetypes, certain categories (which transcend time). If the events in Moscow have meaning this is because they betray a universal human need to identify historical events or persons (things that "really happened") with archetypes and categories. It is hard to imagine how the Moscow trials could have meaning to us living in the twenty-first century. As historians we can show how they follow a logical process, how they are caused by certain factors and give raise to other events, but this still does not mean that they would mean anything to us or that they would affect us personally. For the Moscow trials to have meaning in the twenty-first century requires that we first find out what archetype or category underlies them and then see how concrete historical events manifest this universal archetype or category.

The Moscow trials are only one example of the positive side of Eliade's rejection of historicism. He will follow the same method in his many other writings. What we find in Eliade is an impressive attempt to develop a genuine hermeneutics through his rejection of historicism. Hermeneutics is not a tool that can be used to solve specific problems. It must be universal in that it must claim to be universally applicable. It is thanks to Eliade's nonhistoricism (to phrase his rejection of historicism somewhat less negatively) that we can have the feeling that the Moscow trials do matter to us as well. With regard to some events and the persons involved in the near past it may not be too difficult to feel something. We may still feel something of the terror felt by the people who lived the events of the fifties. When we study what happened four thousand years ago in Mesopotamia or in some remote tribe on the Amazon, this will be less the case. It is at this point that Eliade's approach proves its value and that it becomes clear why he rejects historicism. The reason why Eliade tries to locate this identification of historical persons with eternal archetypes, of historical events with eternal categories, is none other than to render them intelligible, a task the historian of religion shares with the hermeneut.

In 1952, three years after the publication of *The Myth of the Eternal Return*, Eliade's study of Hegel seems to have made a great advance and to have significantly contributed to Eliade's own understanding of historicism. The last chapter of *The Myth of the Eternal Return*, which contains Eliade's rejection of historicism, already contained some intuitions but was in need of further elaboration. Eliade's continued study of Hegel would help him to identify the historicists more accurately (*Journal I, 1945–1955* 74–75).

First of all, who were the historicists of Eliade's days? We have seen that Eliade includes among the historicists people ranging from the Marxists to the existentialists. What do these people have in common? Eliade does not really answer this question in *The Myth of the Eternal Return*. For a satisfying answer Eliade will have to study Hegel more profoundly. One moment in the development of Hegel's thinking drew Eliade's special attention. Eliade claims that from 1800 onward Hegel had reconciled himself with his time in that he took the decision to transcend the dichotomy between the absolute finitude of his inner world and the equally absolute infinitude of the outer world.[3] This change in Hegel's thinking—this acceptance of the world and the things that are happening in it—Eliade observes—shows striking similarity to a great number of contemporary philosophies. "Our generation," as Eliade calls it, shows a strong tendency to "integrate itself in the historical moment." Nowadays, there is a widespread fear among many to find themselves thrown in the "trash can of history." People are afraid of the "abstract" and of the "irreal" in which they might end up if they do not adhere to the present moment of history. To the extent that these currents of thought are mindful of any form of escapism, they are justified. But the fact remains that their adherence to the "Spirit of the time" (in Hegelian terms) conceals an inability to cope with the historical moment. But are the historicists not, on the contrary, precisely those people who feel all too comfortable with regard to the historical moment? Eliade would agree. However, his point is that they are unable to attain a degree of freedom with regard to the historical moment in which they are living. Freedom with regard to the historical moment means that one is able to live in history while holding the perspective open toward a transcendental dimension. Eliade's ideal is that of the "integral human being" (*l'homme intégral*, which he opposes to the "historicist"):

> [O]ne cannot regard as "evasive" or "unauthentic" the fundamental experiences of love, anxiety, joy, melancholy etc. Each of these makes use of a temporal rhythm proper to itself, and all combine to constitute what might be called the *integral man*.

To be an integral human being is a matter of the right attitude with regard to the historical moment: "the *integral man*, who neither denies himself to his historic moment, nor consents to be identified with it" (*ne se laisse pas non plus identifier à lui*) (*Images and Symbols* 172 n.13, italics in the French added).

Eliade saw this attitude also exemplified in Indian yoga mysticism. His books on yoga read as a reminder to modern people who have lost the ability to adopt an attitude of freedom with regard to their historical moment. Eliade, moreover, believes that this desperate clinging, caused by an equally desperate attempt to save oneself from dropping out of history, is no less than a betrayal to the vocation of the intellectual. Eliade opposes the intellectual to these people who are completely led by their fear.

THE ITALIAN HISTORICIST CRITICISM

Storicismo Assoluto or "Absolute Historicism"

Benedetto Croce is the father of a particular form of historicism: "absolute historicism" (*storicismo assoluto*). Croce's point of departure is the status of the historian. As with many other branches of learning of his time, Croce found the autonomy of historiography threatened by the predominance of natural science. In the nineteenth century natural science seemed to offer a perfect paradigm for historiography. It had a methodology, laws to establish meaningful relationships between facts of the past, and, above all, an undisputed authority in which the historian was all too willing to partake. Within this context Croce tried to restore the autonomy of historiography. What makes historiography distinct from other sciences? The answer to this question would determine whether historiography has any right to maintain itself as a valid means to gather knowledge. It also will determine whether there is such a thing as "history" which is the source of this knowledge.

Croce's ideas of history are integrated in his larger work on the history of Italy and its culture. Nonetheless, two main steps can be distinguished in his developing a specific concept of history. First, Croce subsumes history under another source of knowledge; art. After that he shows how history needs to be conceived to be valid by virtue of itself.

The first step, subsuming history under the idea of art, dates back to 1893, to Croce's *laurea* thesis: *La Storia Ridotta sotto il Concetto Generale dell'Arte* ("History Subsumed Under the General Concept of Art"). Science studies the general, historiography the individual. Science sees its objects as instances of general laws, whereas the historian merely describes what is seen. By its descriptive character, historiography distinguishes itself from science. Historiography grasps things in their individuality. Anything the historian sees is something that he can and must "relive." For Croce historiography is "art" in the most literal sense of the word for, like art, it is intuition followed by representation of what has been intuited. History and art are identical in their concreteness. Art does not seek to express the things it sees in terms of abstract concepts. Neither does historiography. The historian does injustice to the things he studies when he sees them merely as functions of general laws. The law of causation, for example, notices only those things that can be either cause or result. The rest it dismisses as outside the scope of the historian or simply ignores it. This way of writing history overlooks a number of things to which the historian of religions pays special attention. How, for example, can nature matter religiously if it does not literally cause religion?

Subsuming historiography under art is only a provisional move to safeguard historiography from being modeled after the natural sciences. It does not yet establish the autonomy of historiography. Croce's theory of history culminates in the idea that there are two types of historiography and hence two types of history (*Teoria e Storia della Storiografia* 113–20). One type adopts the method of natural science and produces an "abstract" idea of history. This is not really history. It is "pseudo"-history, "quasi"-*storia* and relates to the other kind of history as a corpse to a living body. This type of historiography proceeds by way of generalization and analysis.

Through abstraction it distils "types" and all sorts of classifications from the data it studies. Croce calls this kind of history "history of nature": it takes the situation outside the mind of the historian merely as it is, as "nature."

Another type of "history" is spiritual. Since historiography deals with the individual, it is descriptive and, because of its descriptive nature, it cannot be science. "Descriptive science" is a contradiction in terms. Historiography and science are totally different. But Croce does not end up just affirming what seems to be a truism. In the history of philosophy, he observes, we notice a resolution of the realist conception of "nature" into the idealistic conception of "construction" (*Construktion*). Idealism holds that a given situation around us ("nature") arises as the human spirit "construes" it. In German idealism this process is designated with the technical term *construction*. Croce discusses the idealist treatment of nature to draw attention to what happens when we consequently hold to the distinction between concrete and abstract history, living and dead history, "history of nature" and "history of the spirit." We end up in a sort of agnosticism, Croce says, in which history has been confined to the realm of the human, of which we can have genuine knowledge, whereas all the rest has become the object of "meta-history" and hence is thought to fall outside the scope of human knowledge. Croce refutes this agnosticism for it implicitly assumes that human thinking has two objects: man (knowable) and nature (not knowable). This dualism is artificial and therefore untenable. Human thinking (*pensiero*) never ceases "thinking" history (hence Croce's famous dictum that "all true history is contemporary history"; *ogni storia è storia contemporanea*, 4). Beyond human thinking there is nothing. We can have no knowledge of an object that would exist in isolation from human thinking. Any such an object would immediately become a "myth," which for Croce means nothing less than an illusion.

Storicisto Critiques of Eliade

For a representative sample of a *storicisto* critique of Eliade we, obviously, have to turn to Croce himself. We may suspect that his critique of Eliade will consist of more than simply the observation that Eliade devalues history. Two aspects of this critique merit a closer look: the contemporaneity of all history and the overcoming of the dichotomy between thinking and its object.

"All True History Is Contemporary History"

Soon after its publication in 1949, *The Myth of the Eternal Return* was reviewed by Croce in his journal *Quaderni della Critica*. Croce's first point of criticism is that Eliade's idea of the restoration of a primordial time beyond history is in fact not an idea but a "sentiment." Sentiments cannot be conceptualized nor do they stand for "historical realities." For an idealist such as Croce history is the product of a creative human mind. Beyond the mind of the historian there is nothing. "History" is, in the first place, a concept. Contrary to this, the belief that history develops in perfect autonomy with regard to the historian, or the belief that facts become historical out of themselves, cannot be conceptualized. Croce puts Eliade's "antihistoricism" on a par with this form of practicing history. Both prevent us from conceptualizing the idea of history: the former, by hypostatizing history; Eliade, to the contrary, by simply denying history any value at all.

However, it needs more to be a distinctly Crocian *storicisto* than a concept. In addition to "sentiment" and "concept," Croce introduces a third term, which will give his critique of Eliade a distinctly *storicisto* flavor: "life." It may be asked, says Croce, whether Eliade's "terror of history" really differs from the terror imposed upon us by life. Our life is a concatenation of events that oppress and torture us. The suffering experienced by individuals hence is not only the result of history at its macro-level. The picture sketched by Eliade in his final chapter of *The Myth of the Eternal Return* may be true, but it is one-sided. Man not only feels oppressed by the events that occur in the public sphere of history. This feeling of being oppressed may be something completely private as well. The despair that arises in us as a result of the irreversibility of historical events has no less right of existence when we cannot immediately point to historical events at its origin.

De Martino's investigations into the nature of magic would be an attempt to understand magic in similar terms (*Il Mondo Magico*). Man resorts to magic at the point where he feels his existence to be endangered. When external factors (e.g., certain events) threaten to alienate him from an authentic existence in the world (from his *Dasein*, following Heidegger) man resorts to magical practices, including such practices as the ritualized return to a mythical time beyond history. Despair, for De Martino and for Croce, need not be the same for everyone. It is not because I feel threatened in my being-in-the-world that anyone would have to share my feeling. This position is different from Eliade's. Eliade sees a more direct and more causal link between historical events and our regular need to return to the primordial time before history. It seems that for Eliade we almost cannot but feel as if we have to return to this primordial time. The nature of the historical events in his days may somehow account for this. There was despotism in Eastern Europe, large-scale oppression, and the constant threat of atomic war. Not to seek refuge from these events in a primordial time would have seemed almost impossible for any reasonable human being witnessing them.

In his critique of *Le Mythe de l'Éternel Retour* Croce points out that despair may be aroused by events that would not cause despair to anyone other than myself. The course of my private life may as well oppress me as the irreversible course of events on a world-scale. A major difference, however, is that it seems less easy to escape from history at its smallest scale, that is, from our private life, than from world-scale history. We may believe that is possible to abolish history, but we cannot abolish life. We would be entitled to abolish life if we were somehow able to conceptualize this act of abolishing. It is clear that this does not make sense: we are thrown into life; we cannot abolish it. Even by committing suicide we do not abolish life. That is to say, suicide does not detract from the realness of life (quite the contrary!).

Now, we may ask ourselves: Is Croce reasoning analogically from life to history? Is he establishing the realness of history in the realness of life on the basis of an analogy? We need not agree with Croce's criticism of Eliade if history and life are really parallel. But does "life" only mean what it says? "Life" has a philosophical connotation, which we need to take into account if we want to fully appreciate Croce's critique of Eliade.

We already referred to the *storicisto* principle that "all history is contemporary history." This implies "solidarity" between discrete histories. Our history is also the history of the Chinese. History is always "thought" history (*storia pensata*). Our only means of dealing with the history of the ancient Chinese is through reconstructing it in our own minds as historians. To write history is always to appropriate it. The *storicisto* view transcends both the dichotomy between the past and the historian as well as the dichotomy between the different culturally bound "histories."

Is this contemporaneity merely a philosophical option? Does its plausibility depend on the philosophical system in which it fits? Or can we make it plausible on other grounds as well? Are there other arguments for the contemporaneity of history than strictly philosophical ones? It seems to me that "life" is the most convincing argument for the contemporaneity of all history and that it is also used by Croce in this sense.

Eliade posits a strict distinction between religion of the "primitive" people and religion of "modern" people. Primitive people try to transcend history; modern people bear the burden of history. Although Eliade would insist on the presence of an archaic substrate of religiosity in modern people, the separation between cultures is not really overcome as it is in *storicismo*. For Croce the distinction between "primitive" and "modern" is baseless. Contrary to what one may expect, Croce does not adduce the mere rejection of history by primitive man (or by his interpreter, Eliade) as an argument. This would not suffice to convince an Eliadean. Instead, he refers to the fact that in abolishing history no new form of life arises. Life precedes history. We must be able to conceive of primitive people as standing in a particular relationship to the world (in other words, as "living" beings). If representatives of primitive cultures become lifeless, they are no longer human. Whether they abolish history or cling to it does not matter any more then.

That life is the most inalienable characteristic of human beings creates solidarity between ourselves, modern people, and primitive people. Our conception of how primitive people situate themselves with regard to history may become a phantom of our own mind. For it is a fact that primitive people have no history in our sense of the word: they lack any notion of a linear history and a sense of chronology. The idea that one can return to an eternal time before historical time fits well in a linear conception of history. In other cultures, with a cyclical conception of history, the idea is simply tautological and therefore methodologically redundant. If Eliade's attempt to situate primitive man with regard to a history is bound to fail, all that remains is Croce's attempt to see how primitive man situates himself in his world (his "life"). Croce does not present the primacy of life in terms of contemporaneity but is clear that the primacy of life is entirely in line with his principle that all history is contemporaneous history.

Overcoming the Dichotomy between Thinking and its Object

The *storicisto* critique of Eliade may take several forms. The more fundamentally Crocian, the more it will avoid criticizing Eliade in terms of some alleged "antihistoricism." Eliade, Van der Leeuw, and Otto have represented so many opportunities for *storicismo* to articulate itself. More than on Eliade's "antihistoricism" Eliade's reception by *storicismo* throws light on *storicismo* itself.

One of the numerous implications of Croce's *storicismo* is that it changes the understanding of "values" (*valori*); of how we "value" the past as "good" and "evil." To many historians of Croce's days only two ways of conceiving history seemed to be possible (*Teoria e Storia della Storiografia*, in particular 73). Either history was seen as the continuous succession of evil by good (progression). Or, it was the continuous succession of good by evil (regression or deterioration). The only other alternative to these two conceptions of history seemed to be a combination of both: the continuous alternating of evil and good in the course of history.

It would be a mistake to think that we need to choose one of these. Croce's own position is wholly different from these common conceptions. History, according to Croce, is not the transition from one state to another, but "the transition from good to better, in which the evil is the good itself, seen in light of the better." This, too, shows the "absoluteness" of Croce's *storicismo*. "Good" and "evil" do not exist as "values" outside the course of history. Past facts become historical in the mind of the historian thinking them. They are judged—not by the standards of an extrinsic "value" of good and evil. They are qualified ("valued") in one indivisible act of judging in the mind of the historian. This judgment will always be a positive judgment: "A fact which looks merely evil; an era which looks merely decadent, can be nothing else but a *non-historical* fact—that is to say, not yet historically elaborated, not yet penetrated by thinking and still prey to sentiment and imagination" (*Teoria e Storia della Storiografia* 74).

The term *value/valore* recurs often in the Italian literature on Eliade, with or without the philosophical weight it has in Croce. The *storicisto* critique of Eliade very often is a critique of the dichotomy between "thinking" (*pensiero*) and certain religious "values" (*valori*). Of course, this dichotomy is not explicitly postulated by Eliade. We will find it indirectly in Eliade, for example in what he writes on "demythization."

Religion has not disappeared from our modern, profane world. "Residues" of archaic religion live on in a world that, for the rest, seems completely desacralized. On the one hand, Eliade acknowledges the religious nature of, for example, Marxism; Eliade does nothing to suggest that the *homo religiosus* would manifest itself any differently in Marxism than in archaic religion. On the other hand, however, one has the impression that the history of religions is one long process of deterioration. That Eliade does not show a way out of this dilemma is one of his weaker points. To criticize him for it is one thing; to account for it another.

Storicismo is entitled to replace the Eliadean approach in the study of religion to the extent it is able to show that and how Eliade's dilemma is the result of not acknowledging the principles of *storicismo*. In speaking about the "survival" of old myths in our time Eliade creates a dichotomy between our "thinking" (*pensiero*), which appears to be totally desacralized, and some privileged situations in which old mythical elements come to the surface (Andolfi, review of *Mito e Realtà*). Witnessing the marginalization of the sacred and the subsequent appearance of a surrogate for it, we must not forget another important aspect of the matter. The process of demythization is not merely a "transcription" of old mythical elements in modern, rational language (as Eliade seems to believe). Demythization is an integral part of the development of religious ideas and therefore is itself religiously relevant. Occasionally, Eliade does acknowledge the religious function of critical thinking. However, he tends to find the meaning of religious phenomena exclusively in what remains beyond "thinking." This, *storicismo* points out, precludes a real comprehension of modern forms of religiosity.

NOTES

1. Translated from Hegel, "Die Verfassung Deutschlands" 462 (italics added). Eliade, *The Myth of the Eternal Return* 148, has a quotation from the same work of Hegel, although the source is not cited.

2. "Category" is a technical term in Eliade, paralleling "archetype." Historical "persons" may incarnate eternal "archetypes" (the "hero," for example), whereas "categories" are incarnated in historical "events." The distinction is made explicitly in *The Myth of the Eternal Return* 39, 74.

3. Eliade's source for this aspect of his study of Hegel are the texts translated and commented upon by Alexandre Kojève and Jean Hippolyte. (I have been unable to locate Eliade's references in either case.)

V

The History of Religions

Gender Perspectives in Eliade's History of Religions

Katrine Ore

Androcentrism in comparative religions is practiced through the omission of the discussion of gender. The gender question in modern comparative religions proves that gender is a fundamental category in symbols and religious texts. In most textbooks in comparative religions today, gender questions are present in many different ways. This chapter focuses on a hidden gender rhetoric common in universalistic conceptualization of religion. A good example in this respect is Mircea Eliade's way of depicting the history of religions. Eliade was important in the developing of the academic tradition of comparative religions, especially in the United States.[1]

Some scholars hold that Eliade constructed a universal and timeless method for analyzing symbolic systems. Over the years many scholars of the history of religions have discussed Eliade's theory of religion as ahistorical and gender neutral, as illustrated for instance, in *Patterns in Comparative Religion*.[2] Some think of his theory of religion as androcentric and therefore of no interest to feminists. Ursula King calls his way of theorizing about religion *gender blindness*, and she says of Eliade's comparative study of religions: "[O]ne important criticism certainly concerns the complete blindness to gender differences at the linguistic, descriptive and theoretical level" ("A Question of Identity" 238). In my opinion, gender discourses are present in Eliade's writings, especially in many chapters of his books about goddesses, *hieros gamos*, and the androgyne. Eliade deals with feministic issues and themes, but he uses them to think about maleness.[3] This chapter focuses on the connections between the first wave of feminism (c. 1880–1925), and the second wave (c. 1960–1990), which can be identified in a reading of Eliade's books, with a gender perspective in mind.

One prominent question in this context is the relationship between a feminist critical analysis of literature produced by men and a gynocentric criticism in research (Elaine Showalter, *A Literature of Their Own* 25). I distinguish between feminist theories and women's studies; feminists always imagine social change as an extension of their research.

> Feminism is concerned with the shift in roles and the question of rights that have been unjustly denied women. But all of that, however important and essential, is secondary. The main event is epistemological. Changes in what we know are normal; changes in how we know are revolutionary. Feminism is a challenge to the way we have gone about knowing. The epistemological terra firma of the recent past is rocking, and, as the event develops, it promises to change the face of the earth. (Daniel Maguire, *The Moral Revolution* 122)

A feminist perspective is directed toward a rereading of sources, a rethinking of concepts, and reestablishment of traditions. I think of women's studies as research into women's lives carried out by women. From women's studies we get knowledge about women. It is empirical and descriptively oriented.[4] In introductory books on feminism and women's studies one almost always finds the distinction between *Feminism* and *Women's Studies*.

In the comparative study of religions we most often find a descriptive approach to women's studies. A good example in this context is *Women in World Religions*, edited by Arvind Sharma. *Gender and Religion: On the Complexity of Symbols*, edited by Caroline Walker Bynum, Steven Harrell, and Paula Richman, is primarily an attempt to discuss the phenomenology of religion, but it is very closely linked to the empirical side of comparative religion. Another book worth mentioning is *Religion and Gender*, edited by Ursula King, where the authors incorporate feminist epistemologies in their descriptions of religions.

JANE HARRISON AND THE FIRST WAVE OF FEMINISM

The feminism that Eliade expresses is an inversion of first wave feminism. We know from biographical sources about Eliade that he was inspired by gender perspectives in the way Jane Ellen Harrison (1850–1928) expressed them in her writings (*Autobiography, vol. I* 100). In particular, Harrison's thoughts on ritual, matriarchy, women's sexuality, and goddesses are referred to in Eliade's books. Eliade also adopted Harrison's way of combining anthropological knowledge with historical knowledge. The mixing of the ethnographical with the historical was first adopted in Eliade's *Yoga, Essai sur les origines de la mystique Indienne* (PhD thesis 1933/1936) and later in *Shamanism: Archaic Techniques of Ecstasy* (1951). These are the books that gave him fame and fortune in the beginning of his career in Europe.

Harrison published many books on Greek religion; the best known are *Prologomena to the History of Greek Religions* (1903, 1908, and 1921), *Themis: A Study of the Social Origins of Greek Religion* (1912 and 1927), *Ancient Art and Ritual* (1913 and 1947). In addition to philological training, she adopted modern archeological and anthropological thinking on religions in her books on Greek religion. Harrison also developed ideas on woman in ancient cultures, which were introduced by J. J. Bachofen (*Das Mutterrecht: Eine Untersuchung über die Gynaikokratie der alten Welt nach ihrer religiösen und rechtlichen Natur*) and Edward B. Tylor (*Ancient Law*). She read Emile Durkheim's preliminary essay on religion (later published as *The Elementary Forms of the Religious Life*), and began to elaborate her new and pioneering thinking on Greek religion.

In *Prologomena to the History of Greek Religions*, Harrison discusses the hypothesis of a matriarchal goddess-oriented religiosity in Greece in the period preceding the patriarchal religion. In a chapter called "The Making of a Goddess" she focuses on how gender and particularly women are described in the sources. She emphasizes the understanding of Greek Gods, described as anthropomorphic, functioning in a family structure.

> From art-representations Kronos the father is singularly, saliently, absent. We remember the detailed representation of the birth of the child, on the Milan relief, the mother giving birth to the child, the child set on the throne, the child on the back of the prancing goat; always the mother and child, and the animal form of the mother with its totemistic remembrance, but never the father. The myth is a presentation, a projection

of the days when, at first the facts of fatherhood were unknown, and later, but little emphasized; when the Themis of the group was the mother, as mother of initiate youth to be. (*Themis* 493)

In Harrison's opinion, Greek religion was constructed around the principle of the mother. Consequently, she names her concept *Themis* after the Greek goddess of wisdom and maintainer of order. The concept of *Themis* is, according to Harrison, equivalent to Durkheim's concept of totemism.[5] Accordingly *Themis* is accounted for as the simplest form of religion and connected to clan societies. Harrison holds that in antiquity they did not understood human reproduction in modern terms. She concluded that the Greeks must have had the woman, the mother, at their center of their religion because sources other than the Greek refer to her as symbolizing their origin and continuity. Nevertheless, Harrison distinguished between the concepts of matriarchy and matrilinearity. Matriarchy is defined as a state-governing system and an early form of social organization. Matrilinearity refers to women as central to the structure of society within a patriarchal society. The Greeks had according to Harrison a strong matrilinear affiliation.

Eric Sharpe's book *Comparative Religion: A History* is considered to be a credible history of research books produced in the context of comparative religion. He, however, only mentions Jane Harrison in a small footnote (95, n.39).[6] In Sharpe's book Harrison is primarily linked with the growth of evolution-inspired study of religions, extending J. G. Frazer's research on magic. It seems to me that her influence on the subject was probably greater than Sharpe wants to give her credit for here. Louis Henry Jordan mentioned her and other feminist scholars of religion in his book *Comparative Religion, its Genesis and Growth*. He holds that feminist research represents a challenge to the subject, which will take it into a new phase.

Harrison was active in the Women's Liberation Movement in England. In 1913 she wrote her feminist manifesto: *Homo Sum. Being a Letter to an Anti-Suffragist from an Anthropologist*. In this essay she wrote about women's right to vote, to earn their own living, and to choose their own lives. Jane Harrison was also a friend of Virginia and Leonard Woolf. Virginia Woolf describes her in *A Room of One's Own*:

and then on the terrace, as if popping out to breathe the air, to glance at the garden, came a bent figure, a formidable yet humble, with her great forehead and her shabby dress—could it be J. H. herself? (18–19)

The modern history of comparative religions gives Jane Harrison a renaissance, and this renaissance shows that her work was considered important within the community of comparative religion scholars in Europe between the wars, and also, to some extent, in the fifties and sixties.[7] She is often discussed negatively, but considered as a scholar with an influential approach to Greek religion. Edmund Leach mentions her in "Two Essays Concerning the Symbolic Representation of Time, part 1 Cronus and Chronos."[8] The question is whether time is considered as a male or a female category. Harrison, like Frazer, has linked the divine temporal aspect in Greek mythology to vegetation goddesses. Leach, for his part, thinks that it must be Cronus who is the personification of divine time in Greek mythology. Leach holds further that it is the differences between the sexes that creates human time. Leach claims that one must replace Frazer's and Harrison's myth-ritual thinking with a structuralist model. In a feminist reading of Leach's article, it is tempting to understand his presentation of Cronus and Chronos as a way of making the male principle the central symbol of the reproductive capacities in Greek culture. Still, Harrison's presentation of the picture of Chronos sitting on his mother's lap is intriguing, and is not easy to sweep away. (Harrison referred to the "Milan relief" in this respect. See *Themis* 493.) Furthermore, Harrison also depicts Kronos as father, in the expression "king upon earth in the Golden Age.... It is not a heavenly kingdom imagined, it is a definite reign upon earth" (493–96). Still, King Kronos is son of his mother, *Gaia* (Earth).

Another scholar, Geoffrey Kirk, dismisses Jane Harrison as eccentric:

Miss Harrison had an almost physical passion for the ancient past. Her books are lively, learned, yet unpedantic—and utterly uncontrolled by anything resembling careful logic. In this she was, to some extent, only following the precedent of Frazer himself; . . . Frazer tossed in catalogues of vague similarities drawn from a dozen different cultures in apparent support of highly dubious theories, much as textual critics of the old school used to fling in huge lists of supposedly parallel passages selected on the most arbitrary and superficial principles. (*Myth, Its Meaning and Functions* 3)

Despite this "terrible" association with Frazer, Kirk discusses Harrison's concept of myth. Thus he declares: "[M]yth is the *legomenon*, the thing said, ritual the corresponding *dromenon*, the thing performed" (23). Kirk also includes another of Harrison's definitions of myth: "The myth is a fragment of the soul-life, the dream-thinking of the people, as the dreamer is the myth of the individual" (273). Kirk also invokes Harrison's interpretations of Durkheim and Freud in spite of having dismissed her as eccentric and illogical in her research.

Ursula King, who describes Harrison in positive terms, discusses Harrison in the article "A Question of Identity: Women Scholars and the Study of Religion," on female religious historians, and links Harrison to the first wave of female researchers/feminists (*Gender and Religion* 219–44). Harrison's connection with feminism is championed as part of the age of enlightenment project. Jane Harrison was one of the forerunners in both women's studies and feminist studies. She was also a pioneer as a scholar in the study of religions in its formative phase, together with James Frazer.

ELIADE'S UNIVERSALISTIC CLAIMS IN A GENDER PERSPECTIVE

I am concerned, in this context, with the epistemological implications of Eliade's theory, and therefore I will examine the concept of *homo religiosus*.[9] There is much to indicate that Eliade worked with this concept long before he adopted the term *homo religiosus*. *Homo religiosus* is a term that can be traced back to Cicero, who talks about *homines religiosi* (Alles, "Homo Religiosus"). Gregory Alles states that "homo religious refers to a particular religious person within a given (religious) community, that is, to a religious leader" (443). *Homo religiosus* referring to humanity was introduced by Gerardus van der Leeuw in

Der mensch und die religion (1941). The term is always used to describe male figures in Eliade's comparative religion although he is under van der Leeuw's influence. It is used by Eliade to refer to "the universal Man," the prototype of Man conceived in the platonic sense of the idea of Man. In 1927 Eliade had a series of articles in the weekly newspaper *Cuvântul*, which he called *Men from Books* (*Autobiography I* 118). These short articles had as their themes various literary figures such as Sixtine, a feminine figure in a novel *Sixtine* by Rémy de Gourmont (1858–1915), Adam and Eve, Brand (a priest in the play by Henrik Ibsen), Gilgamesh, etc. This series of articles can be considered as the groundwork for his comparative religions, where paradigmatic humankind was given a central place.[10] This is not to say that we can talk of male idols in comparative religions. We can talk about Western concepts of man and religiosity. Eliade's focus is obviously linked to his own contemporary view of gender. At the time Eliade wrote his books, there were not many questions linked to the problem of universality. Simone de Beauvoir says in her book *The Second Sex* that "the description of the world as well as the world itself is men's work; they describe it from their own point of view, which they mistake for the absolute truth."[11] This was not a common remark on universality in 1949, but de Beauvoir's statement has been and is still widely used in the debates about orientalism, human rights, and gender. Rita M. Gross also discusses the problem of universality in conceptualizing theories in the study of religion:

> [I]n androcentric thinking, the male norm and the human norm are collapsed and become identical. That is to say, it is assumed that one standard and one norm really are applied to all humans, both male and female.[12]

I think that this is the case in Eliade's theory of religion. He is identifying the male norm with the human norm in his concept *homo religiosus*. In a universalistic theory of religion such as that with which Eliade is associated, one disregards the particular and local in favor of the essential and global. In this context the link between the concepts *homo religiosus* and "nature hierophanies" becomes a complex relationship. If it is the case that Eliade worked within the framework of a philosophical phenomenology, then one must say that *homo religiosus* is a man who experiences the manifestation of "the sacred" through "nature hierophanies."[13] In the interwar period it was not a problem. That "man" appeared as universal man. Today it is difficult to ignore the difficulties attached to androcentric theories of knowledge.

As Eliade seeks uniform explanations for plurality, this leads him into generalizations about the experience of the sacred. In *Patterns in Comparative Religion*, chapters VII and IX, woman is referred to as a "nature hierophany" together with soil, stones, and the moon. Woman is something that is experienced along the same lines as the different "nature hierophanies" by *homo religiosus*. Eliade himself says about the relationship between man and woman toward the sacred the following:

> Ceremonial nakedness greatly increases the magico-religious power of woman, and the chief attribute of the Great Mother is her nakedness. In her body, by her body, the goddess reveals the mystery of inexhaustible creation on all levels of life in the cosmos. Every woman shares the essence and the import of the goddess in this archetypal nakedness. The ancient concept involved here has never wholly disappeared, even in very highly evolved religions. For the Hindus, for example, every nude woman incarnates prakrti, nature, matter, the primordial substance, and the prototype of women.
>
> Man, on the contrary, increases his magico-religious possibilities by hiding his face and concealing his body. When he puts on a mask, he ceases to be himself; at least, he seemingly, if not actually, becomes another. This amounts to saying that, at least after a certain period in history, a man knows himself as a man precisely by changing himself into something other than himself. By wearing a mask he becomes what he is resolved to be: *homo religiosus* and *zoon politikon*. Such behavior has a good deal of bearing on the history of culture.[14]

I regard this quotation from "Masks: Mythical and Ritual Origins" as an extension and clarification of the thinking one finds about gender in *Patterns in Comparative Religion*.[15] Contextualized within the debates of feminist theory, it is obvious that Eliade defines woman by her female biology and in terms of her reproductive qualities.

Female theologians were pioneers in the construction of feminist theory, and they called attention to a number of important issues for modern feminist scholars of religions.[16] One can say that Eliade adopted some feminist issues and themes that were present in his time, but he uses them to think about maleness. The feminism that Eliade expresses is, in my opinion, an inversion of feminism. On the empirical level it is easy to identify an interest in topics similar to feminist studies, but this turns into an inverted feminism at the theoretical level, caused by conceptualizing the male as universal.

MARIJA GIMBUTAS AND THE SECOND WAVE FEMINISM

This androcentric epistemology became a problem to his female students. Eliade was the dissertation supervisor for Marija Gimbutas and Wendy Doniger, well-known feminists in the study of religions. Feminists in literature and classics refer to his concept of *illud tempus*, or primordial time, and the primordial family. Gilbert and Gubar mention him in their famous book *The Madwoman in the Attic: The Woman Writer and the Nineteenth-Century Literary Imagination*.[17] One can only question what they think of the word *feminism* when they lean heavily on Eliade's conceptualizing of religion.

As an example of the scientific reading of Eliade in a feminist perspective, I shall mention Marija Gimbutas's *The Language of the Goddesses* (foreword by Joseph Campbell).[18] Gimbutas is concerned with finding her way back to an archetypal feminine perspective through the different phases we find in the Stone Age. She is especially concerned with fertility perspectives as she interprets it from her archaeological material. Gimbutas's scientific eye is leveled at archaeological excavations. This is not in itself particularly controversial and she refers to standard works. She also makes references to standard literature in comparative religion. On the one hand, she refers to studies of goddesses in the interwar period. On the other hand, she aims at a liberating feminism that illustrates women's prehistory in an energizing way. It is the mixture of scientific material and her own ideological speculations that forms the basis for her view of the feminine. Gimbutas's understanding of the feminine is similar to what we find in Eliade's books. According to her, a woman can primarily be characterized by her biology. But she wants something completely different from what she is able to achieve with her way of carrying out her studies. Therefore, Gimbutas also needs a concept of a universal man, because otherwise she is unable to say anything about "intellectual" self-awareness in the Stone Age.[19] The problem with Gimbutas's way of writing—what she calls an existentially liberating comparative religion—is that she believes in essentialism/the universal man. She is ahistorical and makes false generalizations on the basis of her material (Martin, "Methodological Essentialism, False Difference, and other Dangerous Traps"). She does not discuss at all the epistemological problems that are associated with adapting Eliade's theory of religion to a project of the kind at which she aims. Despite the obvious continuity between the old and the new feminist studies in comparative religion, Harrison's basic construction of the female aspect of a culture as complementary to the masculine aspect of culture is not found in Gimbutas's work. Feminist interpretations of goddesses and matriarchy emphasize that the myth of matriarchy could have been a myth constructed to legitimize men's power over women (Bamberger, "The Myth of Matriarchy"). Another argument against Gimbutas in this respect is that the presence of goddesses in religions or mythologies does not necessarily imply female worshippers.[20]

CONCLUDING REMARKS

Both feminist research and women's studies in comparative religion adopt a critical attitude toward traditional theoretical categories. It is important in gender studies to identify theoretical assumptions for the collection of data, and analysis and interpretation of the material. Gender studies in comparative religions has turned its gaze toward the research process. Ursula King states that:

> [g]ender is an issue that affects all other topics; it has historical, philosophical, theological and existential dimensions and

is ultimately concerned with the meaning of sexual differentiation, that is to say, what it means to be a person with a gendered self in relationship with other such persons. (285)

June O'Connor asserts in her article "Feminist Research in Religion" that a gender-aware research grows out of "a sensitivity to and criticism of the androcentric manner in which many religions have been shaped and formulated and also the androcentric manner in which religions generally have been studied" (O'Connor, "The Epistemological Significance of Feminist Research in Religion" 46). She then lists five contributions of the feminist study of religion to the construction of new knowledge:

> (1) some measure of suspicion, given the androcentric context and content of inherited sources; (2) attention to recovery and remembrance of women's lives and history, together with efforts to reconstruct the lives of those who had little voice in their societies; (3) criticism, correction, and transformation of given concepts, such as inherited claims regarding what is universally human; (4) efforts to rethink and alter the ways scholarship itself is approached and carried out, given the findings of feminist perspectives; and (5) feminist self-critical examination, part of the process of following questions wherever they lead us and refusing to turn feminist inquiry into an ideology or orthodoxy. (46)

It is obvious that if gender studies are integrated in the comparative theory of religion, the profile of the discipline will alter with regard to the concept of religion, and to the theoretical discourses concerning the sources that form the basis for modern comparative religion research.

The epistemological themes that I have discussed in this context are the transformation of androcentric perspectives on religion in a gender-oriented research. This adaptation of theories, methods, and attitudes in general is an important issue for modern women's studies. For as long as we continue to use inherited traditions and concepts for the study of religion, we will not achieve anything other than that women's studies will become a marginal part of the research environment. If one is to conduct an information campaign and get recognition for it, then one has to establish grounds for the research at an epistemological level (Miller-McLemore, "Epistemology or Bust").

A reasonable understanding of Eliade's books in comparative religion must give an account of the different aspects of traditional comparative religion that are present in his conceptualizing of religions. Despite the fact that Eliade's writings are definitely androcentric, my analysis of his books shows that he is not gender-neutral. The male-oriented thinking in his books does not exclude the discussion of women at the empirical level. Eliade wrote about women in a descriptive way that might even allow us to say that he did women's studies in a weak sense, because he describes women as active and important to religious life. However, he cannot be associated with feminist studies in the strong sense. The political aspects so well known to gender studies (women's studies and feminist studies) are missing in Eliade's writings.

NOTES

I would like to thank Prof. António Barbosa da Silva, Prof. Ursula King, Prof. Kari Elisabeth Børresen, and Prof. Knut Kjeldstadli for discussions and valuable comments on my work on gender perspectives in the writings of Mircea Eliade.

1. Ivan Strenski states that "Eliade has been, in effect, the historian of religions in the United States." Ivan Strenski, *Four Theories of Myth* 70. See also Bryan Rennie, *Reconstructing Eliade* 1–6, and Jonathan Z. Smith, "Acknowledgments: Morphology, and History in Mircea Eliade's *Patterns in Comparative Religion* (1949–1999)."

2. "*Patterns* is a work that founded an influential approach to the study of religion. It is a work that can be thought with or against, but never thought around or away." Jonathan Z. Smith, "Acknowledgments" 315.

3. Not many books or articles have been written about the problems of gender in Eliade's theory of religion. Christ, "Mircea Eliade and the Feminist Paradigm Shift," King, "Women Scholars and the *Encyclopedia of Religion*," and Gross, "Androcentrism and Androgyny in the Methodology of History of Religions" should also be mentioned in this connection. Gross's article discusses concepts that are closely connected to Eliade's theory of religion, but

she does not discuss his theory openly. She does not mention any particular theory at all, and therefore her article is not very clear concerning gender perspectives in the writings of Mircea Eliade.

4. An extensive discussion on this topic can be found in Henrietta L. Moore, *Feminism and Anthropology* 4–10. The distinction between woman studies and feminist studies is also found in Rosi Braidotti, *Patterns of Dissonance* 12–15.

5. Émil Durkheim: *Elementary Forms of the Religious Life*. Harrison probably also read the article "L'Organisation matrimoniale des sociétés Australiennes."

6. Here an observation is mentioned on contemporary research, which Harrison makes in *Introductory Studies in Greek Art* (1885). "The historical instinct is wide awake among us now. We seek with a new-won earnestness to know the genesis, the *origins* of whatever we study," 2 in Harrison, quoted in Sharpe.

Another example, mentioned in Sharpe's book, is Mrs. Rhys Davids (also referred to as Caroline Augusta Foley) (1857–1942), married to the orientalist Thomas Rhys Davids. She worked on Pali texts and Indian religions. She was the president of The Pali Text Society and a closer inspection reveals that she translated, edited, or contributed to more than twenty-four different publications of Pali texts. Her husband is only associated with nine and he became famous! She influenced a large number of researchers in the area of Indian religions by being their teacher. It is supposed to have been said of her that she contributed to people not reading the Indian texts as fundamentalists. A few of her books were even on the syllabus at many places of learning. But she is not mentioned in any way other than in association with her husband. Quoted from Ursula King, "A Question of Identity: Woman Scholars and the Study of Religion," in *Religion and Gender* 229–31.

7. Versnel: "Myth and Ritual. What's Sauce for the Goose Is Sauce for the Gander," *Inconsistencies in Greek and Roman Religion*, and Beard: *The Invention of Jane Harrison*.

8. Edmund R. Leach, *Rethinking Anthropology* 124–36. Also in William A. Lessa and Evon Z. Vogt, *Reader in Comparative Religion* 221–33.

9. This concept is widely used in comparative religions. It is often conceived as "der *homo religiosus* als vorgegebener Idealtyp des Menschen." Kurt Rudolph, *Geschichte und Probleme der Religionswissenschaft* 393. See also Rennie, *Reconstructing Eliade* 41–46.

10. "[T]he only way Eliade proposes to adequately understand religious man is by understanding the structures in which he participates ... *homo religiosus* is not an historical but an archetypal religious man." Robert D. Baird, *Category Formation and The History of Religions* 86.

Archetype in the Eliadean sense is often seen as related to Jung's concept of archetype. Eliade explained his view on this relation stating, "In using the term 'archetype,' I neglected to specify that I was not referring to the archetypes described by Professor C. G. Jung. This was a regrettable error. For to use, in an entirely different meaning, a term that plays a role of primary importance in Jung's psychology could lead to confusion. I need scarcely say that, for Professor Jung, the archetypes are structures of the collective unconscious. But in my book I nowhere touch upon the problems of depth psychology nor do I use the concept of the collective unconscious. As I have said, I use the term 'archetype,' just as Eugenio d'Ors does, as 'exemplary model' or 'paradigm,' that is, in the last analysis, in the Augustinian sense" (*Myth of the Eternal Return* XIV–XV).

11. Simone de Beauvoir, *The Second Sex*. Speaking of religions, de Beauvoir says of the function of the patriarchal religions as legitimizing male power: "Man enjoys the great advantage of having a god endorse the code he writes; and since man exercises a sovereign authority over women it is especially fortunate that this authority has been vested in him by the Supreme Being. For the Jew, Mohammedans, and the Christians, among others, man is Master by divine right; the fear of God will therefore repress any impulse to revolt in the downtrodden female." See also Toril Moi, *Simone de Beauvoir: The Making of an Intellectual Woman*.

12. Rita M. Gross, "Androcentrism and Androgyny in the Methodology of History of Religions." The only reference in her essay is to Simone de Beauvoir's *The Second Sex*.

13. Philosophical phenomenology is used in this context in the epistemological sense.

14. "Masks: Mythical and Ritual Origins," *Encyclopedia of World Art*, vol. 9 520–25. Also in *Symbolism, the Sacred, and the Arts* 64–71.

15. The influence of Jane Harrison's study of religion is very clear here.

16. See for example, Sly, *Philo's Perception of Woman*; Clark, *Ascetic Piety and Woman Faith*; Børresen, *Subordination et Equivalence*; Børresen and Vogt (eds.), *Woman's Studies of the Christian and Islamic Traditions*; and Bynum, *Holy Feast and Holy Fast*.

17. They refer to Eliade twice in their famous feminist manifesto, both quotations are from *The Myth of the Eternal Return* (on Great Time and *Illud Tempus*). Eliade's traditional understanding of the relationship between man and woman is present also in *The Myth of the Eternal Return*.

18. In the Acknowledgments, Gimbutas thanks Eliade for reading her manuscript. Her thinking on women in the prehistoric Eastern Europe was presented in her book *The Prehistory of Eastern Europe*.

19. Eliade talks about religion and religiosity in the Stone Age in *A History of Religious Ideas*, ch. 1, "In the beginning. . . . ; Magico-Religious Behavior of the Paleanthropians" 3–28 and ch. 2, "The Longest Revolution: The Discovery of Agriculture- Mesolithic and Neolithic" 29–55.

20. King, "Religion and Gender," in *Turning Points in Religious Studies* 282–83. A similar argument can be found in Arvind Sharma (ed.), *Women in World Religions*.

VI

The Dialectic of the Sacred and Creative Hermeneutics

Mircea Eliade's Dialectic of Sacred and Profane and Creative Hermeneutics

Chung Chin-Hong

If one examines Eliade's argument, one can see that he takes as the axes of his discussion two elements. Expressed in the form of questions, one axis is: "What does the term *religion* indicate?" And the other is: "How can religion, thus understood, be interpreted?" Eliade's discussion of the first question shows how he prepared the apparatus for perceiving that which he designates religion. While this is Eliade's founding concern, it is also an epistemological matter. In contrast to this, the second question attempts to provide an analytical framework for understanding what meaning is invested in certain previously described sources, clarifying the structure of the object revealed through that analysis while seeking to interpret the meaning of that object's existence. Thus, this question is a hermeneutical one.

These two questions, epistemological and hermeneutical, are not totally separate for Eliade. The key thing is that these questions establish the integrative axes of his study of religion. What will be done in this chapter is to understand Eliade's study of religion through these questions.

TO WHAT DOES THE TERM *RELIGION* REFER?

Eliade's study of religion begins by stating that the discussion of religion refers to a reality. However, it is important that he clarifies the fact that the series of phenomena that human culture has since ancient times recognized as religion is the category of the sacred. In so doing he is distinguishing this from other realities, but it must be noted that not all things that exist and are called religion are the sacred. Eliade limits what he calls the sacred to that single reality that reveals itself as sacred. In other words, for something to be the sacred, it must manifest itself as such. For Eliade, to the extent that something does not reveal itself as the sacred, it then becomes the reality of the non-sacred.

When contemplating such a reality, one can say that it is such that if something is the sacred then it appears as sacred, while if this intentionality is not invested it does not appear as the sacred. When this intentionality is not invested, that reality appears as the absence of the sacred, and in such a case this absence can be called the profane. Eliade clarifies this latter case as the experience of a reality in which the sacred is not manifested. Accordingly, the existence that he calls either sacred or profane is a reality in the sense that it is a mode of being or an existential circumstance one experiences in the course of one's life. The sacred is that which exists as a mode of being that one accepts as one's own and experiences in the course of one's life, and which has the position and structure of the non-profane. In contrast, the profane is that which exists as a mode of being that one accepts as one's own and experiences in the course of one's life, and which has the position and structure of the non-sacred (*The Sacred and the Profane* 11–14). However, even though the sacred and profane may be viewed as realities, for Eliade they are not realities in the sense of an essence.

The existence of neither the sacred nor the profane corresponds to the naive, objective realism of the here and now. While each is revealed as a mode of being, it is not something that itself actually exists—and thus it would be mistaken to take the sacred and profane as two objects that exist separately. The sacred and profane are empirical realities that are revealed only through intention; to put it in phenomenological terms, the sacred and profane are the two modes of being that constitute the existential predicament of human life and which are the sort of thing that can be termed "life experience." Accordingly, in this vein, this experience can be referred to as a function of consciousness. This becomes clear in the following passage in which Eliade explains the sacred, which is "an element within the structure of consciousness, not a stage in the history of consciousness" (*Quest i*). We can estimate from this what sort of epistemological basis Eliade constructs for the reality called religion.

What can be confirmed from this may be summarized in two points: First, Eliade categorizes religion in terms of an object of study as the sacred. Second, even while categorizing religion in this way, Eliade makes no clear reference to the sacred as an objective reality. If one examines his writings, his references to the sacred appear to deny its objective existence. However, Eliade predicates his argument on the sacred as something that exists and despite his suggestions to the contrary, the fact that he argues for the essentiality or irreducibility of the sacred seems to support a totally different interpretation (*Patterns* xiii). A correct understanding of the sacred demands it be seen as an incontrovertible substance that exists in the here and now (*Cosmos and History* 4). Moreover, when Eliade refers to the relationship between the sacred and the profane, he points out their qualitative difference. According to him, the sacred appears as something that possesses ontological status. Thus, in my reading of Eliade's arguments this series of facts inevitably becomes a whirlpool of confusion.

This confusion can be surmounted by organizing things in the form of a simple question: the question that can be asked is whether religion as the object of understanding is a so-called objective substance or, if not, whether it is a subjective phenomenon of consciousness.

To answer this question it is necessary to examine what Eliade means by the term *empirical reality*. Let us take an example: Eliade divides human life into two realms—life in the sacralized cosmos and life in the desacralized cosmos. This distinction is of course another way of stating the fact that a single being or existence can appear either as the sacred or as the profane. However, the important thing is what Eliade says about the reason for this distinction.

First, Eliade stresses the *oughtness* of this classification and that this division is unavoidable. At the same time, he states that all facts originate from a singular mode of being, namely that because people are religious beings (*homo religiosus*), things appear in this way (*Sacred and Profane* 17–18). This stipulation that sees human nature as a religious existence can only be enunciated from an existential horizon. What he means by the concept of empirical reality can be inferred from this aspect of Eliade's argument. The notion of experience to which this refers is not the experience of some particular object. Rather than saying that people experience something, what Eliade is arguing is that because people are religious beings from the start then we inherently live a life that is religious and this is necessarily reflected in our consciousness. In other words, the two realities of the sacred and profane constitute the lifeworld of *homo religiosus*.

However, it should be noted that the lifeworld as a phenomenological concept is neither a naive objective reality nor a subjective structure. There is only the transcendent subject of an objective structure and the concrete object of that subject (Sinha, *Studies in Phenomenology* 50–67). And from this it can be inferred that the question whether religion as the object of study of the discipline Eliade is advocating is an objective substance or whether it is a phenomenon of subjective consciousness is quite inappropriate. Eliade's epistemology is apparent from the orientations in which the relationship of substantial object and conscious subject is always formed, first by positing the object of knowledge as a substance and then entering into the realm of that substance from outside of it. To initiate this particular mode of discourse, Eliade has chosen a particular term to indicate religious phenomena: the hierophany (*Myths, Dreams, and Mysteries* 124).

The difference between the hierophany and the sacred must be stressed. Hierophany is simply the manifestation of the sacred, which reveals itself in the lifeworld. Yet there is also in the lifeworld that which is not the manifestation of the sacred: the profane. When it is said that a manifestation of the sacred is a hierophany, this means that the hierophany is a phenomenon of the lifeworld. But the lifeworld is itself not something that is either sacred or profane. It is, rather, the place where the direct perception of the sacred and profane is possible. And this perception itself is possible because people are religious beings (*homo religiosus*). Of course, as it was seen earlier, it is clear that Eliade argues that the sacred and profane are essential realities. At least, this is what his statements on this seem to indicate. But if one reinterprets this from the perspective just described, one can understand that it, in fact, refers to a reality in the form of a latent possibility in which the affairs within the lifeworld can be understood respectively as the sacred and also as the profane.

This is not to say that it is impossible to distinguish between the sacred and the profane. Even if the lifeworld in itself is neither sacred nor profane, the encounter with it either takes the form of the manifestation of the sacred, or in the absence of that, it takes the form of the profane. Thus, the distinction does not originate in the parallel existence of the sacred and the profane, nor is it made possible because the sacred and profane are parallel. In conclusion, while it can be indicated that the principle of distinction is found in that parallel structure, what makes such an assertion possible is the fact that the sacred and profane first manifest themselves in the lifeworld: it is, in other words, made possible in the first instance because of the hierophany.

The hierophany does not allow anyone to distinguish between the sacred and profane because it is the sacred; rather, because it is a manifestation of the sacred it establishes the latent possibility of the two and so provides a basis for distinguishing between them. Eliade expresses this thing by saying that that latent possibility is established from out of the coexistence of the sacred and the profane within the process of sacralization, which he refers to as the intentionality of hierophany (*Patterns* 11, 125).

The important fact here is the intentionality possessed by the hierophany, which Eliade views as its structure. It is this structure that permits the hierophany to exist. Eliade explains this as an event that, even while continuing to remain part of its original cosmic environment, becomes a vessel for the sacred itself, and in so doing breaks the bounds of the mere event (*Images and Symbols* 84). Finally, Eliade distinguishes the sacred and profane according to the hierophany, while at the same time seeking to understand them in such a way as to preserve their intersubjectivity and to recognize that intersubjective relationship.

What I have stressed is the way that the description of the relationship of the sacred and profane is structured by Eliade in terms of a science of religion that studies the hierophany. If the structure of the sacred and profane can be inferred from the above discussion, one can see that in defining a religious phenomenon as a hierophany and at the same time establishing this as the domain of religious studies, Eliade does so for the following reasons: the hierophany as an object is not something that exists "out there" but is an intentional correlate bound up with the subject. And so, because the hierophany must be explained from within the bounds of correlative realism, it is the sort of thing phenomenology refers to as a world-building creative subjectivity. In other words, stemming from the reduction of the sacred to the hierophany, the task of religious studies as a discipline is the confirmation of its particular sort of academic subjectivity together with its corresponding object of knowledge.

However, this inquiry has been constrained by the form of the traditional problematic, which asks: "What is religion?" But the questions that religious studies must now pursue are those related to the problematic defined by the question: "What is meant by religion?" And so the important thing that is discovered here is not what is the object of knowledge characteristic to the discipline Eliade describes. It is, rather, the way that a change in problematic gives us a whole new sense of what that object is. It is mistaken to think that the question "What is religion?" can be answered with factual statements. And yet any religious phenomenon perceived as an object within this cognitive logic must inevitably reconnect with the realm of understanding. For such an object is a world-constructing object, the object of a creative subjectivity.

HOW IS RELIGION TO BE INTERPRETED?

The discipline of religious studies does not merely delineate so-called religious facts, but seeks to understand them by pursuing the meaning they possess. This emphasis takes the form of a self-consciousness on the part of religious studies about itself and is one that the field has consistently pursued throughout its history. This emphasis within the field of religious studies, moreover, emerges methodologically in close connection with an epistemological concern with the object of knowledge and inevitably comes to appear as the formation of a hermeneutics.

In this sense, Eliade becomes an important focus of interest. This is because, as has already been seen, at the same time as he intends the delineation of facts, he expects that narration itself gives birth to an understanding that in turn becomes an experience of meaning. In other words, Eliade seeks a single grammar that makes it possible to register both the narration of facts and their meaning.

This problematic appears most clearly in Eliade's discussion of the hierophany. As has been seen, hierophany is the manifestation of the sacred. And according to Eliade, it is precisely because of this that it offers people insight into the essential meaning constitutive of religious phenomenon: hierophany reveals a special sort of religious fact as well as the whatness and structure of religious phenomena in general.

Yet the hierophany is a concept. Hierophany as a phenomenon, however, quite differently from the abstract distinctness and unity of the concept, is quite definitely not a singular thing. It has various origins and forms and is necessarily quite diverse. And yet despite this, all of these diverse hierophanies possess in common a single pattern and transmit a clear meaning, which can be collectively identified as hierophany. Eliade registers two points in this regard: hierophany points to an archetype (*Cosmos and History* viii–ix) but, secondly, as the form and structure of the hierophany arises out of that archetype, it also indicates a system (*Patterns* 9).

What Eliade wants to emphasize through the descriptive notions of archetype and system is the fact that even though all hierophanies manifest differently, they are nevertheless oriented with a particular intentionality. It thus can never remain the mere object of perception, but is an object whose intention must be interpreted. Here, much as Eliade has chosen hierophany as a means for perceiving religious phenomena, he has chosen the notions of symbol and symbolism as a means to understand religious phenomena (*Patterns* 446–47). An object of perception and not a concrete object of knowledge, the hierophany is for Eliade a source to be interpreted—a symbol.

Given that the hierophany must be interpreted in this way as an intentional mode, what must be considered here is why Eliade conceptualizes it as symbolic. This choice on Eliade's part is clearly unworkable except in light of his particular gloss on the notion of the symbol. To get at this, one must first come to a conceptual understanding of the way Eliade customarily employs the term *symbol*. In general, when one terms some object or event a symbol, the word refers to a quality of opacity. When a single event is comprehended as a symbol it becomes a reality possessing a multitude of meanings; it is polysemic. One could even say that symbols are trapped within plurality. Moreover, there is no necessary answer to questions such as why red can mean authority, or why the same red can mean love. The symbol, confronted with this sort of question, "Of all things why this?" can only offer its own arbitrariness as an answer. The only way to explain the reality possessed by the symbol is to admit that it is that by accident. Accordingly, the symbol is not something that can be understood in terms of a causal analysis but is the sort of thing that must be interpreted.

Yet the symbol understood in this way also has a fundamental problem. Such notions as opacity, arbitrariness, and the dependence on interpretation all express the epistemological conundrum of the symbol. Eliade, however, takes this aspect of the symbol as its characteristic logic. The symbol is precisely that autonomous mode of cognition preserved in such things as opacity, cultural arbitrariness, and the dependence on interpretation. Because this is so it is possible to see that they possess a logic and suitability of their own, and this in turn makes it possible to derive a single consistent system out of a diverse variety of symbols. Premised upon this understanding of the symbolic, Eliade can therefore propose a system for interpreting symbols; or more fundamentally, Eliade expresses the consciousness of the intentional mode of the hierophany as a symbolic system. He explains religious symbolism as that which can reveal the structure of a world that cannot be clearly distinguished from within the bounds of direct encounter. And so that world, rather than being something perceived as a purely objective reality, is something more deep and mystical—it is a reality that is naturally interpreted. Thus, such symbols are dependent upon how they are read. Precisely because of this polysemy, religious symbolism can be understood as a system integrating those diverse meanings into a totality. Each disparate meaning adheres to a concrete event, but founded upon this is a larger connectedness of total meaning. Viewed in this way, however, one sees that it is inadequate to say that symbols are dependent upon how they are interpreted, for the symbol also enforces its own deeper structure and meaning—and, precisely because of its ability to unify or systematize, the symbolic is able to represent paradoxical situations that can be expressed in no other way. And as a result, these symbols inevitably possess an existential value (*Patterns* 98–103).

However, the problem one confronts here is not informed by the question of how Eliade explains religious symbolism. Rather, what is of consequence is how he develops his argument, which moves from the hierophany to the symbolic, and which posits the hierophany as the object of consciousness and the symbolic as the structure of understanding. The logic of the symbol is the conclusion of that process of development. It is precisely here that one can begin to pursue an understanding of Eliade's notion of the phenomenological procedure. For example, one encounters the moon or sun, which have become religious phenomena, in the lifeworld. The moon and sun, however, are not the sacred itself. Rather, they are things that have the possibility to be the sacred—in other words, when they become the contents of religious experience, they become hierophanies that reveal the sacred. In such a scenario, Eliade collects the various incidences when sun or moon become hierophanies and seeks for the invariant core that they share, composing out of it a sort of fabric. With this fabric, Eliade reintegrates the diversity of the hierophany, or in this case the varieties of lunar and solar hierophanies. This reintegrated hierophany he defines as solar or lunar symbolism. And these symbolic systems are revalorized in conformity with the existential realm. This revalorized symbolism is for Eliade the meaning of the hierophany—which he argues is the kind of description and understanding religious studies ought to have of religious phenomenon.

Yet this kind phenomenological process is not one directly influenced by the phenomenology of traditional philosophy. Eliade is, of course, not unaware of that tradition, nor does he overlook it: he merely unfolds his own epistemology within the tradition of religious studies. Yet it is also possible to attempt to reconstruct Eliade's efforts in accordance with the concepts and theories of philosophical phenomenology, for this is the most effective way to achieve a consensus with the various views critical of religious studies.

First, it can be said that Eliade himself executes what is known as free variation on those materials objectified as hierophanies. This practice is comparable to the phenomenological reduction that seeks to exclude empirical reality. In other words, this practice has the constitutive function of recognizing each hierophany as an initial structure, while at the same time symbolizing those hierophanies and then re-systematizing them once again. It can be said that Eliade's symbolism is an essence obtained through a phenomenological reduction, yet this undergoes another procedure of conscious internalization.

This practice of revalorization effects a transcendental reduction in order to ground this essence nominally within consciousness. Accordingly, if one sees the perception of hierophany as an aesthetic intuition, one can see the intuition of the symbol as a categorical one. This is because at the same time as a variety of symbols is intuited individually, the unified object or category they form can also be intuited. Eliade represents the contents of this intuition as the discovery of structure.

It must be pointed out here that the unfolding of the logic, which begins with hierophany and arrives at the symbolic at this point, takes on yet another form. Eliade's concept of the hierophany from its inception indicated a perceived and experienced historical fact. And so it can be said that the hierophany is historically conditioned. However, the structure Eliade discovers via this categorical intuition possesses its own continuity and universality irrespective of any particular historical condition or temporal factor. The discursive transformation of the hierophany into the symbolic can be seen as a process in which the continuity of structure supercedes historical conditioning, and as the linguistic expression of the results of that supercession for the purpose of cognition. Accordingly, when through symbolization one perceives an event's structural solidarity or system of association, this is not the reconstruction of that event. Put differently, this is not a reconstruction within historical terms but rather is the reintegration of an event's historical representation and structure, returning it to unity.

What Eliade is proposing through this argument is a hermeneutic alternative to the historical-evolutionary hypothesis that has grown out of contemporary religious studies. Thus, the aforementioned structural system of symbolic association, with its characteristics of autonomy, coherence, and universality, provides a framework within which it is possible to recognize and understand religious phenomenon. Eliade concretizes this view in his notion of the morphology of religion. However, Eliade does not mean by morphology a voluntary act of consciousness that invests the materials of academic study with a certain preconceived form. Morphology for Eliade is instead the product of reading the structural system of religious symbolism in accordance with its characteristic grammar. What Eliade seeks to argue from this point is that, if one can consent to this description of morphology, it enables a very different interpretation than that which is based on historical-evolutionary hypotheses; it opens up the possibility of an interpretation based on the system of symbolic association.

This argument also shows how Eliade sees religious structures as fundamentally atemporal and ahistorical. If this view is granted to be correct, one may also go on to observe that Eliade has an antihistorical attitude—that his argument is only possible from an antihistorical attitude. Yet if one reexamines Eliade's logic, which begins with his discussion of religious symbolism and arrives at his religious morphology, from there developing into an interest in the meaning of religion, one sees that this critique of antihistoricism is based on an understanding limited solely to this aspect of his argument. For Eliade pursues a range of larger arguments whose development neither begins from nor concludes with the notion that religion is a suprahistorical reality.

Nevertheless, if it is recognized that people may judge Eliade's religious structuralism, as it derives from his theory of the symbolic, as only possible from a suprahistorical perspective, then it is necessary to explore this issue more fully. And moreover, it is important to consider this problem more concretely because it is elemental to the hermeneutics Eliade proposes for understanding religious phenomenon. In this regard, two issues can be emphasized. First, how does Eliade define the notion of free variation, which has been described above as the phenomenological procedure? Second, how does he explain the relation of the symbol with the realm of existence?

As for the first point; the notion of free variation, which was understood as the work of reduction of traditional philosophical phenomenology, has generally been established without reference to historical conditions or facts—it has been established only in accordance with a pure intuition of a phenomenon's essential structure or meaning. However, for Eliade, what has been called free variation, the act of finding the invariant core of hierophany and weaving it into a fabric, is something established within historical sources. Consequently, while the free variation of phenomenology can be termed an imaginary variation, that of Eliade can be termed an actual variation. It is, in other words, a movement from historical particularity to structural universality; a phenomenological movement inclusive of both history and structure that already originates from the action of that variation.

This, then, is quite different from something understood as anti-, or a-historical. Accordingly, just as one considers this operation to be the reduction of all meanings to a single common denominator, one can understand the actual variation established in this way as the reconstruction of historical fact. However, as it has been mentioned above, Eliade argues that this is not a process of reconstruction but one of reintegration (*The Two and the One* 201). So, for Eliade, the real character of free variation is not only the movement from historical particularity to structural universality but also includes a separate phenomenological movement from universal structure back to historical particularity.

This operating procedure can be viewed as an effort to preserve equilibrium between history and structure. But this simple resolution of the problem is not the one Eliade intends, for he emphasizes that specific social and historical moments clearly make for opportunities in which an atemporal structure is revealed. This is to affirm that without historical time there could be no manifestation of structure. But Eliade also argues that even though this may be so, history in this sense does not fundamentally modify or determine symbolic structure. Of course, history invests the symbolic with value and thus the reevaluation of the symbolic arises in historical circumstances. But it must be noted that for Eliade the investment of new value or revalorization is conditioned by the basic structure of the symbolic, and so it cannot be said that the various relations among hierophanies—the structural system of symbolic association—accord with a particular historical order. This is the ahistoricism Eliade advocates.

So, in this light, criticism of Eliade as antihistoricist is unreasonable. Such criticism is erroneous because it is based on a limited understanding that overlooks the structure and history—in other words, the interpretation of structurally expressed empirical reality—that Eliade is anxious for others to understand.

Secondly, one thing that must be recalled related to this critique is that Eliade's discursive analysis of the symbolic constitutes an existential concept that surpasses that analysis itself, and through this is concretized as meaning. Among Eliade's statements related to the symbolic, it ought to be noted that the symbolic possesses the quality of existential intentionality. Eliade says that the symbolic is always oriented toward a circumstance or reality that impacts on human existence. Accordingly, because of this characteristic of the symbol, it must not be confused with the merely conceptual. Because the symbolic is bound up with the existential dimension in this way, the existential dimension toward which the symbol is oriented in turn becomes the basis upon which the meaning of the symbol is interpreted.

Eliade's argument, just as it begins from the symbolic and arrives at the formation of existential concepts, employs a series of logical devices whereby, beginning from introspective structures, it arrives at existential structures. Understanding for Eliade also achieves its consummation in the end only in terms of existential reality. The structure or meaning Eliade finds is not the least bit ahistorical or antihistorical: structure and meaning are not discovered within particular facts but are instead positively interpreted and also formed according to historical facts. So the question that has been asked about how Eliade interprets religion can finally be answered as follows: Eliade first recognizes the independent validity of the sacred, and while describing the hierophany that expresses the sacred, he structurally or morphologically analyzes and also integrates the intentional symbolism revealed by the hierophany. This he then interprets existentially and in so doing comes to a grasp of religion itself.

I have shown that Eliade's argument does not merely adopt epistemological, structural, or morphological theories of religious phenomena. One can see that he has a specific agenda in the way he develops his epistemology. The symbols he refers to are not simple revelations but either have some ontological function or make normative statements about the situation of human existence in the world. When one asks the question of how religion should be interpreted, in the case of Eliade, this is not fully exhausted by such things as simply comparing different religions and confirming their similarities and differences, or by structurally delineating the various aspects or religious culture. To the extent this question must be answered based upon existence, it requires a sort of metaphysics.

To put this differently, if ontological structure is left undetermined, it becomes possible to argue that Eliade's logic of understanding is unable to reveal any of the transhistorical-religious meanings of symbols. In point of fact, if Eliade had been unable to include in his theory mechanisms for revealing this meaning or if he had failed to develop this logic, his science of religion would be little more than a means for differentiating between religious phenomena. In saying that all this is not the case, one comes to the topic of Eliade's hermeneutics. For example, when Eliade speaks of tribes who became cannibals, he argues it is not a result of instinct but of "a theology and a mythology." He continues to note that "the historian of religion, if he truly wants to understand, is obliged to relive that situation and all the rest of man's infinite series of existential positions in the world" (*Ordeal by Labyrinth* 120). This "reliving of events" is immersed in the problem of how religious phenomena are to be interpreted. Interpretation is the extraction of meaning grounded in existence. Reliving is just that orientation, and the logical structure of that orientation is none other than hermeneutics. However, the form this argument takes is after all not very important. What is clear, nonetheless, is that Eliade proposes a norm based upon discovered meaning, and he argues such normativized, discovered meaning is ultimately capable of leading to the creation of new cultural values.

Eliade's statements on the role and mission of religious studies do not end with this epistemological interest in the duty of hermeneutics. Eliade's views on academic disciplines themselves also have a normative dimension related to his epistemology. A discipline is not something that fulfills itself when it repays the price for the luxury of creativity through analytical writings but, inversely, only achieves its reason for existence from the moment it becomes able to have a creative impact upon humanity. In this sense, Eliade sees the hermeneutic role and function of religious studies as providing a way to read the meaning of existence and the intention of phenomena, something other disciplines cannot provide. This, then, is the logical end of religious studies, which both focuses upon and begins from the lifeworld ("Cultural Fashions and the History of Religions" 21).

FURTHER PROBLEMS

Thus far in my consideration of methodological issues I have followed Eliade's arguments, and two points have emerged through this process.

First, when one explains Eliade's argument using the structures of phenomenological methodology as found in traditional philosophy, one can appreciate their logical consistency and coherence. Even though Eliade may not explicitly employ them, the thematic concepts of phenomenology, such as intentionality, consciousness, essence, experience, the self, and the world, as well as its operative concepts, such as epochē (or reduction), direct intuition, construction, reflection, or explanation are all not only fundamental to his argument but it is only through such concepts that the various aspects of his system can be shown. It is, accordingly, only natural that he is categorized as a phenomenologist.

Secondly, however, what can be seen as related to this is that Eliade's argument lacks a process of clarification. This sort of statement can also be seen as a contradiction of the previous point and although it seems clear that there are correspondences between Eliade's argument and phenomenology, his arguments, seen from the perspective of philosophical phenomenology, show traces of unclear logic and vague concepts that are hard to define as the development or application of the traditional concepts of phenomenology. In fact, in order to evaluate his argument as phenomenological, it is first necessary to rewrite it, striving to translate it into phenomenological terms. From another point of view, the fact that Eliade's argument has required translation reveals the fact that his method cannot be wholly subsumed under that tradition of phenomenology known as the phenomenological movement. This can indicate either an omission or deviation on Eliade's part, or else it can be taken to indicate his originality; and, of course, Eliade falls into this latter category.

One must really stop to consider what import these two points have for today and the problems they raise. To do this one must analyze and evaluate each point in turn. And what is even more urgent is viewing these points as providing a problematic for contemporary religious studies. In this sense, this helps us begin to appreciate what contribution Eliade's argument can make as the basis of a new science of religion. Accordingly, one ought to clarify one's understanding of what the themes are of Eliade's overall arguments about religion. To do so, one must review Eliade's sense of problematic; his perspective on why he felt he must restructure that field of concern to which only religious studies can speak.

So, what are the main concepts that Eliade adopts in his overall argument? Three can be listed: consciousness, structure, and history. These sorts of concepts continually surface in the phenomenological movement and so they must be retranslated from their technical meanings into their phenomenological ones. What is found in Eliade is that these themes are not developed through being directly grafted onto the phenomenological tradition. Such concepts, rather than serving the purpose of providing religious studies with methodological rigor and theoretical accuracy, are instead conceived by Eliade as a means of expressing his own problematic—as concepts that can lay the theoretical as well as the practical foundation for the field of religious studies.

Keeping this fact in mind, let us try to redefine Eliade's position. What then could possibly be the system put forth by the themes of structure, consciousness, and history? One can try to answer this with the notion of the model: these themes establish an integrated system that one may christen a model. However, what is meant here by model is something metaphorical, symbolic, or figurative (allegorical) and not something set or fixed. It is, rather, analogical and open-ended. Of course, that which reveals the enduring structural elements within whatever phenomenon one is intending is none other than a model. Accordingly, in this sense the model is neither the written depiction of reality nor a useful fiction. It is, rather, something that might be called a symbolic reality (Barbour, *Myths, Models, and Paradigms* 27). Understood in this way, it can be said that it is finally only the model that offers a means for structuring experience and interpreting the world.

I have shown above how the model, formed out of the epistemological concepts of phenomenology that themselves were established in the form of questions, became the theoretical basis of religious studies. In a related way, the notion of the paradigm can be categorized as the practical basis of religious studies.

The term *paradigm* indicates a standard of academic effort that becomes an index or guide. It is constituted by conceptual, methodological, and metaphysical assumptions. Thus, unlike the model, which is considered to be a symbolic representation, the paradigm names traditional facts conveyed by historical exemplars (Barbour 93–118). This is why the paradigm provides a standard for academic effort or for the delineation of arguments. A single academic collectivity is governed by this paradigm, which naturally takes the form of a sociohistorical reality. A paradigm is both shared and transmitted, and it is precisely because of this fact that paradigm change can be discussed.

Looking at it in this way clarifies Eliade's hermeneutic concepts. His creative hermeneutics is not a mode of those forms of hermeneutics pursued by phenomenology but is what can be called a form of poetic imagination. For the poetic imagination is that which begins from symbolic realism and, via the mechanism of the model, arrives at a cognitive claim (Ricoeur, *The Symbolism of Evil* 13, 24). In other words, it is a process of making something in this world exist directly for oneself, rather than a speculative vision of something that does not exist. Yet Eliade, in developing this hermeneutic procedure, is doing so to lay the practical basis for religious studies, and religious studies at the deepest level, it seems, is itself formed through this process of paradigm change.

Eliade's overall argument can be mapped as in the figure below. That region of Eliade's argument that can be directly translated using phenomenological concepts corresponds to the shaded area, A, while the blank region, B, is that region of concepts particular to Eliade and which exceed or transcend the limits of phenomenology. In saying this it should be noted that Eliade himself does not discuss these two regions using any special logic. Eliade, by developing his discussion on B, which subsumes the space of A, distinguishes himself as an independent and original phenomenologist. At the same time, he establishes a foundation for religious studies as an autonomous discipline. In so doing, Eliade prepares the very groundwork upon which he can be recognized as a scholar of religious studies.

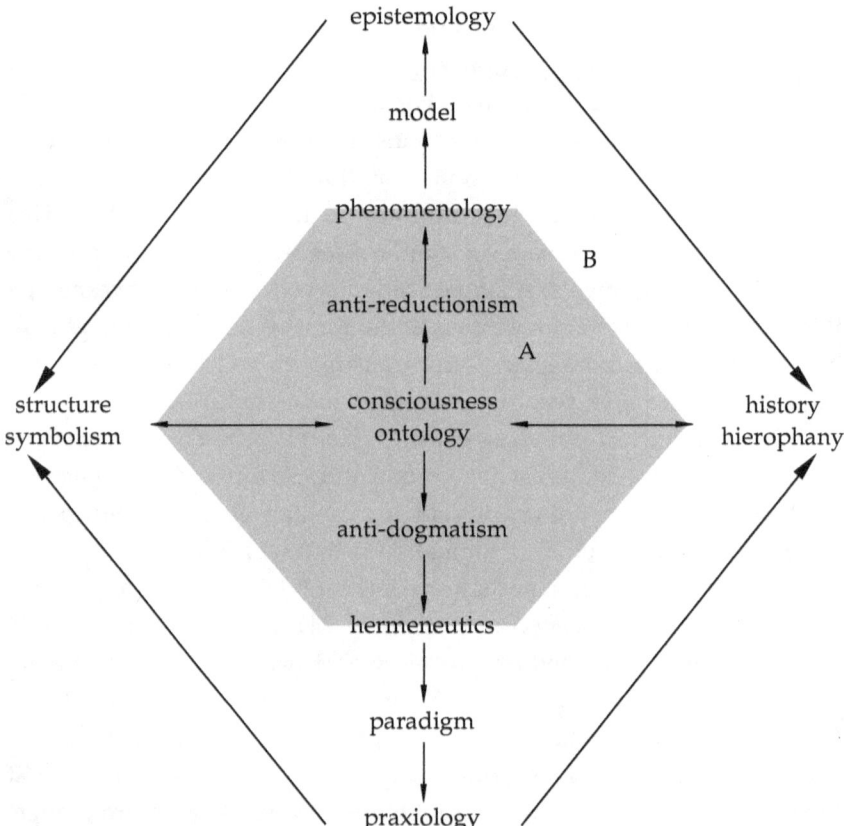

Figure 10.1. Eliade's Overall Argument

So saying, the theme becomes clear: in Eliade's creative hermeneutics—what might be called the surplus of phenomenology—is found not a new proposition intrinsic only to Eliade but what is at once the founding and ultimate objective of all the traditional concerns of religious studies. In this, it begins to appear what today's religious studies must become.

VII

Mysticism and the Orthodox Tradition

The Origin of the Concept of *Mysticism* in the Thought of Mircea Eliade

Wilhelm Dancă

As a historian of religions, Mircea Eliade was formed in the framework of his own time. It is obvious that his interest in religions must have had to do with the wave of religious renewal that had made itself felt in Western Europe at the end of the nineteenth century and had reached Romania after World War I. At the same time, the effects of the war on Romanian society in the twenties could not fail to impress him. Allow me to recall some of them: the loss of hundreds of thousands of human lives led to the search for a more just relation between the individual and the multitude; the unity of the Romanian historical and spiritual identity was sought in relation to both nation and Orthodoxy; the desire grew for restoring values that were no longer perceived as traditional, but received as fundamental axes. Romania's role as victim, its Latin origins, its innocence as a small power, were all rhetorically reaffirmed, as well as its capacity to synthesize the Orient and the Occident, and its privileged status as an heir of Byzantium. These themes, which circulated in 1848 and were taken up again in 1878, reappeared in the writings of historians and politicians who, consciously or unconsciously, cultivated the ambiguity between religious factors (Orthodoxy) and political ones. During the entire period between the two world wars, the confusion between religion and politics was axiomatic.[1]

However, Romania's relationship with foreign cultures was strong, and it influenced a new movement, animated by the will to know and the drive to produce. The motto for that period was "Everything is possible." Finally, the distinctive characteristic of the twenties was nationalistic militantism, promoted at Iași by Corneliu

Zelia Codreanu and his comrades, as well as by Professor Ion Cuza, who created a party of Christian national-socialist inspiration in Bucharest, which became part of the philosophical climate due to the influence of Professor Nae Ionescu. Author of the theory of life for life's sake, the latter was convinced that Europe was entering a new epoch of spirituality that was to replace the lay morality introduced by the Renaissance into modern society. Professor Ionescu located the sources of Romanian spirituality in Orthodoxy, which, in his opinion, had always differentiated the Romanians from Catholic and Protestant Europe and had determined for it a different course of development (Hitchins, "Desăvârșirea națiunii române" 351–484, 426). One of Nae Ionescu's recurrent themes is the denunciation of Anglo-Saxon hegemony. He was highly suspicious of the ecumenical openings effected by the Church of England in the early twenties. The philosopher moved in the direction of a mysticism according to which the Christian has to accomplish the painful sacrifice of his intellect (*Roza Vînturilor* 26–27). Ionescu fascinated his disciples, Mircea Eliade, Mircea Vulcănescu, Mihail Sebastian, and Emil Cioran; he was convincing in his style, his elitist exigency, and oratorical talent (Durandin, *Istoria românilor* 198–214).

However, the paths followed by Nae Ionescu's disciples were various. For example, Emil Cioran did not let himself be deluded by Orthodox mystical philosophy and, in his book *The Transfiguration of Romania*, repeated again and again, "I can love Romania only if I grow delirious" (*Schimbarea la față a României*). Mircea Eliade found out with sadness that Romanians have retained of mysticism "only the initial taste: the irrationalism, the passion, the urgency, the need for total transformation" ("Cele două Românii" 169). Although they followed different paths, the professor's disciples continued to owe much to the philosophical and religious ambience of the twenties, when an Orthodox spirituality asserted itself, inspiring an organic state based on anthropological and spiritual ethnicity.

In this chapter I am tracing the genesis of the concept of *mysticism* for Mircea Eliade against the background of what he owes to Professor Nae Ionescu.[2] This study has three parts:

1. Romanian mysticism for Nae Ionescu;
2. The primacy of the spiritual for Mircea Eliade;
3. The language of mystical experience.

This research deals only the academic writings of Mircea Eliade's youth.

ROMANIAN MYSTICISM FOR NAE IONESCU

Mircea Eliade spoke more than once about the part played by Nae Ionescu in the life of his generation.[3] For some, his influence was felt in the political sphere; in Eliade's opinion, the professor modified the trajectory of a generation through the religious and theological issues discussed in his lectures as well as through his new approach to the religious phenomenon ("Profesorul Nae Ionescu" 258). It should, however, be said that even before he met Ionescu, the *religious* orientation of Eliade's studies was already visible ("Jurnalul tipilor din clasă," in *Cum am găsit piatra filozofală* 601) and he was interested in political life only so far as it revealed a spiritual attitude (Sebastian, *Journal* 2 March 1937).

From Nae Ionescu's religious profile, Eliade first of all retains the two fundamental callings between which the human soul has always wavered: *sympathia* and *soteria*. Sympathy—closeness to people, even fusion with them (remaining in history)—and *salvation*—separation from humankind, the search for God, fusion with the divine Being (the exit from history, "Și un cuvânt al editorului" 437–38). Second, Eliade sticks to Ionescu's method, according to which the similarities among religious phenomena, both in content and in form, are not ascribable to reciprocal influences (as Raffaele Pettazzoni would advocate) or to exterior ones, but "to the fact that they are all the outcome of the same causes exerted on identical materials (human souls)" ("Raffaele Pettazzoni: I misteri" 59). Through this method *causal explanation* is refused and correlations and parallelisms between various aspects of life are established that can lead to the discovery of the whole spiritual configuration of an epoch (Ionescu, "Individualismul englez," in *Neliniştea metafizică* 138 n.1). In this sense, what is crucial is "the way in which the relationship between humanity and God is conceived ("Individualismul englez" 138)." Ionescu says that this method is used by modern religious science and comes from Hermes Trismegistus, who "set no causal link between the world of the essences and the world of perceptible reality, but simply said there were correspondences, correlations between these two worlds" (*Curs de metafizică* 141). However, this does not mean that he shared the magical point of view, the tribulations of freemasonry, of theosophy (*Curs de metafizică* 143), or that he was in solidarity with the anti-intellectual crisis and the religious renewal of humankind at that time. His point of view was eternal (*Prelegeri de filosofia religiei* 11–12). To this we add that Ionescu's method has no psychological, but rather a phenomenological character. That is, it takes religious phenomena out of space and time in order to study them in their own essence and not in their immediate realization, for he treats empirical phenomena as types before he looks at them (*Prelegeri de filosofia religiei* 29).

Finally, Nae Ionescu applies this method in his many courses of lectures on the philosophy of religion,[4] with an aim to discovering the essence of Romanian Christianity, "*a Christianity that is ours*, beyond any dogma and any church, *a Christianity of atmosphere*" ("Forme româneşti ale problemei religioase," in *Opere*, vol. VI 438). In this sense, he argues that, unlike the Catholic Church, where there do not seem to be any direct links between humanity and God ("Individualismul englez," 138), for the Eastern Orthodox Church, the problem of solitude before God is more acute. In the East, this consciousness of individuality in the religious sphere manifests itself through asceticism as an ideal of religious life ("Reforma bisericească" in *Opere*, vol. VI 253–56), through a feeling of brotherhood and a specific conception about love. In the social and political sphere, this kind of consciousness caused the asocial character of Orthodoxy on the one hand and, on the other hand, a lack of creative values in politics ("Individualismul englez" 141). However, this does not mean that the experience of solitude before God is specific only to Christianity: "[M]ysticism is a general attitude of the human spirit, which can lead to several solutions that are all historically possible" (*Curs de metafizică* 152).

As for the mystical manifestations of his time, Nae Ionescu saw them as expressing a desire for *something else*. In this sense, the way toward Romanian mysticism can only be opened by eliminating Cartesian rationalism, although mysticism is not contrary to true rationalism. "Mysticism supposes a discipline of mind and attitude" ("Sufletul mistic," in *Roza Vînturilor* 23–25), and "that is why mysticism is not an instrument for the realization of the absolute which can be used by anyone (*Curs de metafizică* 20)."

Mircea Vulcănescu considers that Ionescu's way of interpreting Romanian Christianity is false and paradoxical (Vulcănescu, *Nae Ionescu* 43). To the students attracted by the ethical dimension of Christianity as preached by the English missionaries Ionescu presented a stern, asocial Christianity, completely oriented toward the hereafter, a metaphysical Christianity that lived only by the liturgical contemplation of an ecstatic God (*Nae Ionescu* 43–44). For Ionescu, Christian religion is not moral (as opposed to Nietzsche); it goes far beyond the limits of such concerns by its metaphysical interpretation of the whole of existence ("Juxta Crucem," in *Neliniștea metafizică* 156–57).

Finally, it is worth adding that Nae Ionescu was first of all a logician. The permanent subject of his academic activity was the teaching of logic[5]—a philosophic discipline, which is empirical and formal at the same time. For him, experience, that is, the direct living of reality, constitutes the fundament of knowledge. But this experience is individual and ineffable. In order to be shared, it has to be formulated, and the instrument for this purpose is logic. Logic does not create reality; its main function is communication (*Curs de logică* 7–13). Although his teaching had a realistic touch, Ionescu thought that the virtual was more full of existence, more real than the actual, that passing from potentiality to action was a loss and not an increase in being.

Nae Ionescu also spoke of an Orthodox logic, in which the fact of knowing would explicitly refer to the Fall and to the Incarnation. In other words, the attempts of the human mind to formulate truth are affected by the Fall of the whole universe and therefore incapable of surpassing its weaknesses without contradiction. Therefore, the effort of the human mind toward the truth shares in the whole pining of the world for God, while *the correction of the mind* has more to do with prayer and with the saving work of God than with the natural process of mathematizing rationalization and of moralizing universalization through act, which Descartes, Spinoza, and Kant had substituted for holiness.[6] Hence Ionescu's criticism of modern rationalism.

THE PRIMACY OF THE SPIRITUAL FOR MIRCEA ELIADE

In the preface of his book *Primauté du spirituel*, Jacques Maritain wrote: "Si je suis amené à traiter ici de questions qui intéressent à la fois la politique et la religion, on voudra bien penser que ce n'est ni pour essayer, ce qui serait ridicule, d'usurper sur le domaine de l'Église enseignante, ni pour quitter le terrain philosophique pour celui des contingences de l'action pratique, auxquelles je désire plus que jamais rester étranger."[7] We think these words could constitute a motto for Mircea Eliade's youthful writings, as they mirror both his concern for the connection between the spiritual and the temporal and his interest in the general primacy of the spirit.

As I said before, Eliade's introduction to the world of religions was through the political and cultural environment of Romania in the twenties and it started in earnest after his encounter with Nae Ionescu. It is true that as early as his last year at high school Eliade had already decided to specialize in theosophy ("Jurnalul tipilor din clasă" 601). But the professor himself had shown an interest in this area a year before ("Ce e tezofia?" in *Opere*, vol. VI 427). In his opinion, theosophy was a spiritual technique having a magic character, as the fundamental engine of magical activity is the will (*Curs de metafizică* 140). The same magical perspective was to be found in the new trend of thought then prevailing in America and England—in freemasonry, in Rosicrucianism, in the Jewish Kabala, in democracy, in liberal individualism: in short, in all the activities that aim at strengthening the personality, at better defining individuality, and which recognize the existence of divine forces in cosmic reality. For Mircea Eliade, magical beliefs represent a stage in the evolution of human spirit and they coexist or survive alongside religious beliefs. Their existence is confirmed by metapsychic research.[8]

Among spiritual techniques, Nae Ionescu thought that alchemy was something distinct. Alchemy was a mystical operation, a therapeutic for perfecting the human individual, while magic was a technique for transforming reality external to the individual. The position of alchemy is transcendentalist, while the position of magic is demiurgical (*Curs de metafizică* 182). Therefore, alchemy differs from magic. Eliade's position is more subtle. To begin with, "alchemy was and remained a spiritual technique" (*Alchimia asiatică* 22), but eventually it acquired a strong *mystical* accent, to such a degree that it became asceticism and prayer (*Alchimia asiatică* 35). So, for Eliade, alchemy continues to be linked with magic and religion, fulfilling a spiritual function: immortality, liberation—the eternal motive of mysticism everywhere (*Alchimia asiatică* 42.58). Then, even if the vocabulary and the technique of alchemy acquired polyvalent meanings, an alchemical operation cannot be integrated into the "liturgical spirit":[9] "[I]n alchemy there is too much cosmology and a rather *personal* mysticism, while the liturgical spirit has above all a universal, catholic structure" (*Alchimia asiatică* 164–65).

As for theosophy, Eliade sees in this occult science "a certain kind of impure and sometimes deviant mysticism" ("Teozofie?" in *Profetism românesc 1* 47). In this field what interests him are the occult faculties, which are put to use by theosophy.[10] His readings from Schuré, Mieli, Blavatski, Flammarion, and Steiner convince Eliade that, besides rational faculties, humanity has also faculties that are *occult* because of their not being used: permanent intuition, clairvoyance, telepathic communication, etc. While through rationalistic means we seize the exterior, formal aspect of things (by means of our senses), through occult means we can get into contact with reality directly (without the help of our senses). Nevertheless, there is a difference between occult sciences, mysticism, and theosophy: "[A]n *occultist* is a man who *consciously* seeks to develop those qualities sleeping in his own being which can lead him to the knowledge of truth; *a mystic* is the man who abandons himself rather *unconsciously* to the ecstasy which makes him break loose from forms and get near to the same truth, while a theosophist is a man who studies all the occult ways, especially in Oriental science, never distancing himself from *morality*."[11]

The study of occult powers is important for Eliade, because they constitute other *means of knowing* reality,[12] which illustrate a new attitude before the need to know reality, a method based on other laws and other human senses and through which another aspect of reality can be known ("Clasicii ocultişti," in *Misterele şi iniţierea orientală* 112). Occultism also shows a certain mentality, certain mystical tendencies ("Clasicii ocultişti" 113). But going deeper into the study of occult sciences has an initiating and purifying role, as Eliade's aim is orthodoxy, the holy faith and the holy rules of the Church ("Teozofia?" 48). For him and for his generation, mysticism is "a *reality*—more confused or more lucid, more undifferentiated from vitalism and aestheticism, or more purified," but in no way "a morbid phenomenon, or an autosuggestion or a pose, neither is it a metaphysical creation" ("Misticismul," in *Profetism românesc 1* 51). In this context, theosophy or anthroposophy are pathways from "*philosophical* materialism to Christianity" ("Teozofie?" 48–49).

Last but not least, Eliade distinguishes between the inferior forms of manifestations of mysticism in magic and occult sciences and true *mystical experience*. In the first case one speaks of the so-called *everyday irrationalism*, that is, of the *metapsychic phenomena*, which assert the *possibility* of religion as a self-sufficient reality, while *mystical experience*, the functional actualization of religious reality, is the only effective one. Such an experience is reached as a result of the emotional and rational needs of our consciousness, as an outcome of our soul's nature, which longs for harmony and unity. Thus, religion—but not the essence of mysticism—can be attained following roundabout ways: reason, metaphysics, logic, metapsychics. Following in the footsteps of Maine de Biran,[13] Eliade contends that the effective necessity of consciousness is the vehicle that actualizes the divine ("Misticism" 52).

After his Indian experience, Eliade insists even more upon the role of consciousness. In his doctoral thesis, *Yoga, Essai sur les origines de la mystique indienne*, he argues that in India consciousness has a different value from the one ascribed to it in the West and that it is *experienced* in a totally different way (*Yoga, Essai sur les origines de la mystique indienne*). To work on consciousness means to get into direct contact with *life*, to remain in the *concrete*. Eliade also shows that the history of the matrixes of yoga is the history of the conflict between mystic and asceticism, between contemplation and meditation. In fact, the conflict between the *magic structure* and *the mystical structure*, between asceticism and prayer, between meditation and contemplation is a permanent conflict of human spirituality (cf. Noica, "Yoga și autorul ei," in Eliade, *Yoga* 5–10).

Thus, for Eliade, the term *mystical* has multivalent significations and therefore it is analogical, but it always refers to transcendence, to something *beyond*. Mystical forms can be divided into impure and pure ones. The former are inferior because they reflect a magical, self-centered attitude: alchemy, theosophy, anthroposophy, occult sciences in general, yoga techniques. The pure forms mirror a theocentric attitude and they express the natural necessity of the consciousness to have a relationship with the divine.

THE LANGUAGE OF MYSTICAL EXPERIENCE

Pure mysticism can only be known by experience, because "religious fact is not a fact of knowledge, but an *experience*. We do not know an outside reality by means of our rational faculties, but we *feel* God, we *melt into* a being that transcends our senses. And this melting is an ecstasy—therefore a loss of consciousness" ("Experiența religioasă" in *Misterele și inițierea orientală* 219–20). Mystical experience turns the subject who lives it into an actual *presence*.

However, Eliade finds that term *experience* as used by Vittorio Macchioro somehow vague and says that a more appropriate one would be *living*, the German *Erlebnis* (Romanian *trăire*) which is so rich and suggestive in meaning. However, this living does not mean simply to let oneself be carried away by the equilibriums of life, which are always variable, contingent, and therefore limited. When you let yourself be carried away, you no longer live, but *are* lived, at random. I think that the entire mystery of *experience* lies in this perfect coincidence with the term (which may be an event or a state of mind) that is outside yourself, and, at the same time, in transcending it, in liberating yourself from it (*Oceanografie* 49–50).

Speaking of an abandonment of one's own self, the problem is how to get inside this mystical experience, which is neither a dialogue nor a discourse.[14] For Eliade, access to the experience of the ultimate meaning is the study of spiritual language, which is differs from philosophical, or conceptual. As a matter of fact, religious experience is actualized by *rites*; a rite is not an exterior act, but the influence it has over the consciousness ("Experienţa religioasă" 220). Thus, although experience is a subjective fact, it can be objectified into a formula, an allegory, or a symbol. The formula in itself does not contain the religious fact, but if, starting from the formula, one imposes a religious attitude upon oneself, one makes *the same* experience. In other words, the formula serves for the *communication* of experience, hence its function of *disciplining* religious experiences, of bringing consciousness to unity, of imparting it to the same rhythm and evolution ("Experienţa religioasă" 221–22).

Among these formulae, Eliade prefers the symbol because it is something more than a sign of reality: it is its essence. As Nae Ionescu used to say, symbolic language "is an essentially analogical language, or an essential reality, analogous to the reality it expresses. This analogy facilitates our direct communication with reality" (*Curs de metafizică* 165). Therefore, through the symbol, the consciousness that knows identifies itself with the object to be known.

Moreover, Eliade finds that the symbol is an essential object of the mind (*Oceanografie* 14) and is different from the other forms of knowledge because it "makes possible the coexistence of the meanings and, at the same time, it maintains *the diverse, the heterogeneous*" (*Alchimia asiatică* 87). The sense of the symbol is "to continuously integrate the individual into an order that transcends him," both horizontally and vertically (*Fragmentarium* 107). Through this integration into the transcendent, into *the whole,* one becomes truly free. One can really know human life. One can become complete. But this *whole* is not a panoramic landscape, neither is it a mirroring of the whole in the soul, "but its *coincidence* with anything" (*Oceanografie* 51).

As for the mystical allegories—*love, wedding, engagement*—they are another proof that the supreme experience of human consciousness is mystical experience, which is founded on humanity's capacity to love God. In this case, love means loss of self and living in God alone. The fact that the concrete living of God's presence in the human soul has been expressed in concrete terms demonstrates how natural is humanity's thirst for knowing and loving God.[15] Since mystical experience is a transcending of the consciousness into another sphere, certainly a mental one, into an alien universe, this actual escape to *the world beyond* is achieved by love as well as by contemplation. If here love is a self-effacement in the divine, contemplation is a spiritual exercise, an instrument of knowledge through which humanity gets to know certain realities beyond his senses.[16] Adopting the position of Dionysian theology, Eliade claims that mystical experience cannot be translated into words, causal relations, notions. It reflects itself in the usual consciousness, transfigures it, gives it a different structure. In fact, "mysticism boils down to the seeking and finding of God" ("Misticism" 54).

The ineffable character of mystical experience is noticeable also in the way humanity has envisioned God, as a totality of attributes, as a *sum* in which all contraries coincide. "This coincidence of oppositions cannot be *understood* by human mind, in the same way as it cannot be apprehended by human experience" ("Mitul reintegrării," in *Drumul spre centru* 341–42). But mystical experience does not mean only the dwelling of the divine presence in the human soul, but also that humanity cannot approach divinity otherwise than by becoming perfect, by becoming again an archetype, by becoming again the Adam-Eve of the beginning ("Mitul reintegrării" 386). As for absolute reality, Eliade says it cannot be borne by the present human condition; however, one has to achieve the experience of the sacred, that paradisiacal state, be it only for a moment, because this means for him real existence, *the new life*, which is the way to the center or returning to the center, to ultimate reality ("Comentarii la legenda Meșterului Manole," in *Drumul spre centru* 442).

How can this merging between the human and the divine be achieved, be it only for a single moment? Eliade claims that "any religious act, like any magical act is nothing else than a *rupture of plane*; reality coincides with non-reality, the whole with the part, the eternal with the ephemeral etc. Obviously, this *rupture of plane* occurs according to certain norms, rituals, which are mythical or metaphysical. We have to do with *meaningful* experiences, oriented and consumed inside reality" ("Comentarii la legenda Meșterului Manole" 445–46.). In other words, "man can only take possession of power and of reality either through direct contact with the sacred or by imitating the acts and the attitudes of those who pre-eminently embody the sacred, that is, of the divinity" (452).

However, the archaic theory of the archetype and of participation comes near the platonic theory of Ideas, and Plato, the Pythagoreans, and Aristotle have neglected to state what such a participation or imitation actually consists in.[17] Nevertheless, the theory of the archetype has borne fruit even when it was degraded to levels of valorization that were lower and lower.[18] The value of this theory is confirmed by Christian religion, which not only assimilates, but *saves* it. "By absorbing a popular custom or an archaic theoretical scheme, Christianity restored their spiritual meaning, transfigured them in case they had been disfigured, increased their content" ("Comentarii la legenda Meșterului Manole" 476).

As far as Oriental mysticism is concerned, Eliade's opinion is that it has remained unimpaired in Orthodoxy. In the West, except for the Spanish mystics, religious experience takes place *outside the theological divine* and becomes psychism, vitalism, moralism, *Christian science*, Gidism, religious pragmatism, theosophy, etc.[19] At that time, Eliade was convinced that "whatever path it took, European consciousness was bound to reach Orthodox Christianity," because pure mysticism is only to be found within Orthodoxy. Specific to this tradition is "the fact of *seeking*" ("Ortodoxie," in *Profetism românesc* 34; *Șantier* 152). Orthodoxy is the goal of everybody, since the deification it proposes is a mystical process starting from the reality of creation into which the Unique God descends "in order to show man the way, the technique, the secret of becoming God, . . . but this is not so much the outcome of Grace, as the result of the religious will of the individual, who totally surrenders to the Divine" (*Soliloquii* 60). In this context, "prayer is the purest act of religious life," since "in prayer the drama of human condition is summed up: its great powerlessness and its ardent hope." Together with Otto, Eliade says that at every time and wherever in the world, man felt the need for religious experience and had a knowledge of God, even if obscure. His act of adoration has always been profoundly religious, even if its object was not divine. We are interested in the act of adoration itself—that is, in the act of total surrender of man before an invisible power, his act of subordinating himself to a divinity. It is out of this act of subordination that prayer was born.[20]

Finally, the dramatic condition of man causes him to constantly return to the *inferior forms of mysticism*: when man can no longer *lose himself in God*, he loses himself in alcohol, opium, collective hysteria; when he can no longer lose himself in the Holy Trinity, he loses himself in the *mysticism of the tractor*; when he no longer believes in Paradise, he starts believing in spiritism. But even in such situations, humanity's instincts remain intact, especially his thirst for salvation, which is part of the natural order of things (*Fragmentarium* 155–56).

CONCLUSIONS

Mystical experience holds a central place in the writings of Eliade's youth. The term *mystical* has an analogical meaning and mainly refers to the search for the divinity or for what one identified as divine. Mystical experience means humanity's merging with the divinity, loss of self, total commitment to the divinity. In its pure or impure forms, mysticism always implies the experience of an unspeakable link with what lies *beyond*, with the transcendent. At the same time, it reflects a spiritual attitude and a particular mentality, historically and anthropologically important. Being a fact of life, mysticism cannot be understood without the concepts of experience and symbol, the latter having a function of communication. Within mystical experience, Eliade lays stress upon the consciousness of the religious subject, upon the individual character of the relationship between humanity and divinity, leaving aside the problem of the irruption of ultimate sense in human consciousness. That is why he says that the final expression of mysticism is prayer.

Eliade's way of interpreting mysticism has something in common with the cultural, political, and religious environment in Romania during the twenties, when the confusion between the religious and the political was almost universal. In an initial moment Nae Ionescu's influence was felt; the professor gave the term a metaphysical-Christian interpretation and he underlined the ecstatic-liturgical dimension of the encounter between humanity and the divinity. But Mircea Eliade did not distinguish between mysticism and magic as did Ionescu. For Ionescu, mysticism has a theocentric character, while magic is egocentric. For Eliade, religious beliefs coexist in humanity; thus, he gives to understand that there is a common tradition shared by the whole of mankind.

After his Indian experience, his point of view on forms of mysticism has a historical and morphological character. However, his relationship with the environment of his formation and with his own Christian tradition remains constant and has grown deeper. From the Oriental Christian doctrine of Platonic-Augustinian-Dionysian inspiration, he excerpts a few elements that are characteristic of the mystical, religious mentality and with their help he considers other beliefs and spiritual techniques that are not Christian. The theory of the archetype and of the symbol, the rupture of plane, the coincidence of opposites, the ineffable subjective aspect of religious experience are some of the elements with which Eliade wants to demonstrate that everywhere the supreme experience of human consciousness is the experience of seeking God.

The religious morphology adopted by Eliade is based on Hermes Trismegistus's conception—resumed by Nae Ionescu—according to which there are certain correspondences between the world of the essences and the tangible world. With this method, Eliade identified spiritual structures and attitudes as moments of humanity's history on earth and demonstrated that religion is an autonomous, natural fact, coming only from the structure of the human soul. Other arguments in favor of this thesis are offered by the metapsychical phenomena, which are studied by the occult sciences, which Eliade dealt with in his youth. Thus, the thorough study of the mystical techniques in theosophy, occultism, and alchemy opened for Eliade a gate to the Orient and eventually to the history of religions. The stress laid on the anthropological dimension of mystical experience caused Eliade to overlook certain terminological ambiguities: he sometimes mixes up mysticism with religion, magic with alchemy and religion, the sacred with the divine. Nevertheless, the validity of his contribution to understanding human destiny is unquestionable. From this perspective, Eliade's youthful writings anticipate not only the great themes of his later academic work, but also those of contemporary debate in the field of what has been called philosophy of religion or philosophical anthropology.

NOTES

1. Alexandrescu, *Paradoxul român* 223–68, 241. The consequence of this attitude of derealization of reality and therefore of self-deception was the political blindness demonstrated by Nae Ionescu, Nichifor Crainic, Emile Cioran, Eliade, and many others.

2. I have dealt with the links between Eliade and Ionescu in my doctorate paper: Wilhem Dancă, *Mircea Eliade. Definitio sacri* 25–96. Approved and published in Italian in 1996 at the Gregorian Pontifical University in Rome, the thesis is entitled: *Mircea Eliade. Definitio sacri*, its subtitle being: *Il sacro come il significativo ed il destino e la sua relazione col metodo storico-fenomenologico nell'opera di Mircea Eliade*.

3. "Şi un cuvânt al editorului" 426: "Ever since 1922, Bucharest students have been living under the spiritual influence of Professor Nae Ionescu, an influence that goes beyond the walls of the Faculty of Letters." Concerning this subject, see also Eliade's *Yoga, Immortality, and Freedom* xxii; *Autobiography*, vol. I passim; "Prefaţă," in *Alchimia asiatică. Cosmologie şi alchimie babiloniană*, 75; "Profesorul Nae Ionescu" 256–59; Dancă, *Mircea Eliade. Definitio sacri*, 34–37.

4. According to Diaconu, Ionescu delivered the following courses of lectures on the philosophy of religion. *Metaphysics: Philosophy of Religion—Philosophical Solutions to the Problem of God (theism, pantheism, atheism)* 1920/1921; *Philosophy of Religion—Metaphysics and Religion* 1923/1924; *Philosophy of Religion—The Phenomenology of the Religious Act* (mimeographed) 1925/1926; *Metaphysics—the Problem of Salvation in Goethe's* Faustus (mimeographed) 1925/1926; *The Philosophy of Protestantism* 1927/1928; *The Philosophy of Catholicism* 1928/1929. Cf. Diaconu, "Bibliografie," in Ionescu, *Curs de istorie a logicii* 246–66.

5. Nae Ionescu obtained his doctor's degree in 1919 at the University of Munich (Germany) with the paper *Die Logistik als Versuch einer neuen Begründung der Mathematik*. Cf. Ionescu, *Neliniştea metafizică* 5–56.

6. Vulcănescu/Constantin Noica, "Introducere," in Ionescu, *Curs de istorie a logicii* 18–34.

7. ["If I am led to treat here questions which address politics and religion by turns, it would be well to realize that it is neither an attempt— which would be ridiculous—to usurp the sovereign domain of the Church, nor to relinquish the philosophical terrain for that of the contingencies of practical actions, which I desire more than ever to leave alone"—ed.] Jacques Maritain, *Primauté du spirituel* 3.

8. Eliade, "Magia și cercetările metapsihice" in *Misterele și inițierea orientală* 75–77. According to Eliade, "metapsychics" is a science about abnormal phenomena of the soul, which the senses couldn't perceive, an unknown phenomenon until then.

9. The external, canonical, sacralized act *operates* on the consciousness with more religious effectiveness than meditation or personal prayer can do.

10. "Rudolf Steiner," in *Misterele și inițierea orientală* 131–41. Eliade points out that theosophy should not be confused with the Theosophical Society founded by Blavatski and Olcott.

11. "Știință și ocultism," in *Cum am găsit piatra filozofală* 246. The use of the word *morals* in this text shows that Eliade did not want to separate morals from religion as the Renaissance had done. For him, morality is not *lay*; an active morality is a religious one, it is the actuation of spiritual values and urges. Cf. Eliade, *Contribuții la filosofia Renașterii* 46.

12. "Pe marginea unor cărți metapsihice," in *Misterele și inițierea orientală* 29–30; "Cunoașterea viitorului," in *Misterele și inițierea orientală* 50; "Rudolf Steiner," in *Misterele și inițierea orientală* 134–35.

13. François-Pierre Maine de Biran: a French philosopher (1766–1842) who influenced Eliade to some extent. Author of: *Mémoire sur l'habitude*; *Mémoire sur la décomposition de la pensée*; *Essai sur les fondaments de la psychologie*; *Note sur les deux révélations*; *Note sur l'idée d'existence*; *Nouveaux essai d'anthropologie*, etc. According to Maine de Biran, it is possible to sustain a phenomenology of the concrete human being, divided into three parts: animal life, human life, spiritual life. Accepting the spiritual life, which surpasses human life, Maine de Biran explores the value of interior experience concerning the problem of cognition. So, the Kantian distinction between phenomenon and noumenon, or in the words of Maine de Biran, between the plane of cognition and the absolute plane of existence has no place within the consciousness of the ego; the actuality of the ego implies a necessary belief in the existence of the soul as a virtual force that exists absolutely. Maine de Biran attempted to maintain an equal distance between ontologism and psychologism.

14. Baruzi, "Introducere în cercetări asupra limbajului mistic," in Davy, *Enciclopedia doctrinelor mistice*, vol. I 27–39.

15. "Mistica primâverii" (radio broadcast, April 19, 1938), in *Taina Indiei*, 190.

16. "Contemplația" (radio broadcast, 1935), in *Taina Indiei* 97.

17. "Comentarii la legenda Meșterului Manole" 478. Cf. Plato, *Parmenides* 131 e; Aristotle, *Metaphysics* 987 b 13.

18. In the light of the theory of archetypes, Eliade elevated to the rank of religion all beliefs, from the primitive to the most modern. Cf. Constantin Noica, "Cei șapte pași ai lui Buddha," in Eliade, *Yoga* 18.

19. "Între Luther și Ignațiu de Loyola" (1927), in *Profetism românesc 1* 56–57. According to Eliade, Rudolph Steiner's anthroposophy is to be recommended to the souls that have not yet found the Church.

20. "Despre rugăciune" (radio broadcast, March 9, 1935), in *Taina Indiei* 81.

VIII

Eliade's Fiction

Camouflage and Epiphany:
The Discovery of the Sacred in
Mircea Eliade and Ōe Kenzaburō

Okuyama Michiaki

With the death of Mircea Eliade in 1986, scholars were faced with the task of evaluating his legacy as a whole and the contribution he has made to the field of religious studies in particular. Although Eliade wrote his scholarly works chiefly in French and spent the last thirty years of his academic life based in Chicago, assessment of his work solely from a Western perspective can only cover part of the picture. Religious studies in the East will have its own appraisal of what Eliade has meant to the intellectual history of the twentieth century. The following discussion is a contribution to that appraisal.

THE CAMOUFLAGE OF THE SACRED IN MODERN MYTHS

Set against the backdrop of Japan's contemporary cultural scene and its reflections in the literary world, Eliade's idea of the camouflage of the sacred takes on special significance. To illustrate this, I begin with a comment from the 1976 preface to the first volume of *A History of Religious Ideas*, which foreshadows the conclusions in the final chapter of the final volume of this massive work:

> Consciousness of this unity of the spiritual history of humanity is a recent discovery, which has not yet been sufficiently assimilated. Its importance for the future of our discipline will become manifest in the last chapter of the third volume. It is also in this final chapter, in the course of a discussion of the crises brought on by the masters of reductionism—from Marx and Nietzsche to Freud—and of the contributions made by

anthropology, the history of religions, phenomenology, and the new hermeneutics, that the reader will be able to judge the sole, but important, religious creation of the modern Western world. I refer to the ultimate stage of desacralization. The process is of considerable interest to the historian of religions, for it illustrates the complete camouflage of the "sacred"—more precisely, its identification with the "profane." (*A History of Religious Ideas*, vol. 1 xvi)

Here the camouflage of the sacred through its identification with the profane is localized as a creation of the modern Western world. In a 1978 interview with Claude-Henri Rocquet, Eliade replies to a question concerning the meaning of the idea of the "death of God" by reiterating the point in much the same words (*Ordeal by Labyrinth* 151).

These statements do more than simply repeat his familiar dichotomy of the sacred and the profane; they introduce the mediation of "camouflage." By tracing the development of this concept in tandem with Eliade's thinking, the importance of this strategy as a comment on modern religiosity should emerge in clearer relief.

Already from the time of his 1949 work *Patterns in Comparative Religion*, the relation between the sacred and the profane becomes a focus of concern. Once the dualism is established, Eliade is able to introduce his particular understanding of "hierophany." He begins by setting forth the manifold varieties of hierophany and then proceeds to what he calls "the dialectic of hierophanies." By *dialectic* he means that "the sacred expresses itself through something other than itself," and that "the sacred manifests itself limited and incarnate" (*Patterns* 26). At this time, however, no mention is made of the idea of "camouflage." In a later section Eliade alludes to modern religiosity in treating the transformation and "corruption" of myth and the survival of mythic patterns or functions in history (section 165). These ideas will figure prominently when he comes later to introduce the idea of camouflage.

The first chapter of his 1957 book *Myth, Dreams, and Mysteries* treats communism and Nazism as examples of political myths, which leads Eliade to wonder: "[W]hat now interests us above all is to find out what it is in the modern world that fills the *central* position occupied by the myth in traditional societies" (27). Clear mention is made of camouflage in the French original, although it is obscured in the English translation:

> It seems that a myth itself, as well as the symbols it brings into play, never quite disappears from the present world of the psyche; it only changes its aspect and disguises its operations [*camoufle ses fonctions*]. Would it not be instructive to prolong the enquiry and unmask the operations of myths [*démasquer le camouflage de mythes*] on the *social plane*? (27–28)

After identifying what he sees as the mythical structure and function of modern festivals, Eliade suggests that the exemplary models or paradigms set forth in formal education and imitated in cultural fashions can be seen as the functional equivalents to myths. This same process is to be found in the visual arts and in reading. Not only have archaic mythical themes and archetypes survived in the modern novel and modern entertainment, but the latter enable people to escape from the limitations of secular time. They are transported to a kind of "concentrated time," a time of heightened intensity, which is nothing less than "a residuum of, or substitute for, magico-religious time" (34).

The suggestion of camouflage at work in the myths of the modern world appears in another book also originally published in 1957, *The Sacred and the Profane*. In the final section of the concluding chapter, entitled "Sacred and Profane in the Modern World," Eliade remarks that "nonreligious man *in the pure state* is a comparatively rare phenomenon, even in the most desacralized of modern societies. . . . [T]he modern man who feels and claims that he is nonreligious still retains a large stock of camouflaged myths and degenerated rituals" (204–205).

In addition, he refers to "nudism or the movements for complete sexual freedom" in which one can detect traces of the "nostalgia for paradise." Similarly, he sees modern people repeating scenarios of initiation, especially scenarios of "ordeals" characterized by the symbolism of "death and resuscitation." He concludes that "in the case of those moderns who proclaim that they are nonreligious, religion and mythology are 'eclipsed' in the darkness of their unconscious" (213). In a subsequent monograph dedicated to the subject of initiation he sees it as an example of the camouflaged mythology of the modern world, observing that "initiatory themes remain alive chiefly in modern man's unconsciousness" (*Rites and Symbols* 127, 134).

Later, in a 1963 volume *Myth and Reality*, the theme of camouflage of myths appears in the title of the final chapter: "Survivals and Camouflages of Myths." The section deals, among others, with "the myths of the modern world." Eliade sees the preoccupation of early modern European nationalism with securing "a noble origin" as the quest for an "almost magical" prestige, in much the same way as mythical or ritual repetition of cosmogony provided archaic societies with a renewed sense of community. He also touches on the eschatological and millennial structures of communism, as well as what he sees as the mythical structures at work in contemporary mass media. Finally, he turns to modern art and literature, which he dubs "the myths of the elite" to stress the difficulty—as in initiatory ordeals—of participating in the creation of novelty. Once again he refers to the survival of mythical themes in literature, to people's longing for paradigmatic models, and to the mythical function of the "escape from time" achieved through reading (*Myth and Reality* 162–93, esp. 187ff.).

Clearly, then, Eliade employed the notion of camouflage as a tool to locate and decipher "myths in the modern world," or more precisely their functional equivalents. That said, from the 1950s on Eliade also used the idea of camouflage for a different purpose, namely, to reflect on his own literary activities.

THE SACRED INTERPRETED/THE SACRED INVENTED

In *Imagination and Meaning: The Scholarly and Literary Worlds of Mircea Eliade*, the editors, Norman J. Girardot and Mac Linscott Ricketts, included Eliade's "Autobiographic Fragment," originally published in 1953 as a contribution to *Caiete de Dor*, a Romanian cultural review published in Paris (*Imagination and Meaning* 113ff.). Eliade composed the piece in response to the request by the editors of *Caiete de Dor* for an article on the relation between his philosophical and scientific works and his literary works. In it Eliade characterizes his scholarly works as philosophical rather than scientific. Regarding the relation between philosophical occupations and literary creation, Eliade notes that he has written in both genres from the outset, adding that his literature has been both realistic and fantastic. He admits a certain complementarity between the two genres, pointing at "a real dependence of some literary writings on theoretical ones, and vice versa" (123). He gives as the most obvious example the direct connection between his 1936 study *Yoga: Essai sur les origines de la mystique indienne* and his 1940 novel *Dr. Honigberger's Secret*.

He elaborates on this relationship with reference to his 1937 novel *Şarpele (The Serpent)*, recalling that he completed the work in some ten nights (123). While writing it, he did not consult reference works, despite the considerable quantity of folkloric and ethnographic material at his disposal on the symbolism of the serpent. He argues that had he consulted the scholarly literature on the subject, literary invention would have been disrupted. This experience convinced him of two things: "1) that theoretical activity cannot *consciously* and *voluntarily* influence literary activity; and 2) that the free act of literary creation can, on the other hand, reveal certain theoretical meanings" (123). Regarding these "theoretical meanings," he notes that

> only after I read *Şarpele* in book form did I understand that in this book I had resolved, without knowing it, a problem which had preoccupied me for a long time... and which only in *Traité* did I expound theoretically—namely, the problem of the unrecognizability of miracle, the fact that the intrusion of the *sacred* into the world is always camouflaged in a set of "historical forms," manifestations which do not *apparently* differ in any way from millions of cosmic or historical manifestations (a *sacred* stone is not different, *apparently*, from any other stone, etc.). Much more might be said about the dialectic of *hierophanies*, but this is not the place for that. (123–24)

Eliade found in a novel he had written fifteen years previously an anticipation of "the dialectic of hierophany," that is, the unrecognizability of miracle, or the camouflage of the sacred in history and the cosmos.[1]

The ideas of dialectic and camouflage that emerge from Șarpele led Eliade in two directions. On the one hand, he was drawn to a scholarly study on the "fall into History" and on the other, to the literary creation of a then unfinished romance, *The Forbidden Forest* (published in 1955). "Both roads lead," Eliade adds, "eventually to the same problem: the unrecognizability of the transcendent camouflaged in History." He summarizes:

> Summing up, I could say that all these works try to uncover the same central mystery of the rupture provoked by the appearance of Time and the "fall into History" which followed of necessity. Each of them is permeated, more or less explicitly, by the nostalgia for Paradise, for the reintegration of the primordial unity, for the "emergence from time." (*Imagination and Meaning* 124)

Here we see an important theme for Eliade: the recognition of a transcendent camouflaged in history. His "Autobiographic Fragment" establishes the concepts of "camouflage" and "dialectic" as the pivotal point in his scholarly and literary writings. The camouflage of the miracle in history would be taken up in his novels, while his theoretical works focused on the dialectic of the sacred in history and the cosmos. At the same time, the fragment does not present a clear idea of how he understands the relation between "the dialectic of hierophany" and "camouflage." Rather, as another example will show, he seems to conflate the two. Consider the following excerpt from his *Journal*, dated 3 May 1976:

> I correct and complete the text of my interview dealing with initiation that is to appear in *Parabola*, and as usual I come up against the same difficulty. We live in an age of radical desacralization, where initiatory scenarios survive only in oneiric and artistic realms. But do they only survive there, and there alone? If one agrees with what I've called the "dialectic of the camouflaging of the sacred in the profane," one must also admit another possibility: The initiatory phenomenon could well be perpetuated in our time, before our eyes, but in

other forms, so well camouflaged in the "profane" that it would be impossible for us to recognize them as such. All the same, to render this paradoxical situation intelligible, I'd have to develop considerably what I understand by "dialectic of the camouflaging of the sacred," and that would take a good sixty pages. (*Journal III* 227–28)

Keeping in mind the idea of hierophany developed in *Patterns in Comparative Religion* and that of camouflage, the "dialectic" in which the sacred manifests itself through the profane, seems to mean that the sacred remains camouflaged in the profane for those who cannot recognize the manifestations of the sacred. As noted earlier, Eliade speaks of the dialectical manifestations of the sacred through the profane, at the same time as he acknowledges the difficulty of recognizing its camouflage in the profane. In short, the sacred camouflaged in the profane will manifest itself as such only to those who are prepared to recognize it; for the others it will remain hidden.

Rereading the relevant passages in Eliade's works, I find him coming back continually to the importance of mythical motifs surviving in the modern world, almost as if he had taken it upon himself to prevent the realm of myth from disappearing in history, and to help today's world see through the camouflage. At the same time, there is no discounting the possibility that the manifestations of the sacred he was writing about were recognizable only to him. In this connection, we may note the following comment on hierophany in a 1978 essay entitled "Literary Imagination and Religious Structure":

> Any religious phenomenon is a hierophany, i.e., a manifestation of the sacred, a dialectical process that transforms a profane object or act into something that is sacred, i.e., significant, precious, and paradigmatic. In other words, through a hierophany, the sacred is all at once revealed and disguised in the profane. (22)

He then adds that the sacred is "disguised for everyone else outside that particular religious community." If I understand Eliade's idea of the role of the scholar in the modern world correctly, such manifestations of the sacred are to be deciphered by the scholars in religious studies and then conveyed to others. But the concept of camouflage does not seem to require that recognition of the sacred be closed off to everyone but scholars of religion. Does not Eliade himself as a novelist engage, if only unconsciously, in camouflaging the miracle of the sacred in a world of fiction? And when he shifts roles to become an interpreter of the camouflage of the sacred, do not the ideas of "hierophany" and "the dialectical manifestations of the sacred" lose some of their objectivity to become a rediscovery of something whose presence he had assumed or even planted there from the beginning?

The concept of "hierophany" left us by Eliade looks to be a two-edged sword. We are given a conceptual tool for deciphering the sacred in an apparently profane world, while that same tool cuts into the unquestioned assumptions of a sacred reality hidden in a profane world. Clearly, we are up against a problem that cannot be resolved merely within the framework of Eliade's own work. If we grant that the problem is not just something peculiar to Eliade's own thinking, we must take recourse to other avenues of inquiry in order to come to terms with it.

A VIEW FROM THE WORK OF ŌE KENZABURŌ

In the foregoing I have suggested that certain of Eliade's ideas open up a new perspective that can help us uncover previously unrecognized dimensions of modern religiosity, but at the same time open themselves up to the charge of a self-fulfilling prophecy by those who do not share his assumptions. To parry this criticism, I would like to turn to the contemporary Japanese novelist Ōe Kenzaburō (1935–).[2] With Ōe's receipt of the Nobel Prize for Literature in 1994, he has been catapulted onto the international scene. I would like to consider his notion of "epiphany" as it relates to Eliade's notions of "hierophany" and "the manifestations of the sacred."

As to the multifaceted nature of Ōe's writing, Faye Yuan Kleeman sums up in 1991 as follows:

> Ōe Kenzaburō is one of the most prolific and talented authors on the contemporary literary scene. Having attained great

success at a fairly young age, Ōe has been producing top-quality fiction, essays and critical writing consistently for the past three decades. It is hard to categorize Ōe's writing into a certain genre because his career spans three decades and he has produced such diverse works as *Kojinteki na taiken* (A personal matter, 1964), a novel with autobiographical elements, a series of fictional works dealing with socio-political issues, highly theoretical essays analyzing the essence of fiction writing such as those collected in *Shōsetsu no hōhō* (The methodology of fiction, 1978), down to his most recent work of science fiction, *Chiryōtō* (*The Tower of Healing*, 1990). (187)

In recent years Ōe's novels, particularly after *Dōjidai Gēmu* (*The Game of Contemporaneity*, 1979), have turned to a more or less obvious preoccupation with the question of "the salvation of soul." But rather than focusing directly on their religious or spiritual aspect, I would like to approach them from another angle, in pursuit of a comparison with Eliade's ideas.

I take my cue from a collection of essays about everyday life composed between 1983 and 1984, and published in 1985, as *Shōsetsu no Takurami, Chi no Tanoshimi* (*Contrivances of Fiction, Pleasures of Knowledge*).[3] As he says of himself, since the time of his late thirties he has concentrated his reading, in two- or three-year cycles, on the works of one particular author. He describes himself as devoting the majority of his daytime hours to a careful and studied reading of his chosen author, as far as possible in the original language, after which he turns to his own writing, interrupted by the occasional swim to relax. This is the routine he had when he read the works of Eliade, as he explains: "Mircea Eliade has become the axis around which my days rotate now.... I had read him before, but this time around I felt drawn to him through my continual reading of [William] Blake and scholars of Blake. I will face the texts of Eliade calmly for the years to come" (*Contrivances of Fiction* 76).

Ōe comments in several places in these essays on Eliade's *The Myth of the Eternal Return* and *Ordeal by Labyrinth*. He also writes that he was profoundly impressed by *Journal II* (a version of *No Souvenirs*) and derived a great deal of inspiration from it. For example, he was touched by Eliade's reflections on W. N. P. Barbellion (1889–1919) after reading *The Journal of a Disappointed Man* (London, 1919). I cite the relevant passage from Eliade's journal, dated 10 January 1961:

> This morning I'm leafing through Barbellion's *Journal*. His enthusiasm after reading (December 22, 1912) *Ancient Hunters* by Sollas [impressed me]. The perspectives opened to him toward the Paleolithic consoled him in his miseries and his illness. Even better, it revealed to him the certainty of his *indestructibility*—as matter but also as "epiphany." He writes: "For nothing can alter the fact that I HAVE lived; I HAVE BEEN, if for even so short a time." It is indeed what I would call the indestructibility of human existence as epiphany. But B. adds: "And when I am dead, the matter which composes my body is indestructible—and eternal, so that come what may to my 'Soul,' my dust will always be going on.... When I am dead, you can kill me, burn me, drown me, scatter me—but you cannot destroy me.... Death can do no more than kill you." B. wrote that because he was a naturalist. But I have met similar experiences, expressed almost in the same terms, among numerous "mystics" (cf. especially the experience of "cosmic consciousness"). (*Journal II* 120–21)

These words helped Ōe realize that it was his son (the composer, Ōe Hikari), who, having been disabled from birth, represented for him the indestructibility of human existence as epiphany. After his son's birth, his novels struggled with the meaning of leading a life with his new son. As he explains, everything he had written prior to the birth of his son seemed useless for his present situation and of no help for the future. He therefore began to write novels that might serve him in his new life with his son. In the struggle to reform himself as a writer, the chief catalyst was the indestructibility of human existence as epiphany that he saw every day in his son. He continues:

> To put it more concretely, I might paraphrase the words of Barbellion: Nothing can erase the fact that *he* (this disabled child)

has lived, the fact that *he has been*. I became convinced of that fact the more I wrote the novels about the life of this child.

Moreover, I had a premonition that if I continued writing novels about life with my disabled son, I would come to know that very indestructibility of human existence as epiphany. (*Contrivances of Fiction* 114)

The phrase "indestructibility of human existence as epiphany" was to become crucial to Ōe and in fact gives the title to his final essay in *Contrivances*.[4] An examination of novels written around this period testifies to the importance of his notion of "epiphany."

EPIPHANY IN THE FICTIONAL WORLD OF ŌE KENZABURŌ

THE GAME OF CONTEMPORANEITY

In 1984, at the time Ōe was composing the essays that would eventually make up *Contrivances of Fiction, Pleasures of Knowledge,* the paperback edition of *The Game of Contemporaneity* appeared. Immediately after the book's original publication, Ōe tells us, he had embarked on a new novel tentatively entitled *Matriarchs and Tricksters* as a companion volume to *The Game of Contemporaneity* (*Contrivances of Fiction* 179–80). Although he finally abandoned the project, it reemerged in a new form as a novel entitled *M/T to Mori no Fushigi no Monogatari* (*The Tales of M/T and the "Wonder" of the Forest*), in which the earlier idea of "matriarchs and tricksters" survived as the abbreviation "M/T." In a postscript to the 1990 paperback edition of the work, Ōe explains the meaning for him of writing novels:

> When I think of what a novel is and what it means to me to write, it all comes down in the end to the narrative, that is, to the way the story is told. Whenever I am at the point of completing a novel, I find myself in crisis, alarmed at the fact that this is not narrative I really need right now. I always finish writing my works thinking that my attempted narrative is quite different from the one that I should really have created.

> In fact, this gap between the narrative I wrote and the one I needed to write leaves me groping about for a next novel. (*The Tales of M/T* 410)

For Ōe the clearest example of the gap between these two narratives shows up in the contrasting modes of narration in *The Game of Contemporaneity* and *The Tales of M/T and the "Wonder" of the Forest*. Both novels are based on the foundational myth and the ideas of life and death found in the folklore of his native land, a village in the forest of Shikoku (one of the four main islands of Japan). The different way each work establishes the narrating "I" strikes me as helpful for understanding what Ōe means by epiphany.

The Game of Contemporaneity is constructed in the form of six letters written by the narrator to his twin sister.[5] The first person narrator is a Japanese scholar teaching history at a university in Mexico. His letters show him accepting as his personal destiny the task of recounting his native land's history and myths, whose character he believed to be so distinctive that it would not allow simple identification with the larger surrounding nation of Japan. In view of this partial independence, the narrator's homeland is referred to as a "village=nation=microcosm." It is set deep in the wooded mountains of Shikoku and traces its history back to the "primordial age" when a figure known as Kowasu-hito (the Destroyer) smashed to pieces a gigantic rock that had blocked the mouth of a foul-smelling swamp basin, draining the water and leaving in its place the habitable land of the "village=nation=microcosm."

The narrator's mission of recording the history and myths of his homeland was entrusted to him by his father, a Shinto priest who had been dispatched to that region as a religious official of the state. (Shinto had been the state religion in Japan's early modern period.) Although an outsider, the young priest grew interested in the history and myths of the area, so much so that he devoted his years to studying local folk traditions known to diverge from the orthodoxy of institutionalized State Shinto. He passed this same devotion on to his son whom he drilled in the local lore in the hopes that one day the lad would grow up to chronicle the tradition formally. This hope is embodied in the six letters that make up the book.

Regarding the use of the epistolary form for the narrative, Kleeman explains:

> By marshalling historical, mythical, and folkloric elements in a synchronic manner rather than in a diachronic narrative, as most narratives tend to do, the author is able to exercise his freedom of imagination, merging events from different times and places, juxtaposing seemingly impossible combinations of history and myth, and presenting a unique view of his own account of myth and cosmos. (231–32)

The use of the term *contemporaneity* in the title points to this synchronic juxtaposition. Ōe recalls that in composing the novel his principal concern was with *what* to write rather than *how* to write it. He had wanted to include more of the actual myth and folklore of his native land. As he struggled to complete a work he was already dissatisfied with, the narrative method required to write his next novel became clear to him (*Tales of M/T* 412). Although to some extent the relationship between the Shinto priest and his son, whereby the understanding of the father is completed through his son, contains the seed of Ōe's attempt to see the indestructible human in his own son, it is in the narrative technique of *The Tales of M/T and the "Wonder" of the Forest*, I suggest, that the meaning of epiphany comes clearly to light.

THE TALES OF M/T AND THE "WONDER" OF THE FOREST

The Tales of M/T and the "Wonder" of the Forest is obviously a retelling of the material of *The Game of Contemporaneity*.[6] But, in the retelling, mythical and historical figures from the folk tradition of the village are arranged by the narrator into two groups: the Matriarchs and the Tricksters. One of the latter is Kamei Meisuke, who is said to have played an active role in the latter days of the Tokugawa Shogunate. Legend has it that he reincarnated after death to play an important part in an uprising against the tyranny of the Meiji Government. And so it is that in the course of time Meisuke came to be revered by the local population, who had a statue of him placed in a recess alongside the Shinto altar in their homes. Incidentally, Meisuke is said to have had a scar on the back of his head, a hint of things to come in the novel.

The narrator "I" of *The Tales of M/T* is a writer from Shikoku, now living in Tokyo. He is referred to by others as K, leaving little choice for the reader but to identify the character with Ōe himself. When he was a child, K would be summoned by his grandmother, who would oblige him to listen to her repertoire of tales and legends that blended the history and myths of their native village. Looking back, the narrator recalls the vague sense that his role as listener would be too heavy a responsibility for him to assume, especially if he would be expected one day to write down what he had heard about the "whole" village. With the death of his grandmother he felt free of that obligation; as if a great weight had been lifted from his shoulders. That is, until the day he almost drowned in the river.

One day in early summer when K was swimming in the river, he dived deep under a big rock to watch a school of dace swimming against the current. While underwater his head got wedged in between the rocks and would have drowned had his mother, keeping guard over her son at play, not pulled him up to the surface at the last moment. The incident left him with an injury on the back of the head. It also freed him from his fear of the task he had known all along was his. Henceforth he became a willing listener of the lore recounted by the elders in the village.

After retelling the myths and history of the village in four chapters, the narrator confesses at the start of the final chapter that he has never been quite sure of the basic meaning of his role (*Tales of M/T* 344–45). He then begins to write about his own family. At this point the narrative method of *The Tales of M/T* contrasts sharply with that of *The Game of Contemporaneity*. He tells us that he named his first son Hikari (the actual name of Ōe's first son), meaning "light," in view of the fear that the child might lose his sight after the operation to remove the growth on the back of his head that he was born with. The son did not lose his sight, although some brain disorder remained. At the same time, he was compensated with a good sense of hearing, which would later serve him as a composer of music. The narrator tells us that he had heard from his sister, who lives with their mother, that the mother had begun to pray before the statue of Meisuke in the belief that the scar on the back of her grandson's head, like that on the head of her son, was a sign of special affinity between the three.

At this point the story jumps twenty years to the time when the narrator and his family pay a visit to his mother in Shikoku for the first time. Soon after that, Hikari expressed the wish to visit his grandmother again—this time on his own—and his father permits this. During his stay, Hikari listens to her long tales, but does not tell his family about it. About half a year later Hikari makes a musical composition and sends a tape recording of it to his grandmother. The narrator tells us that he knew that his son had grasped the spirit of his grandmother's tales as soon as he saw the title of the piece: "Kowasu-hito" (the Destroyer).

Two years later, the narrator's mother is admitted to hospital. On the morning she leaves home, she has her son-in-law drive up to a hill overlooking the village. They get out of the car near the top and feel that they hear faint echoes of the music from "Kowasu-hito." At this point it is as if something has broken through this otherwise ordinary scene. When we hear her explain the meaning of the music, we understand this to have been a kind of "epiphany."

Later, from her hospital bed, the mother sends a tape-recorded message to her son in which she remarks that the strains of "Kowasu-hito" sounded to her like a bright light illuminating everything around her and within her. It was as if it had caught the sounds of "the 'Wonder' of the Forest," emanating from the very *source* of the birth, life, and death of the people in the village: *the One* that envelops all individual lives and to which individuals return once when their souls have been purified.

Having recounted the long tales of the "Matriarchs and Tricksters," the narrator finds that listening to the music of his son and hearing his mother's reflections on their homeland, he felt as if at last the meaning of his mission as a storyteller had been revealed to him. Given Eliade's understanding of the sacred as something real, meaningful, and powerful, one could call this revelation a "hierophany," a manifestation of the sacred. In contrast to *The Game of Contemporaneity*, in *The Tales of M/T and the "Wonder" of the Forest*, the narrator brings his son and mother into the story, which in turn makes it possible for him to articulate these moments of climactic breakthrough of "epiphany" and "hierophany."

To take this a step farther, we might say that just as the narrator understands the sign that he and his son have on the backs of their heads as a sign of a common destiny and mission to transmit the essential spirit of their homeland, so, too, has Ōe Kenzaburō come to understand his own vocation as a writer. The first person narrator and the author become one, precisely at the point of recognizing the indestructibility of human existence as epiphany. And, if mother and son are thus made to embody M/T, they do so in a kind of camouflage wherein the author conceals the central "epiphany" of the novel as if he himself were also a trickster like Meisuke with a scar on the back of the head. These conclusions are supported, I believe, by reading Ōe in the light of Eliade's ideas.

As noted earlier, Eliade occasionally uses the term *hierophany* interchangeably with that of "camouflage of the sacred." Clarification of the idea of "camouflage" makes Eliade open to the possible charge of arbitrariness in his "rediscovery" of the sacred in the modern world. Taking Ōe Kenzaburō, who acknowledges his debt to Eliade, as one example of literary creativity, a good case can be made for the utility of the notion of camouflage and epiphany. Ōe not only uses the notion of epiphany to interpret his own life with his disabled son, but also camouflages the moments of epiphany in his *The Tales of M/T and the "Wonder" of the Forest*. Just as Eliade characterizes modernity as the period when West meets East and the archaic world, here in the modern literary world in Japan we see Western concepts from Eliade meeting the literary imagination of one of its brightest representatives, an encounter that has given Ōe a new style of narrative and at the same time challenges the criticism that Eliade's hierophanies are no more than self-fulfilling prophecies.

NOTES

I wish to express my gratitude to Professor James W. Heisig of the Nanzan Institute for Religion and Culture, whose detailed comments were of great assistance in the preparation of this chapter.

1. On this issue, Eliade refers to *The Serpent* also in his diary (24 June 1963). When a student came to see him after he read *The Serpent*, Eliade spoke with him about the conception of the fantastic in literature. He continues: "I reminded him that this conception has its roots in my theory of 'the incognizability of miracles'—or in my theory that, after the Incarnation, the transcendent is camouflaged in the world or in history and thus becomes 'incognizable' " (*Journal II* 191).

2. Japanese names are given accordingly to the convention of family name preceding given name.

3. In his afterword, Ōe describes the book: "*Contrivances of Fiction, Pleasures of Knowledge* is a collection of essays in which I probably expose my life and inner mind more openly than ever before. I might call it the definition of a novelist living in the nuclear age" (251–52). As a novelist Ōe is well known for his keen sensitivity to the problems of the nuclear age after Hiroshima. In this chapter I shall have to omit this side of his work.

4. In this essay again, Ōe reflects on himself, taking Eliade's idea as a clue. Cf., *Contrivances of Fiction* 245–46.

5. The contents of these six letters are summarized in Kleeman 223–32.

6. The " 'Wonder' of the forest" is another important topic in this novel, but as I am focusing here on the concept of epiphany, I shall refrain from discussing this and other elements of the work.

Men and Stones

Mircea Eliade
(translated by Mac Linscott Ricketts)

ACT I SCENE I

The stage represents the immense vault of a cave, only partially lighted by torches, with the profile changing constantly. At the right, rock walls are guessed, forming a sort of gigantic amphitheater, whose lofty ceiling cannot be seen from anywhere in the audience. A huge rectangular stone is situated at the base of the amphitheater. In the corner at the right, close to the floodlights: a puddle of water, into which heavy drops fall from time to time with a metallic sound, echoing and reechoing. In the rear: walls of solid rock and boulders, strange shapes and colors constantly changing, depending on how the light is diverted or diminished. To the left the cave narrows, allowing one to imagine a narrow, twisting corridor.

Toward the center of the stage, carefully placed on a low rock, are two knapsacks crammed full, two unlit flashlights, and two alpenstocks with steel tips. Beside them are two large, round objects that glow; their purpose will be revealed only later: they are spools of very thin, phosphorescent metallic thread.

As the curtain rises, ALEXANDRU is in the middle of the stage, watching with a kind of youthful bliss the play of shadows and shapes produced by the torch at the slightest movement of his arm. He is a tall, light-haired young man, quite handsome, perhaps thirty or thirty-five years old, though he does not look it. The extreme mobility of his face and the fervor that pervades his voice, looks, and gestures give him an adolescent grace, especially in the first scene. Often he falls silent, absorbed by the forms and happenings that only he can see. In such intervals of silence, he does not have the air of a man lost in vague reveries, but wears an expression of supreme concentration, as though he were listening to something he cannot fully comprehend.

A few seconds later, from the right, preceded by a cloud of magnesium smoke, appears PETRUȘ, endeavoring to close up a large camera. He is a dark-complexioned man, well-built, with a thick head of black hair slightly graying at the temples. He could be forty, but looks older. A curiously mixed athletic type who in no event could be mistaken for a pedant. He is not handsome, but his face is noble, his brow and chin strong-willed, his eyes clear, and his gaze long and gentle, yet capable of being ironic when he wishes. He speaks softly. When he laughs, he laughs heartily. Sometimes, when pronouncing certain technical terms, he seems to do so apologetically, having no others available. His entire being conveys strength, calm, serenity.

Both men are wearing ski suits.

ALEXANDRU (*gestures with torch*): You don't know how many times I've dreamed about this! . . . Look at it! See how it looks! Just the way I knew it would! It's a shame Adria's not with us!

PETRUȘ (*closing up the camera*): A shame indeed. She'd have taken better photographs than I.

ALEXANDRU: And see how beautiful it is! It's awesome! . . . Look there! (*He lifts the torch and the decor changes.*) Up high! In the back! See what curious forms! Look at that one over there (*gestures with torch*). It looks like a man . . . an old codger. No—it's a woman, standing stooped over . . . beside a man . . . one with a beard.

PETRUȘ (*looking*): I think it looks more like a group of women. Don't you see? Two in front, bending over . . . and others, more in the shadows. It depends on how the flame trembles.

ALEXANDRU: Ah, if only I were a painter!

PETRUȘ: And Adriana envies you for being a poet. You artists are all alike!

ALEXANDRU: . . . Because you don't suspect what power a painter has under his control! Poets are a dime a dozen. Poets like me, I mean. Small, anemic, timid. How would you describe this cave in words? You'd have to be a genius, to have courage! Like Dante, Milton! Nothing half-way would do!

PETRUȘ (*walking around, examining the walls*): But, meanwhile, I see that the cave suits you! You're in fine fettle! As though you weren't five or six hundred meters under the mountain... Bravo, poet! I like you! I thought I'd have to give you some pervitine[1] after the first half-hour... and now I see that I can't keep your mouth shut...

ALEXANDRU: It's so beautiful, it's awesome. And when you think... All this, in just a few hours...

PETRUȘ: You said it! In just a few hours' time. I've been searching for it since I was thirty-three... and I'm still searching. And you see, I was right. It was where I said it was... I could tell by the echo, by the spring...

ALEXANDRU (*mostly to himself*): Think of it—to be able to describe all these things! To be able to write about them, as they are, as you feel them...

PETRUȘ: But I don't see you taking any notes. You'll get these mixed up with other things later on. You'll forget them.

ALEXANDER: This vault—never! I know! I've told you, I dream about it at night too.

PETRUȘ: Adriana laughed about that.

ALEXANDRU: She wouldn't believe me, but I *do* dream it, as it is... For a long time I've wanted to write a book about caves. But what can you say in a book? How can you describe these columns?

PETRUȘ (*gesturing*): And they're not even columns!

ALEXANDRU: True. I said "columns" because I couldn't think of anything more suitable... But if I had been able to *paint*...

PETRUȘ: Yes, maybe that would have been better. Then you could've copied these markings, these signs. Anyhow, we'd have had them on paper. With measurements, done right. (*with fervor*) Ah, Săndel, if only I could be sure they're Paleolithic, if I knew that we'll both be famous!... That is, I'm speaking mostly about myself, since you, with your love poems and your metaphysics, you are, so to speak... (*He breaks off, examining the signs again.*) I'm no expert, but they *seem* to be from the Paleolithic... You see, the question of the Paleolithic in the Carpathian Bow[2] is awfully controversial.

ALEXANDRU (*who has ceased looking at the vault*): But nothing except these markings. No treasure...

PETRUȘ (*smiling*): If you think those poor unfortunates had time to hoard treasure—! They knew nothing about such things. They didn't know metals, they didn't know anything. They were just a bunch of poor human beings... and maybe not even that.

ALEXANDRU: Right, but I wasn't necessarily thinking of treasure in that sense. I was thinking of pottery, of tools made of bone and stone. Maybe if we dug here, right here, we'd discover some skeletons, skulls, or who knows what...

PETRUȘ: Maybe..., although this cave was undoubtedly a cultic site. Probably this stone was an altar. It might be possible to find skulls and other bones of animals, maybe even bear skulls, if these signs do indeed belong to the Paleolithic Age. The cave bear, you know...

ALEXANDRU: Do you realize how thrilled I am?

PETRUȘ: About what?

ALEXANDRU: About everything, about all these things around us! You've got to admit, it's impressive. To be the first persons to enter such a cave after who knows how many thousands of years...

PETRUȘ: Maybe only a few hundred years. Or, maybe tens of thousands of years. It depends on how many earthquakes there've been. And how the structure of the cave has been modified... Look, a subterranean spring used to flow here at one time, and later it stopped. That is, it changed its course.

ALEXANDRU (*in another place*): But look, there's water over here too.

PETRUȘ: That's from seepage... It would be interesting... (*Bends over*) I don't think so, but anyhow, let's try it... (*Bends down again*) No, don't bring the torch any closer. I have my camera light.

ALEXANDRU (*returns to center stage, stares*): It's awful! To be able to evoke all this! (*He lifts the light above the altar. Among the stones, several men are seen, gathered around an enormous bear.*)

A MAN: This bear, real bear.

ANOTHER: Big, very big.

ANOTHER: And strong. Strongest bear.

ANOTHER: He brings luck. From now on, our hunts will be lucky.

ANOTHER: We'll have plenty for ourselves and our women.

ANOTHER: We will eat!

THE BEAR: Why do you brag about bringing me down? How many of you were there? I was alone, and I was sleepy.
A MAN: The poor beast complains because we caught him.
ANOTHER: But you see, he's not dead.
ANOTHER: These bears never die. Feed on them and they still live.
ANOTHER: Bears don't die. That's why they're good luck!
(PETRUȘ *appears. Alexandru, pensive, moves the light.*)
PETRUȘ: Why so quiet? Were you dreaming?
ALEXANDRU: No, I was thinking... I was imagining. What a life!
PETRUȘ: Hard, my friend, very hard.
ALEXANDRU: To stay here, to live here, without fire.
PETRUȘ: Without anything... But it's not certain that that this part was inhabited. Probably they came here for the cult. Or, maybe, they closed their dead up in other corridors. Those poor souls had a lot of absurd beliefs!
ALEXANDRU: Do you really think they buried their dead here?
PETRUȘ: They didn't *bury* them, in any event. They threw them on top of one another and piled stones over them... To keep them from coming back. Poor benighted souls.
ALEXANDRU: Nothing to look at here.
PETRUȘ: We shall see farther on... We've had some truly good luck. Although, with so much humidity, it's hard to believe that anything would be preserved. As I told you, the Paleolithic in this region is problematic. (*He bends over.*)
ALEXANDRU: What're you looking for?
PETRUȘ: To save time, I'm collecting a few rocks. You take some too. Whatever you find. We can't tell here if they were used by people or not. Experts will examine them in the light, in laboratories. Let's do our duty.
ALEXANDRU: But we're not going to carry them with us all the way, are we? How could we do that?
PETRUȘ: We'll collect them and leave them here. We'll leave a marker and pick them up on the way back. But to keep from confusing them, we'll mark the bag number 1. I shall baptize this cavern "Cave Number 1."
ALEXANDRU: You ought to give it another name. Call it Adria, for example.

PETRUȘ (*smiling*): Very well, we'll call it that, to flatter her. But scientifically this cave is and will remain Number 1.

ALEXANDRU: —Although, God only knows if there were ever any women in here.

PETRUȘ: Why not? Plenty of dead ones, but maybe living ones also entered ... What do we know about all those confused beliefs?

ALEXANDRU: To stay here, almost naked ...

PETRUȘ: Naked, they were not ... You, with your artist's imagination, can't think of them otherwise, so you see them that way. But in fact they covered themselves as best they could: with animal hides, or, in warmer climates, with leaves.

ALEXANDRU: Really, what a lot of fantasizing it takes to imagine them as they really were!

PETRUȘ: Yes, that's very hard. With some approximation, a paleontologist who was also an artist might be able to make a less obscure image of them. But how they *really* were, no one will ever know. (*He puts several stones in the sack and sets it down on a high spot. A group of women, almost nude, appear. Some are carrying children around their necks, as monkeys carry their young.*)

GIRL: Where are you taking me?

A WOMAN: To Bear. We take you to Bear. He wants you.

GIRL: I'm afraid of him. Bear eats people.

ANOTHER WOMAN: You, no. You have a warm body. Bear wants you.

GIRL: He's old.

WOMAN: He strong. He the strongest bear. He does not die!

GIRL: I like a man.

WOMAN: You have no choice. You belong to Bear. He wants *you*. The other one won't touch you.

ANOTHER WOMAN: I'll make him mad and he'll go away.

ANOTHER: We'd be left without any meat.

ANOTHER: And we'd perish. And our children will miscarry and go after Bear.

GIRL: But I like a man.

WOMAN: What man? Who?

GIRL (*pointing at Alexandru*): Look there; him! (*She looks him in the eyes. All the women stare at him. Alexandru, smiling, wipes his hand across his face. The group vanishes.*)

PETRUŞ: The cave, I see, inspires you. To what? An epic poem or a dramatic one?

ALEXANDRU: It's awful! Those shadows make you dream.

PETRUŞ: That depends, my friend. Some they frighten, others they cause to dream, others still—a very few—they set to thinking.

ALEXANDRU: What are you thinking about here?

PETRUŞ: Well, for example, speleology.

ALEXANDRU: That's absurd! I have the impression that things like that lose all importance here. To investigate the fauna of caves . . . ! That's nonsense!

PETRUŞ: You're right. I was just joking. But still, you can think of other things, more important things. Life, prehistory, history . . .

ALEXANDRU: How can you *think*? To me the past seems to oppress you too much here. It crushes you. Nothing functions anymore but the capacity to fantasize . . .

PETRUŞ: For those who have it, it functions. But what do you do with someone like me?

ALEXANDRU: Don't you *see* anything?

PETRUŞ: Of course. I see stones, water, markings . . .

ALEXANDRU: And nothing else? Doesn't this stone altar say anything to you? Can't you imagine anything?

PETRUŞ: Only to a very limited extent. I just feel a sentiment of pity for those unfortunates who lived then. A sentiment of boundless pity. How those people suffered! What humiliation!

ALEXANDRU: And yet . . . But who knows?

PETRUŞ: No buts about it. They were brutes, impoverished. And they were the weakest of the brutes. A cave bear could best them. Ah, but later the tables were turned! They began to be masters of the bears. (*with satisfaction*) And they exterminated them, down to the last one.

ALEXANDRU (*ironically*): It was, at any rate, a victory . . .

PETRUŞ (*firmly*): A very great one, indeed. Do you think it was easy?! With a stone like this (*points*). By the way, where did you put the stones you picked up? (*Gestures*) Bring them here . . . You know, it would really be something if we discovered a complete Paleolithic station! So what do you say to that?

ALEXANDRU: What do you mean by a complete "station"?

PETRUȘ: With burials, my friend, with skeletons... Now, if we were to discover one, we'd leave it intact. I'd photograph it, that's all. For others to come, specialists in prehistory... We'd become famous just for discovering it. As a geologist, I'd be satisfied with even less. But Adriana—she'd be awfully proud.

ALEXANDRU (*absently*): Yes... I'm sure of that. But where are we going to find skeletons?

PETRUȘ (*with craving*): Ah, if only we do find them! (*Sighs*) Come on, put your pack on your back (*gestures*). We're just getting started. (*Turns around*) No, wait a minute. I'll check our signs at the entrance again. I have my methods, friend!

ALEXANDRU (*smiling, picking up his pack*): Better safe than sorry!

PETRUȘ (*who has gone off to the right*): Very true. If we're not back in three or four days, they'll come looking for us.

ALEXANDRU: But what if the phosphorous gives out?

PETRUȘ (*off-stage*): Impossible. The way I prepared it, it'll last at least ten days.

ALEXANDRU (*to himself*): It will last...

PETRUȘ: All right, everything's set. Now, let's go. How do you feel?

ALEXANDRU (*smiling*): Inspired. (*The stage darkens.*)

SCENE II

A vaulted cavern in a gallery of the cave. The torches are extinguished. A diffuse, green light comes from one of the flashlights set on the ground in the middle of the cavern. The luminous thread runs toward the right of the stage. One of the spools is used a little; the other, still unused, lies beside it. PETRUȘ, using a flashlight, leans on a stone and writes. ALEXANDRU, at the mouth of the cavern, gazes intently, toward the interior. PETRUȘ does not see or hear anything.

THE GREEN GIRL: No use for you to look any farther! People were never here. Here there are only dwarves.

A VOICE (*sharp*): And Baba Dochia! And Muma Pădurii![3]

THE GREEN GIRL: But they're old women, and wicked. Dwarves aren't wicked. Do you want to see the dwarves?

VOICES: Show us! Show us!

THE GREEN GIRL: Why so pensive? Don't you like dwarves?

VOICES: Show us! We like them!

THE GREEN GIRL: Look! (*With a gesture she reveals a group of dwarves with beards down to the ground, bowing deeply. Alexandru looks at them incredulously, smiling.*) Don't you believe they're dwarves? I swear they are! Look at them closely. They look the way you know they do. Don't you believe they're real?

ALEXANDRU (*Moving his head slowly, he lifts his eyes from the dwarves and fixes them on the girl. He speaks in a sad voice*): They're not dwarves.

THE GREEN GIRL (*stepping nearer to him, smiling*): You've aged, Săndel! You don't see anymore! You don't believe! It's a pity you don't see them, Săndel... They really were dwarves.

ALEXANDRU (*starting*): Where are they?

THE GREEN GIRL (*very close to him*): Look! (*The same gesture, but the dwarves do not reappear. The place where they had been is empty, sad, lighted only by a bluish glow.*)

ALEXANDRU (*after staring with a painful effort*): I don't see them now. They're not there any more. (*Ignoring the presence of the girl, he speaks to himself.*) Oh, to be done with this! Over and done with it forever! There was no sense to it anyway. Baba Dochia, Muma Pădurii, fairies, dwarves—so banal, banal! Pseudo-poetry, cheap "literature"! Folklore! Cheap, cheap...

THE GREEN GIRL (*continues to smile, placing her hand on her hair*): A pity, Săndel, a pity that you've grown so old. You'll never again be able to write what you *could* have written now!... If only you'd kept your youth, your genius. Like Shakespeare, like Milton.

ALEXANDRU (*with a bitter voice*): Those are great men. They alone are great. If you can't be like them, then there's no point staying in the business.

THE GREEN GIRL (*with the same gesture*): A pity! You could have been able... If only you'd had the courage not to grow old!... To stay as you were at first. Unchanged from the way you were in the beginning... You won't see me again. Look, I'm starting to fade away...

ALEXANDRU (*annoyed, speaking out loud as the girl disappears*): Humph! Fairies and dwarves! Cheap literature! Trite, much too trite! Something else, you can see something else, something new. Not seen by anyone before. Not imagined by anyone!

PETRUŞ (*who, at Alexandru's first words spoken out loud, lifted his eyes from the notebook*): Pick up that pen, man, and *write*! Or else you'll forget these things!

ALEXANDRU: Ah, but what is there to write now? And for whom?

PETRUŞ: What do you mean, for whom? In the first place, for yourself. And for us, for others, for me, for Adriana, for the whole world! Pick up that pen!

ALEXANDRU: What is there for me to write? I've nothing to say. The same story, the same old story! Cheap fantasy, fit for films, for children's books ... All written by mature men and women who don't believe a word of it. What can I write about this cave? Fairies, dwarves, Muma Pădurii, Baba Dochia?! Stale subjects!

PETRUŞ: Yes, but you have imagination: create something new, something more beautiful!

ALEXANDRU: That's what I *want* to do. To see something else in this cave ... Especially since we're the first people who've been in here for who knows how many tens of thousands of years!

PETRUŞ: Ah, about that we can't be so sure, but it *is* certain that for a very long time, for several centuries at least, no one's set foot in this place.

ALEXANDRU: That's it! That's the thing I want to say. Not dime-a-dozen stories with fairies and dwarves.

PETRUŞ: I see you're terribly opposed to dwarves. Why do you bring them up?

ALEXANDRU (*smiling, but furious nonetheless*): Because they keep popping into my head, appearing before my eyes! Dwarves and a fairy ... the inevitable fairy and her dwarves ... What anyone sees who goes inside a cave. The same old things! As if I had no imagination of my own, as if I weren't a poet. (*Bitterly*) And it's very probable, I'm not ... since I see the same things everyone sees. I'm not a poet! I'm not, and that's that.

PETRUŞ: Well, Adriana is of another opinion.

ALEXANDRU: Yes, and she is, in large measure, the author of my poetic genius! Adriana and you. You two declared me a genius. You put it in my head that I'm a genius. Well, you're going to be bitterly disillusioned. When you read what I write about this cave.

PETRUȘ: If your verses are good, you can write about any subject. Even dwarves!

ALEXANDRU (*sarcastically*): What would you say to a story about a fairy transformed into a rock and a Prince Charming with hair of gold who kneels beside it, weeping?

PETRUȘ (*smiling*): What, no dwarves? None?

ALEXANDRU: Don't you see how absurd it is? It's the same story, repeated a thousand or a million times, with so-called "personal" interpretations. Prince Charming, for example, grows old embracing the block of granite—instead of abducting the fairy on a miraculous horse and throwing combs behind them.

THE GREEN GIRL (*who has reappeared a few seconds earlier, looking at him sadly, with a faded smile*): Săndel! Săndel! How you've fallen! How you've destroyed your luck!

ALEXANDRU (*more furious*): That's what it is: dime-a-dozen literature! Don't ask me again why I'm so angry. And I'm not angry anyway. Just depressed, that's all. I'm depressed at suddenly discovering that I have no calling, no spark of genius in me!

PETRUȘ (*calmly*): My friend, you're upset over nothing. This is a passing mood. Maybe it's the darkness, the dampness that's depressing you.

ALEXANDRU: No, it's not that. *Here* you understand better what you are and what you're not. Outside, everything seems different: you see things through rose-colored glasses, they look more interesting. The question is, what do you do and what do you think in a new situation—one you've never been in before and will never be in again, in your whole life. As has happened with us, now. We have had this unique good luck...

PETRUȘ: I've told you, it wasn't just luck. In the first place, it's the result of our investigations, our persistence.

ALEXANDRU: Yes, of course. But anyhow, we find ourselves in a new and unique situation. In the first place, as a human experience.

Not everyone has the courage to engage in an adventure like this.

PETRUŞ: But it's not an adventure at all! It's a carefully calculated action.

ALEXANDRU (*irritated, frenetic*): For me it *is* an adventure! That's what drew me here—adventure. The uniqueness of the experience. I was sure that it would produce a fundamental change in me, that it would unleash all the wellsprings of inspiration locked up in my soul, that I'd see something great, fantastically great, of gargantuan proportions, of Promethean power, that would shatter my horizons. I *should* have been able to, Petruş. If I'd had any genius, *I could have*. I'd have written something truly great, comparable to the great poets. Not with fairies and dwarves—something I could have written at home, in front of the stove... I should have been able to *see* something else...

PETRUŞ: But wait, you're wrong. In the first place, we're just getting started and we don't know what lies ahead. Maybe we'll discover something big. It's not impossible. Maybe we'll come upon a prehistoric burial site. And in the second place, inspiration sometimes comes only after—how shall I put it?—after the experience has been lived.

ALEXANDRU (*sadly*): No, no... A revelation—you either have it or you don't. But if your mind is divided up among the same old types, you can't see anything else. For instance, I wish I could escape from that cheap fantastic element of my imagination and be able to *realize* something inaccessible to my contemporaries—to realize, to sense with all my soul and being, what those people of the Stone Age felt when they penetrated deep into this cave. To feel again their fear, their terror of the darkness, to believe in their beliefs, to see the world as they saw it. To love and hate as they did...

PETRUŞ (*indifferently*): Do you think that would be so interesting? They felt nothing but fear. That was the only truly human thing about them. Fear, terror, as you like to call it. The rest of their emotions and sentiments appertain to the whole animal kingdom. But their capacity for fear was greater, it was infinite. This, in fact, was what made them human.

ALEXANDRU: Yes, *those emotions* are what I'd like to feel—so I could express them again.

PETRUȘ: But do you really think they're *worth* expressing again? That fear, which dominated us for thousands of years—does it merit being experienced anew? It would be an act of regression. It would mean a betrayal...

ALEXANDRU: That's because you, as always, see everything through the eyes of a scientist and a moralist. But art is something else—the art of the great ones, of course. Art permits any regression. To the ultimate limit of the consciousness, to the ultimate limit of life itself. You can descend anywhere, and to any depth, provided only that you return fuller and richer, and that you *believe*... That's what I dreamed of doing. A poem of the cave... A new *descensus ad infernum*. A descent to the deepest level of consciousness and cosmic life.

PETRUȘ (*convinced*): Very beautiful. That's very beautiful indeed. And you know you can write it. Only you, Săndel. Listen to me: these are trifles, these periodic depressions of yours. Take it from me; I know you! All great poets have doubts. And you're one of the great. If you don't believe me because I'm a geologist, then believe Adriana. She sees things better than either of us. Both as a woman and as an artist, she has an intuition we can't have. Especially since I'm no great expert in literature and you're always moping and nursing your doubts. You're always in a crisis. But you have poetic genius, you really do!

ALEXANDRU (*somewhat moved, but bitter nevertheless*): I *could* have had... Not necessarily poetic genius, but I could have had *genius*. That would be enough for me, just to have been a genius. Otherwise, it makes no sense for one to write. Or to paint. Or to do anything else. I believed once that I had a mission (*looking sheepishly toward PETRUȘ*), or rather Adria put it in my head that I might have a mission: to reveal something, to disclose something to humankind, to people of all countries and all times. The way Shakespeare did. (*Smiling with embarrassment*) How childish these visions seem to me now—the visions of a fifth-rate poet!

PETRUȘ (*exasperated, getting to his feet and gathering up his notebooks and camera*): Why fifth-rate? You're exaggerating. Why not third or second?
ALEXANDRU (*profoundly disgusted*): It's all the same—fifth or second! A matter of fairies and dwarves! If there's no revelation, there's nothing . . . and in that case, it's better to keep your mouth shut!
A VOICE (*harsh, sharp*): Then shut up!
ANOTHER: You're deafening us!
ANOTHER: Because you won't shut your mouth!
ALEXANDRU (*surprised, smiling with embarrassment*): Pardon, gentlemen, pardon me!
FEMININE VOICE: If you talk too much, Săndel . . .
ANOTHER: If you won't listen to what's happening around you . . .
ALEXANDRU (*to himself, annoyed*): Nothing's happening. That's the trouble—nothing's happening!
VOICES: Yes, there is! Yes, there is! Listen!

(*ALEXANDRU remains stationary in the middle of the stage. From the vault above we begin to hear, very softly, the strange, sweet music of harps and other stringed instruments. Then, from a dark corner, several indistinct forms, in long white shrouds, arise, moving toward the gallery that extends toward the left stage.*)

A DWARF (*appearing suddenly beside Alexandru, he motions to him*): They are the dead . . . the dead girls . . .
ALEXANDRU (*smiles bitterly and makes a gesture as though trying to drive away the images and stop the sounds*): I believe that this too has been said before! It's been said a great many times . . . and infinitely better. (*While he was speaking, the music ceased and the forms and the dwarf disappeared.*) When the stones begin to move and the vault of the cave becomes animated—just the stones, without any human profile, without anything being added to them—then, maybe then, I'll begin to see . . . and to believe . . .

DARKNESS

SCENE III

A corridor in the cave. The lower cupola seems to be starting to press downward. To the right, the luminous thread fades away into the darkness. The first spool is almost spent; the second still intact. The large flashlight spreads the same greenish, diffuse light. The two men are resting: PETRUȘ pensive and calm, ALEXANDRU fidgety, bored.

ALEXANDRU (*crushing out a half-smoked cigarette*): It has absolutely no taste. *Senza nessuno gusto,* as my friend in Port Said used to say. Now, *there* was a real comedian!
PETRUȘ: By the way, what ever happened to that fellow?
ALEXANDRU: I believe he committed suicide. The idea had obsessed him for a long time. But he lacked the courage. He had just enough courage to admit to himself and others that he lacked courage. (*Swallowing bitterly*) *Senza nessuno gusto! Senza nessuno gusto!*
PETRUȘ: It's the humidity. Nothing more fragile than tobacco.
ALEXANDRU (*breaking into a short, almost hysterical laugh*): Bravo, Professor!
PETRUȘ (*smiling*): What are you laughing at?
ALEXANDRU: At your philosophy about the fragility of tobacco.
PETRUȘ: Oh, you know it's so... It's not a philosophy. Tobacco's a delicate thing. Maybe "fragile" is too strong a word. But it *is* delicate.
ALEXANDRU (*shrugging; tired and wanting to change the subject*): You're right... maybe you're right. But I think you said something a little while ago about speleology that sounded interesting, but I didn't follow you.
PETRUȘ: Well, it had come to me to philosophize about the darkness... But we'd better take it easy now. I believe too much talking now wouldn't be good for us. We're in a rather unsafe corridor—not well-ventilated.
ALEXANDRU: As you wish... although they were interesting things. I didn't understand you too well... mostly, I guessed, but they were interesting. You were saying that we, here, are contemporary with

a species of living fossils. In the waters of these caves forms of life that lived in the middle of the Tertiary or even in the Secondary Era have been preserved.

PETRUȘ: Yes, the business about the troglobites. Dr. Racoviță has demonstrated it definitively. Archaic periods, Tertiary—the majority are Tertiary, but some are from the Secondary... And these primitive zoomorphic groups can't be fossilized. That's why the fauna of the caves is of utmost importance and this science of speleology is so very important. It makes available to us, directly, forms of life that otherwise we couldn't reconstruct, because they aren't fossilizable.

ALEXANDRU (*shuddering*): It's awful, Professor, to be neighbor to these living fossils, to live in their environs, to have exactly the same experience they do!

PETRUȘ: How can you say so many foolish things in one sentence?! How could you have the experience of these troglobites? (*Points toward the bag with the camera*) You, first of all, are a man. No matter what cosmic milieu you find yourself in, you're a man.

ALEXANDRU: Nevertheless, it's awful—to know that you have them as neighbors...

PETRUȘ: But on the outside you have a lot of "neighbors" who are humble enough. You just don't look at them. You pass them by, you step on them... But they're your neighbors; they're your contemporaries. And there are thousands of them that are downright exciting. In Brazil, for example...

ALEXANDRU: Oh, never mind about Brazil! I'm talking about *this cave*. Here, life is confined to your troglobites. They're the only things living. We're just visitors. It's horrible when you think that all life has been reduced here to troglobites. And they have such an awful name!

PETRUȘ (*smiling*): But they didn't call themselves that!

ALEXANDRU: It's a fine name for them though! Listen: troglobites, living fossils, from the Tertiary, from the Secondary—the way life began on earth! It's horrible!

PETRUȘ: Ha! It's good that it *did* begin that way. Everything proceeded economically for tens of millions of years, if not more, and eventually we arrived at man.

ALEXANDRU: At us, at men, human beings... At you, at Adriana, at me, at Onuţ! I can't believe we're as old as that. Besides, from what I've heard, this matter of the evolution of the species is not so certain as it was thirty or forty years ago. But, be that as it may, it's awful. To know that life was content with *this* (*points around him*). To know that from *this* there awoke the first living cell on earth, that it propagated itself here in this misery... in this darkness! And probably this environment suits the troglobites very well. Because they've endured here for millions of years, they don't want to leave.

PETRUŞ: Why should they leave? In a sense, they've lost the great battle of life. They can't evolve anymore. So they defend the positions they've won. They want to survive. And you see—they're succeeding.

ALEXANDRU: Yes, they're a kind of vampire.

PETRUŞ: No, the poor creatures don't kill anything. They just survive, that's all.

ALEXANDRU: That's precisely why I called them vampires. They should have died long ago, but they persist in remaining alive.

PETRUŞ (*philosophically*): Hurrah for them! Wherever there's life, there's Professor Petruş too!

ALEXANDRU: Not I! If *this* is life, I don't need it. I'd rather be a stone, or dirt—or anything else! But not a troglobite...

PETRUŞ (*philosophically*): You *have* been, and you *will* be again—all of those things. Stone, dirt, and troglobite. It's the same cosmic circuit. The only one.

ALEXANDRU (*shudders*): I thought I was going to descend into hell and I would meet monsters, souls of the damned, demons, and shades... and when I was there, it would seem that I was at the bottom of the ocean, where consciousness sleeps and life is reduced to gelatinous vampires...

PETRUŞ: Yes, and that's your own fault. Instead of getting involved in scientific discussions with me, you should be giving your *imagination* free rein, looking down these corridors, remembering those we've passed through. You should be creating, taking notes... But I haven't seen you taking out your notebook once. And you bragged that you'd come back with it entirely filled.

ALEXANDRU (*annoyed*): What sense does it make for me to take notes when I've become contemporaneous with troglobites?

PETRUŞ: Why, for precisely that reason! Because you're experiencing something no other artist has—you're the first to enter a cave such as this, where life is narrowed and reduced to troglobites. You were complaining a few hours ago that you don't like stories about fairies and dwarves. Look, now you have something new. Let your imagination create! Dream, and pay close attention to your dreams, so you can tell them to us, to us who don't dream, or whose dreams aren't so beautiful.

ALEXANDRU (*bitterly*): I prefer fairies and dwarves. They, at least, make no pretense of living in flesh and blood.

PETRUŞ (*saddened*): You see, Săndel, Adriana was right. She was right when she insisted you leave off these speculations. They're sterile for someone like you who wants to be nothing but an artist. She even whispered to me to leave you alone and not to harp on scholarly and philosophical things ... I've always wondered why she would consider me a philosopher.

ALEXANDRU: Because you are! Reduced to ethics and a vague kind of scientific philosophy—but you are.

PETRUŞ: I, a philosopher? You're mistaken. I'm content to think about what I *believe* I know, that's all. I'm sure, however, that it's much less than what a philosopher claims to do ... But that's not the question. That was just a kind of parenthesis. What I want to say to you, and I want to say it very seriously, before it's too late ...

ALEXANDRU (*interrupting him crossly*): What do you call "too late"?

PETRUŞ: Before this exploration of the cave is finished—this "adventure," as you call it. I want to say to you: no more philosophizing, young man! Create! Listen to the life around you!

ALEXANDRU: A terrible life!

PETRUŞ: Life as it is; terrible or not, it's still life. It's one kind of life. Doesn't this life say anything to you—these walls of stone, this darkness? They *must* speak to you! If to me, the professor, they say a great deal, then to you, the great poet ... !

ALEXANDRU: Please, I'm sensitive to bad jokes.

PETRUŞ: Why do you persist in seeing bad jokes where there is only a great friendship? You don't know what your friendship has meant to us, especially to Adriana. I—well, you know how I feel. I have an almost superstitious admiration for you people, you artists, for those who can conceive new things, new beauty; for you who can create and add something to the world and make life even more beautiful than it is. But other than admiration for art, I have nothing. For ten years I labored over the violin, and finally, when I got married ... I gave it up ... To keep from losing Adriana (*laughs*)! I have no talent and that's the end of it.

ALEXANDRU (*bitterly*): I've discovered the same thing about myself. We have, so to say, the same destiny: to be inartistic.

PETRUŞ (*firmly, but a little exasperated*): Now, just you shut up and listen to me! These protestations of a lack of poetic genius I've heard from your lips at least a hundred times. And afterwards you've come back, and you've written, you've written incredibly beautiful things—for which I'm grateful to you, Săndel. I, *Professor* Petruş, not your friend. Because, through you, I've seen something beautiful, something angelic, something from another world ... that only you have shown me—you, and no other artist. I don't know if you're greater than the others, but you've made me see more than the others have ... And you've seen how much Adriana's talent has been heightened!

ALEXANDRU: Wrong. Adriana has improved me. Because she has genius and she creates like a genius. I—I *ought* to be one, but I'm not.

PETRUŞ: You're awful. When the critical spirit takes hold of you, it's impossible for us to get along with each other. Actually, it isn't even a critical spirit—it's negation. This cave has haunted all three of us for years—I don't know how many. You say you even dream of it at night.

ALEXANDRU (*shuddering*): Not this one! The first one, the one with the vault. The Adria Cave.

PETRUŞ: All right, but it's connected to the same thoughts, the discovery of a new cave. You've dreamed of it for years. Adriana, too, in her way, was preoccupied with it. And I, since I was thirty-three, have fretted over it. And now, when so to speak we've seen our dream come true...

ALEXANDRU (*bitterly*): Yes, yes, you say it well...

PETRUȘ: Instead of taking notes, of letting your imagination run free, instead of animating this rock and transforming it into music, poetry, or whatever... you decide to philosophize about troglobites! I've spoken these few words, mostly to myself, thinking they'd make you dream—not react negatively and deny yourself.

ALEXANDRU (*facetiously*): But what do you care *what* I dream anyway? What do you care what I do or don't do with my imagination and my thoughts? You forbid troglobites to me. I forbid my dreams to you. Restricted territories!

PETRUȘ: It's not the same thing... I want you to show me, in your work later, this cave as you see it. I see it as it is for me, very interesting from a scientific viewpoint, but that's all. I want to see it *created by you*! That's why you're an artist—to show us the world as more beautiful than it is... What will you show me when we return?!

ALEXANDRU: I've told you the day I become positively convinced that I have no poetic vocation, I'll withdraw to the country and take up farming. So, when we return, I'll invite you to visit me on my farm!

PETRUȘ (*exasperated, he shrugs, resolved not to respond again*): Very well. We shall see.

ALEXANDRU (*with the same bitter self-irony*): And I assure you that I shan't resemble any of those farmers in English novels. I won't be a character from a book! I'll practice agriculture with no great style, without a vocation, without any gusto—without any gusto whatsoever! *Senza nessuno gusto! Senza nessuno gusto!* The way all things on this earth deserve to be done... by little men, petty men, men cursed by God...

DARKNESS

SCENE IV

A corridor in the cave with a very low ceiling, resembling a mine shaft. The two men are near the center of the stage. Their faces are pale, weary, with several days' growth of beard. They have lost their athletic appearance of the first scene. The phosphorescent thread runs to the right of the stage from the one remaining spool, which is half empty. The large flashlight at ALEXANDRU's feet illumines only a few hollows in the rock walls. The shapes are hard, monotonous, devoid of grandeur. Stones of a vague and sad hue are visible a few steps away from the men. The whole decor must give the impression of desolation and sterility.

PETRUŞ: If you want to, go on back! Look, you can see the string very well. No danger of getting lost. We'll divide the provisions...
ALEXANDRU: Your pills, you mean!
PETRUŞ: They're good for you—you'll see later. The path's not too difficult anywhere. In five hours you'll reach the first depository. You'll see the sign on a post; it's on the highest spot. From there to the vault you go through a corridor. Don't worry; with your empty pack you can even run.
ALEXANDRU: I'm not going back without you.
PETRUŞ: Then we'll press on.
ALEXANDRU: But why? Don't you see it's ridiculous, absurd? You've explored it all, and you've found nothing important.
PETRUŞ: You might think it's nothing important! I've told you, it'll revolutionize speleology!
ALEXANDRU: But who cares about speleology? Who's interested in these senseless stupidities, with or without troglobites? We're risking our lives here...
PETRUŞ: I've told you time and again that there's no risk. Absolutely none... (*lowering his voice*) outside of an earthquake.
ALEXANDRU: We're ruining our eyes, we're dulling our nerves... and for what? For *what*?
PETRUŞ (*grinning*): For the hell of it!

ALEXANDRU: It's idiotic. Admit it makes no sense. Admit at least this much, that we've gotten involved in a folly that has no sense to it.

PETRUŞ: I admit it's a folly, but it's a folly with a purpose. And if you'd listen to me and take two more pills, since you've got a sound heart and nothing can happen to you, you'd understand yourself that it's an extremely interesting and important folly!

ALEXANDRU: Because it will make us famous? Because we'll be photographed and written up in the newspapers, and you'll present scholarly papers and I'll give inerviews to magazines? For that? For glory and vanity? Even here, under the earth, you haven't escaped pride. Not even here have you realized that you're living an illusion, that you're feeding yourself on illusions. Oh, I'm sick to death of human beings! Worms drunk on vanity!

PETRUŞ (*smiling*): Swallow a pill and you'll see that worms can feel good!

ALEXANDRU (*exasperated*): Of course! Opium! You don't even have the courage to forego it and look life in the face. The moment your vitality diminishes, you're frightened, seized by terror, and you take heroin. Why don't you have the courage to look directly into the void?

PETRUŞ (*firmly*): Because there's no such thing as a void. It exists only in your imagination, in your exhausted nerves. If you had tougher nerves you'd see that no void exists.

ALEXANDRU (*looking at him contemptuously*): I'll expect you to repeat this to me when the effect of the pills wears off!

PETRUŞ (*calmly*): That's nothing; I'll just take some more.

ALEXANDRU (*doing his best to laugh*): And then more, and more . . . And so on, to the end of your life! And this is what you call a meaningful existence. While I, and others like me who refuse the pills are crazy!

PETRUŞ (*shrugging*): I didn't say that! I said, and I'll say it again and again, that for me, this madness we're engaged in is worth carrying to its conclusion, and I take pride in it! Yes, yes, I feel very proud of myself!

ALEXANDRU: How many pills have you taken?

PETRUŞ: The number doesn't matter. That's why they were made—to be taken. They're of our making, they're our instruments of defense and action.

ALEXANDRU: "Our"? Who do you mean by "our"? Men of science?

PETRUŞ: Yes, them in the first place, but others too, people in general—it was of them I was thinking. These things are their work, the work of all people. And I'm very proud of such an accomplishment; that's why I keep going forward. Because I sense myself at one with all the people who have lived up to now and who will live after us, until the extinction of life on earth.

ALEXANDRU: What connection do you see between the destiny of humanity and this idiotic adventure we're engaged in? Other than their mutual absurdity, of course, since the destiny of man is quite as senseless as this adventure of ours.

PETRUŞ: All right, what if it is? And I admit you're right. So what? It still merits to be carried through to the end.

ALEXANDRU: You contradict yourself so wretchedly that it exasperates me! Where do you see any merit? In what does the merit of this idiotic adventure consist?

PETRUŞ: Just here, in the simple fact that we're doing it—we, two men. The fact that man is doing it! That we're avenging ourselves!

ALEXANDRU: Avenging ourselves?

PETRUŞ: We're getting revenge for all we've suffered for hundreds of thousands of years, ever since we emerged from stone. All the humiliations we've had to endure when we lived in caves and were naked—and weak, and stupid, and trembled at every shadow, and were frightened by lightning and the night and phantoms. *Now*, we're not like that! *Now*, we're strong. Man has become master, and we're paying back, to the brim and heaped up!

ALEXANDRU: But *whom* are you paying back, Professor? Whom are you paying back?

PETRUŞ: The world around us, that was *hostile* to us and humiliated us. Nature, if you will. We're settling accounts with this cave. These stones which think they're inviolable, these rock walls into which we're penetrating now for the first time, deciphering their secrets. How can we turn back? To prove to them once again that we're weaklings, like the Quaternarians who came here to worship who knows what spirits born out of their own fear? I'd die of shame! Don't you understand there's something else at stake besides our own comfort, nerves, strength?

ALEXANDRU: I understand only one thing: that you cheat—you and the rest of humanity—you *cheat*! If you had entered this cave naked, or at most with a stylus in your hand as the man of the Stone Age did, I'd understand it as a heroic act, and I'd admire it. But I see you're far from naked. In fact, you're very well clothed, defended from the cold and dampness, equipped with a light and a camera. And worst of all, you aren't even yourself, a natural man, the one you are ordinarily. You're drugged. You've taken I don't know how many heroin tablets to stave off sleep, fatigue, and fear.

PETRUȘ: But what did you expect? That I'd come in here like my ancestors from the Stone Age? To be ruled by *Nature* again? To be haunted by ghosts? No, my friend. I defend myself. I obtained those instruments of defense; I invented them; Nature didn't give them to me *gratis*. They're mine. Heroin or Pervitine, the vitamins, the phosphorus—all these I have hammered out of the stone. That's why I say I'm avenging myself by penetrating deeper and deeper into the heart of the mountain—because now I feel strong. No longer am I afraid. I know how to control my nerves. Phantoms have no way of deluding me.

ALEXANDRU: Everything you're saying is absurd! Utterly absurd! But maybe for just that reason it makes no sense for me to turn back. (*Sits down on a rock*) No action and no gesture makes any sense. That's the truth! That's the only truth!

PETRUȘ (*also sitting down*): Why don't you take a rest now? Time passes, and soon we'll be setting off again.

ALEXANDRU: "Time passes" is well said! Very well said, in fact. Perhaps it's the truest thing you've ever uttered. Time passes! It's the greatest cliché imaginable, but it's so! Everything passes, together with time!

PETRUȘ: You utter deep things!

ALEXANDRU: Very deep, believe me! Actually, why should I regret this absurd adventure, this ridiculously useless descent into hell? It's not worth regretting or not regretting. Nothing's not worth anything! ... Ah, it can't even be said; it's impossible to speak it. It's so absurd that language can't convey it. Language, unfortunately, is made for conventional lies, for trifles indispensable to life. The absurd can't be expressed. You feel like howling ...

PETRUȘ: Dear Săndel, listen to me. Take another tablet.

ALEXANDRU: To hell with your tablets! They muddle my brain! I don't need any phony vitality! I prefer to look reality square in the face. And the reality is that nothing is real. Everything's absurd and useless.

PETRUȘ: The reality is that the darkness depresses you, that the cold and the damp are depressing. That this subterranean environment isn't made for the human organism. And so you need one of those pills to compensate for what you lack here.

ALEXANDRU: Ridiculous! And I don't even have any way to convince you of how ridiculous it is. I thought you'd feel it too, that you'd understand: how *futile* everything is, how absurd and unreal! Look, this thought has already begun to obsess me. Maybe it's on account of the darkness, or the cold and damp, as you say. But what's to be done about it?! The truth is that we judge the world better *here* than *there*, where we all deceive ourselves as best we can, any way we can. You'll have to admit this yourself, everything's a continual deception, an endless farce! This absurd cave has done me good in one way, anyhow. It's wakened me from my dreams. That's it: it's awakened me out of illusion. Think of it: only here have I truly sensed that up till now I've been wasting my time on vanities. I feel like howling when I think ... But what can I do? I've wasted it; it's gone.

PETRUȘ: It *seems* that way to you, but it's just an opinion. What could you have done except what you've done—you and us and everybody?

ALEXANDRU: I don't know what I might have done, or what I should have done, but I know I've lost something ... I've lost something, irremediably ... What I'm saying is absurd. Actually, no matter how things might have happened, whatever I might have done, however I might have lived, the result probably would have been the same. Ashes. Nothing has any purpose. Nothing has any relish.

PETRUȘ: It might be better if I refrained from making any comment, but I believe ...

ALEXANDRU: No, no, listen to me, Petruș, I'm speaking seriously. (*With fervor*) Don't keep trying to fool yourself with words! There are only the two of us here. Alone, as we'll never be again. Stop hiding. Admit it. You can't help feeling this thing! Admit it's all a sinister farce, an immense illusion!

PETRUȘ: What do you mean by all?

ALEXANDRU: All you want. All you believe has value. I mean *all*: life, love, science, morality, humaneness ... all, all, absolutely all!

PETRUȘ: Too many things at one time! ... I can't respond. There are some that don't concern me, about which I know nothing. But there are also several that I know for certain are real. I know they're alive and deserve to be believed in. You spoke about life ... I believe in it; it's something that exists, something I participate in with all my being, and I believe in it. I can't doubt life!

ALEXANDRU: Do you believe anything exists beyond this life? Do you believe something awaits us after death?

PETRUȘ: To be perfectly frank, I don't believe so. Maybe I'm wrong, but I don't believe there's anything beyond.

ALEXANDRU: Neither do I. Or, more precisely, I haven't believed for several hours, or several minutes—I can't say exactly—but I don't believe anymore. I believe now that everything ends here (*points*). And if this is true, then everything, absolutely everything, is a filthy lie. Why then have we been born? Why did we come into the world? To live like butterflies for a night? And what sense can life have if everything is reduced to biological existence? Then it's a matter of glands or, as you say, of pills, or I don't know what. Then we'd better all get high on opium and never return to our right minds! Nothing has any sense if life ends with us.

PETRUȘ: But, you see, it *doesn't* end with us. After us come others, and others, endlessly—until all organic life is extinguished on earth.

ALEXANDRU: What the devil do I care about those who come after me? What do my descendants matter to me? What do they have to do with me, I ask you? *What about me? What do you do with me?*

PETRUŞ: Your question is badly formulated and for that reason you'll never find an answer to it. Your case or my case or anyone's case in particular doesn't matter to anyone. Life can't take account of us. It's concerned only with species, not with individuals. So long as the species endures, so long will there exist on earth a human being.

ALEXANDRU: Then it's all a filthy lie! And anything is permitted! When I get back, I'll run wild!

PETRUŞ (*smiling*): You've been doing that pretty much anyway...

ALEXANDRU: No, no. It won't be the way it was before. Take my word for it, Petruş, I'll run wild like no one's ever done before! I'll have no hesitations, no scruples, no pangs of remorse. Otherwise, I'd be a coward, I'd be weak... If *this* is the truth, then...

PETRUŞ: If *what* is?

ALEXANDRU: What I've just now discovered. What the cave's revealed to me with its darkness, cold, and troglobites. And what you've confirmed: nothingness. Life that begins and ends *here*, with us. Ashes.

PETRUŞ: But this is exactly opposite of what I believe and affirm. I told you that I believe in life, I believe in man... You deny them both!

ALEXANDRU (*exasperated, shrugging*): I deny nonbeing and nothingness! That's called negation. Certainly, I deny that which exists only to perish. What else do vanity and corruption deserve? If nothing lasts, if everything ends *here* (*pointing to the cave*), don't you agree that it's better to *negate*, to trample underfoot, to defile?

PETRUŞ: There's no use of our continuing. You're having another one of your numerous attacks of nihilism. It's nothing, it too will pass... Come on, let's go.

ALEXANDRU: It won't pass. I sense that this is the last one, the true one. This one won't pass. *In fine*, I've had a revelation, a "speleological revelation." Now I'm free again, free as the birds of the heavens. Free to run wild! (*Harshly*) And when I do what I want, it will shake the world!

PETRUŞ (*preparing to set out*): That depends. Maybe you'll relent.

ALEXANDRU (*doing his best to sound cynical*): Only fools relent. Only men weak as angels. Only men whose hand trembles when they kill, who turn pale when they rob. But not a philosopher. Not one who has understood all there is to know about the philosophy of glands and internal secretions, of troglobites and vitamins. Who brings us into life and removes us from it like butterflies. From nothingness—into nothingness.

PETRUȘ (*in a hurry*): Get your pack on your back, little boy.

ALEXANDRU (*falsely sardonic*): Get the pack on your back—time passes, Professor! And so does the effect of heroin. And we wake up from our dream ... The troglobites awaken from their dreaming, and they yawn with boredom ...

PETRUȘ (*smiling*): What's that? The Mephistophelian monologue from Act I, Scene IV? The famous monologue with applause as the scene opens? Why not add the part about the victorious worms? It sounds beautiful ... And it's even profound.

ALEXANDRU (*in the same tone*): It is *very* profound! But I prefer the troglobite. This creature doesn't feed on the dead. This one lives only on water and darkness. What a noble ascetic!

PETRUȘ (*leaving*): You see, if you prolong the monologue too much, no one claps.

ALEXANDRU (*in the same voice, leaving*): No matter. Those who understand will applaud ...

CURTAIN

ACT II SCENE I

A corridor. Vague phosphorescent lights. The thread is visible. From the left, walking with difficulty, PETRUȘ approaches, carrying ALEXANDRU in his arms. ALEXANDRU holds the flashlight. A single pack, almost empty, hangs from PETRUȘ' shoulder. Sounds of groaning are heard.

ALEXANDRU: I can't go on, Petruș ... Petruș, put me down, put me down; I can't go on! For a moment, just one moment, put me down!

PETRUȘ (*after a pause*): A little longer, Săndel. Just a little longer. Be patient!

ALEXANDRU: I can't . . . I feel faint from the pain. I can't go on.

PETRUŞ (*another pause*): A little longer. Come on, make an effort! At least for another hundred meters.

ALEXANDRU: No, no, I can't! I can't stand it any longer! Put me down a moment . . . I think my hip's out of joint too.

PETRUŞ: No, it's not. It just feels that way. There's nothing wrong with your hip. I told you it's all right. Only your knee . . .

ALEXANDRU (*moans weakly*): Ahh . . .

PETRUŞ (*stops, looks around, and approaches a low stone on which, with infinite care, he places Alexandru*): Easy does it. Don't move much . . . There!

ALEXANDRU (*groaning*): What rotten luck! That this had to happen to us now! That this had to happen to me!

PETRUŞ (*searching in the bag*): Be still; it will pass.

ALEXANDRU (*breathing more easily*): Give me a little water, please, Petruş. I'm awfully thirsty.

PETRUŞ (*holds out a tablet*): Take another one . . . Wait till I give you some water. (*He pours water sparingly from a canteen.*) You'll see; the pain will leave immediately. These are terrific!

ALEXANDRU: Rotten luck! And I seemed to have a premonition . . .

PETRUŞ (*morosely*): It was my fault too. If I'd listened to you . . . But it's happened . . . Buck up! Grit your teeth and bear it! This is our destiny—to suffer. It's nothing. We'll get out of this one too.

ALEXANDRU (*smiling*): Poor you! Now you've got me on your back too! Luckily, you're stout. You're awfully stout, Petruş, like a bear!

PETRUŞ: No, not really. But fortunately there are other things besides physical strength.

ALEXANDRU: Yes, that's true. There are other things. (*Sighs deeply*) There are a great many other things in the world.

PETRUŞ (*trying to sound cheerful*): In any event, the adventure is now complete. We don't have to add anything to it from your imagination. Just tell what you've seen, what you've experienced, all you went through—and you'll become the most famous and lionized author in the country . . . Not that you aren't famous and lionized now, but then you'll be something else! You won't even look at us ordinary mortals anymore. Adriana and I will have to make appointments to be able to see you! Hum, what do you say to that?

ALEXANDRU (*smiling, rapt in thought*): Poor Adria. I wonder what she's doing now.

PETRUȘ (*still cheerful, though with an effort*): She's waiting for us and grumbling at us... Although, surely she's grumbling more at me. You're a privileged character, whatever you do!

ALEXANDRU: You know, I've been thinking about her ever since I fell. She was right... You know, Petruș, she was right... I've come to believe in premonitions.

PETRUȘ (*laughing*): A good thing you fell! It's settled you down!

ALEXANDRU: No, no, I'm serious. There's something to these premonitions. Don't you believe in them?

PETRUȘ (*unconvinced*): Oh, yes, of course. Why not? There are still so many undeciphered mysteries. Especially relative to...

ALEXANDRU: No, you don't sound too convinced of what you're saying. But they do exist! I'm sure Adria will understand. There exists a kind of instinct, so to say, a curious sort of divination, that we don't have any way of explaining, but it's real, authentic! (*Groans*) Oh, I thought it had left me.

PETRUȘ (*consolingly*): Be patient a little longer and it'll go away again.

ALEXANDRU: I thought so too, but I just felt another stabbing pain. Up here, in the hip.

PETRUȘ: It's nothing. Be patient. It will pass.

ALEXANDRU: It *will* pass—of that I'm sure. But I thought it had already left me. What curious pains! Sometimes I don't seem to feel anything—and then they start up again, and I feel like screaming. Maybe it's something serious...

PETRUȘ: You had a bad fall on your knees, that's all. That's why you're in pain.

ALEXANDRU: At first I was terribly frightened. When I was falling, I had the impression this would be the end of me... that I'd never move again. I wonder even now how I escaped. I fell into a void. Luckily I'd stuck my alpenstock into the slope...

PETRUȘ (*snapping his fingers*): That's it! I knew I'd forgotten something essential! I couldn't think what it was. Now I know—the spike!

ALEXANDRU: That's true. I left mine there too.

PETRUŞ (*chasing away the thought*): It doesn't matter. One can walk very well even without a stick. And I say we ought to get going now; the sooner we arrive, the better.

ALEXANDRU: A moment longer, Petruş. Wait till I recover my senses a little more. You know, when I got up, I had atrocious pains through my whole body. But especially in my hip and knees.

PETRUŞ: All right, we'll stay, but only a moment.

ALEXANDRU (*changing the subject*): It's curious how this particular melody is obsessing me. I can't get it out of my head. I hear it all the time.

PETRUŞ: What melody is that?

ALEXANDRU: I don't know what it's called. But it keeps running through my mind. It's one of those modern songs. They were singing it all winter in Bucharest. It goes something like this ... (*tries to whistle, weakly*).

PETRUŞ: I think I remember hearing it too.

ALEXANDRU: I can't whistle, but it's very beautiful. Adria liked it, and she's particular, you know ... especially about such trifles (*grins*). Strange, but ever since it's been running through my head, I've seemed to feel better. Yet, in a sense, it makes me sad. It's as though all that world outside is incredibly beautiful and wide. And so far away ... As though years had passed since we buried ourselves alive down here. Everything seems unnaturally far away, lost, unreal.

PETRUŞ: You know better than I how to explain these things. Then too, you have to take into account the lack of sleep, the exertion, the fatigue, the pain—all of these.

ALEXANDRU: No, I can't explain them. Neither can you. It's more that this. It's something else. And I can't think what. And yet, in this experience, *knowing counts*.

PETRUŞ: You see, now you've come around to what I said. Every deed counts. Every act of courage, of manliness, of daring. It changes life. It's equivalent to a reeducation ... to a total renewal of the man.

ALEXANDRU (*enthusiastically*): Yes, it's something—something very important! an initiation. Like a revelation. I don't know how to put it. You discover something inside yourself which might have remained hidden from you till the end of your life. You discover something beyond your being—the everyday one that we believe, in an absurd way, we are . . . Something fundamental, something—how to say it?—something that illumines you within and changes everything around you!

PETRUŞ (*listening with rapt attention*): Yes, yes . . .

ALEXANDRU: And this strange experience, this sudden revelation, can't come from just anywhere, out of the blue. Don't you agree? There exists something real that corresponds to it—something fundamentally real . . .

PETRUŞ: Yes. You say it very beautifully . . . That's how it is, the way you say. This is . . . this is what I call life.

ALEXANDRU: No, it's something other than life. It's *more* than life. It precedes it. It comes from another place . . . from beyond.

PETRUŞ (*looking at him steadily*): What you're saying is very interesting. But we've got to be going, Săndel. Time's flying!

ALEXANDRU: No, Petruş, let me keep talking. It eases me, helps me stand the pain . . . I've got to tell you. It obsesses me. Only to you can I say these things. You've been with me here; we were together. There's something obsessing me. I don't know where to begin, or how to begin. Our misfortune is that we see too much, we sense too much, and we can't say it all, we don't have the words . . . we don't have anything. Even though it's something very important, something that changes life, gives it another meaning, enriches it . . . There exists something fundamental, an absolute certitude, that gives meaning to everything. Ah, what a shame that we don't have any way to say all these things . . . I'm ashamed of myself for feeling so perplexed. It's as though I don't know where I am, and yet . . . I have so much to say! Never has anyone, in any book . . .

PETRUŞ (*smiling*): *You'll* write all these things when you get back. That's why we have to leave. Right now!

ALEXANDRU (*as if he hadn't heard*): They can't be written. No one can write these things. No matter how much genius he might have, or how much imagination . . . It's something else, something else entirely. (*Looks toward the left, where the shapes suddenly become animated, sparkling*) It seems as though I'm starting to get dizzy. And yet I feel good. I seem to feel better and better. And I'd like to say something to you—only you. Something extraordinarily important... like a kind of revelation. I don't know how to say it—something that comes from beyond life—and makes it worthwhile... makes it worth being lived... (*exhausted*) in my sight and yours, and in the sight of God... And I don't know how to begin...

PETRUȘ: Don't talk anymore, Săndel. Don't talk anymore. It's an extra effort that tires you... And we have to leave now.

ALEXANDRU: One moment more, please! Wait a moment longer.

PETRUȘ: No, we can't. (*Puts on his pack.*) We've rested long enough. Now we've got to go. Buck up! (*He approaches him and prepares to lift him.*) I know it hurts you, but you must have courage, grit your teeth, and bear it. This is our fate, from the beginning of time—to suffer, to endure.

ALEXANDRU (*groaning*): Ah, as soon as I get up, it's horrible. And yet... I could bear this too, I could bear anything... if only I could tell you... if I knew how to tell you... these things... that are happening to us—that I sense... and see... You have no idea how clearly I see them... But I have no way to tell you about them... This is terrible... that I don't have any way... to tell you... or Adria...

DARKNESS

NOTES

Written between 29 February and 6 March 1944 in Portugal. Published in a collection of Eliade's plays, *Coloana nesfârșită*, edited by Mircea Handoca (Bucharest: Minerva, 1996), 77–109.

1. Pervitine is a form of methamphetamine, a powerful stimulant, in wide use at the time.

2. The Carpathian Bow is a 12,000km (745.5miles) long mountain range, stretching from Slovakia and Ukraine to the NW in an arc through Romania

to Serbia in the SW. It forms an amphitheatre in Romania whose interior is the plateau of Transylvania.

3. In Romanian peasant mythology two "old woman" goddesses. Baba Dochia is associated with the first twelve days of March and its changeable weather. She and her flock of sheep are identified with a rock formation on Mt. Ceahlau in the Carpathians. Muma Pădurii (Mother of the Forest) is an evil being associated with August 20. She and her daughter inhabit woodlands and can steal a child's shadow and cause nightmares.

Works Cited

Eliade's bibliography is notoriously extensive. I make no attempt to be exhaustive here but give only the publication details of works mentioned in the preceding essays.

MIRCEA ELIADE: WORKS IN ENGLISH

Eliade, Mircea. *Cosmos and History: The Myth of the Eternal Return.* Princeton: Princeton UP, 1954. Translated from the French by Willard Trask.
———. *Patterns in Comparative Religion.* London: Sheed and Ward, 1958. Translated from the French by Rosemary Sheed.
———. *Rites and Symbols of Initiation.* (*Birth and Rebirth.*) London: Harvill Press, 1958. Translated from the French by Willard Trask.
———. *Yoga, Immortality, and Freedom.* London: Routledge and Kegan Paul, 1958. Translated from the French by Willard Trask.
———. "Methodological Remarks on the Study of Religious Symbolism." *The History of Religions: Essays in Methodology.* Ed. Eliade and Kitagawa. 1959. 86–107. Reprinted in *The Two and the One*, chapter five.
———. *The Sacred and the Profane: The Nature of Religion.* London: Harcourt Brace Jovanovich, 1959. Translated from the French by Willard Trask.
———. *Myths, Dreams, and Mysteries: The Encounter between Contemporary Faiths and Archaic Realities.* London: Harvill Press, 1960. Translated from the French by Philip Mairet.
———. "History of Religions and a New Humanism." *History of Religions* 1:1 (1961): 1–8. Reprinted in *The Quest*, chapter one.
———. *Images and Symbols: Studies in Religious Symbolism.* London: Harvill Press, 1961. Translated from the French by Philip Mairet.
———. *The Forge and the Crucible.* London: Rider and Co., 1962. Translated from the French by Stephen Corrin.

———. *Myth and Reality*. New York: Harper and Row, 1963. Translated from the French by Willard Trask.

———. "Masks: Mythical and Ritual Origins." *Encyclopedia of World Art*, vol. 9. 1964. 520–25. Also in Diane Apostolos-Cappadona, ed. *Symbolism, the Sacred, and the Arts*. New York: 1985. 64–71.

———. *Shamanism: Archaic Techniques of Ecstasy*. London: Routledge and Kegan Paul, 1964. Translated from the French by Willard Trask.

———. *The Two and the One*. Chicago: U of Chicago P, 1965. Translated from the French by J. M. Cohen.

———. *From Primitives to Zen: A Sourcebook in Comparative Religion*. New York: Harper and Row, 1967.

———. "The Forge and the Crucible: A Post-Script." *History of Religions* 8:1 (1968): 74–88.

———. *Patañjali and Yoga*. New York: Funk and Wagnalls, 1969. Translated from the French by Charles Lam Markmann.

———. *The Quest: History and Meaning in Religion*. London: U of Chicago P, 1969.

———. *Zalmoxis, the Vanishing God*. Chicago: U of Chicago P, 1972. Translated from the French by Willard Trask.

———. *The Forbidden Forest*. Notre Dame: U of Notre Dame P, 1978. Translated by Mac Linscott Ricketts and Mary Park Stevenson.

———. "Some Notes on *Theosophia Perennis*: Ananda K. Coomaraswamy and Henry Corbin." *History of Religions* 19:2 (1979): 167–76.

———. *A History of Religious Ideas*, vol. I. *From the Stone Age to the Eleusinian Mysteries*. Chicago: U of Chicago P, 1978. Translated from the French by Willard Trask.

———. *The Old Man and The Bureaucrats*. Notre Dame and London: U of Notre Dame P, 1979. Translated by Mary Park Stevenson.

———. "History of Religions and 'Popular' Cultures." *History of Religions* 20:1&2 (1980): 1–26.

———. "Indologica, I: A Review Article." *History of Religions* 19:3 (1980): 270–75.

———. *Autobiography*, vol. I. *Journey East, Journey West. 1907–1938*. San Francisco: Harper and Row, 1981. Translated from the Romanian by Mac Linscott Ricketts.

———. "Les Trois Grâces." *Tales of the Sacred and Supernatural*. 1981.

———. "With the Gypsy Girls." *Tales of the Sacred and Supernatural*. 1981.

———. *Tales of the Sacred and Supernatural*. Philadelphia: Westminster Press, 1981.

———. *A History of Religious Ideas*, vol. II. *From Gautama Buddha to the Triumph of Christianity*. Chicago: U of Chicago P, 1982. Translated from the French by Willard Trask.

———. "Goodbye." ("Adio! . . ."). *Imagination and Meaning*. Ed. Girardot and Ricketts. 1982. 162–78.

———. *Ordeal by Labyrinth: Conversations with Claude-Henri Rocquet*. Chicago: U of Chicago P, 1982. Translated from the French by Derek Coltman.

———. "The Endless Column." A play, in *Dialectics and Humanism* 10:1 (1983): 44–88. Translated by Mary Park Stevenson.

———. *A History of Religious Ideas*, vol. III. *From Muhammad to the Age of the Reforms*. Chicago: U of Chicago P, 1985. Translated from the French by Alf Hiltebeitel and Diane Apostolos-Cappadona.

———. "*Homo Faber* and *Homo Religiosus*." *The History of Religions: Retrospect and Prospect*. Ed. Kitagawa. New York: Macmillan, 1985.

———. "Literary Imagination and Religious Structure." *Symbolism, the Sacred, and the Arts*. Ed. Apostolos-Cappadona. 1986. 171–77.

———. "Nights at Serampore." *Two Strange Tales*. Boston: Shambala, 1986.

———. "The Secret of Dr. Honigberger." *Two Strange Tales*, 1986.

———. *Symbolism, the Sacred, and the Arts*. Ed. Diane Apostolos-Cappadona. New York: Crossroad, 1986.

———. *Two Strange Tales*. Boston and London: Shambala, 1986.

———, editor-in-chief. *Encyclopedia of Religion*. New York: Macmillan, 1987.

———. *Autobiography*, vol. II. *Exile's Odyssey, 1938–1969*. Chicago: U of Chicago P, 1988. Translated from the Romanian by Mac Linscott Ricketts.

———. *Journal I, 1945–1955*. Chicago: U of Chicago P, 1989. Translated from the Romanian by Mac Linscott Ricketts.

———. *Journal II, 1957–1969*. Chicago: U of Chicago P, 1989. Translated from the French by Fred H. Johnson Jr.

———. *Journal III, 1970–1978*. Chicago: U of Chicago P, 1989. Translated from the French by Teresa Lavender Fagan.

———. *Journal IV, 1979–1985*. Chicago: U of Chicago P, 1989. Translated from the Romanian by Mac Linscott Ricketts.

———. "Nineteen Roses." *Youth without Youth*, 1988.

———. *Youth Without Youth and Other Novellas*. Translated by Mac Linscott Ricketts. In *Three Fantastic Novellas*. Columbus: Ohio State UP, 1988.

———. *Bengal Nights*. Chicago: U of Chicago P, 1994. Translated from the French by Catherine Spencer. Translated from the Romanian by Alain Guillermou.

———, and Ioan P. Couliano. *The Eliade Guide to World Religions*. San Francisco: Harper, 1991.

———, and Joseph M. Kitagawa. *The History of Religions: Essays in Methodology*. Chicago and London: U of Chicago P, 1973.

———, and David Tracy, eds. *What is Religion?: An Enquiry for Christian Theology*. Edinburgh: T and T Clark, 1980.

MIRCEA ELIADE: WORKS IN OTHER LANGUAGES

Dates in parentheses are the original dates of publication. These are given when that date is known and differs from a later date of publication. Insofar as is possible these works are listed according to the date of original publication. With later collections and anthologies of reprinted works it is not always possible to give the original date, and such works are listed according to the date of publication as a collection.

Eliade, Mircea. *Cum am găsit piatra filozofală: Scrieri de tinereţe, 1923–1925*. Ed. Mircea Handoca. Bucharest: Editura Humanitas, 1996.

———. "Raffaele Pettazzoni: I misteri." *Misterele şi iniţierea orientală: Scrieri de tinereţe, 1926*. Ed. Mircea Handoca. Bucharest: Editura Humanitas, 1998.

———. "Itinerariu spiritual VIII. (Teosofie?)." *Cuvântul* 3:903 (1927). In *Profetism românesc* 1. Bucharest, 1990.

———. "Ocultismul în cultura contemporană." *Cuvântul* 3:630 (1927).

———. *Profetism românesc 1. Itinerariu spiritual. Scrisori către un provincial. Destinul culturii româneşti*.

———. *Contribuţii la filosofia Renaşterii* (1928). Bucharest: Editura Academiei ("Capricorn" Series, 1), 1984.

———. "Cel dintâi yoghin . . ." *Cuvântul* (17 April 1929). In Eliade, *Biblioteca maharajahului*, 1991. 49–52.

———. *Isabel şi apele diavolului*. Bucharest: Editura Naţională Ciornei, 1930.

———. *Erotica mistică în Bengal. Studii de indianistică* (1929–1931). Ed. Mircea Handoca with a preface by Mircea Vulcănescu. Editura "Jurnalul literar," Bucharest, 1994.

———. "Contribuţiuni la psihologia Yoga." *Revista de filosofie*. Bucharest, January–March 1931 52–76. In *Yoga. Problematica filozofiei indiene*. Ed. Constantin Barbu and Mircea Handoca, 1991. 85–110.

———. "Spiritualitate şi mister feminin." *Azi* I:2 (April 1932): 202–205. In *Arta de a muri*. Selected, edited, and annotated by Magda Ursache and Petru Ursache. Iaşi: Editura Moldova, 1993.

———. *Soliloquii* (1932). Bucharest: Editura Humanitas, 1991.
———. *India*. Bucharest: Editura Cugetarea, 1934.
———. *Întoarcerea din rai*. Bucharest: Editura Națională Ciornei, 1934. Ed. Mircea Handoca. Bucharest: Rum-Irina, 1992.
———. *Lumina ce se stinge*. Bucharest: Cartea Românească, 1934. Reprinted in two volumes, Bucharest: Casa Odeon, 1991.
———. *Oceanografie* (1934). Bucharest: Editura Humanitas, 1991.
———. "Un reprezentant al tradiției hinduse: Sri Aurabindo." *Memra* I (January–April, 1935): 19–20.
———. "Revolta contra lumii moderne." *Vremea* 8:382, Bucharest, 1935.
———. *Șantier. Roman indirect* (1935). Bucharest: Editura Rum-Irina, 1991.
———. "Cele două Românii" (1936). *Profetism românesc 2*.
———. *Profetism românesc 2. România în eternitate*.
———. "Și un cuvânt al editorului." Nae Ionescu, *Roza Vânturilor*, 1936. 421–44.
———. *Yoga, Essai sur les origines de la mystique indienne*. Paris: Librairie Orientaliste Paul Geuthner. Bucharest: Fundația pentru literatură și artă "Regele Carol II," ("Bibliothèque de philosophie roumaine"), 1936.
———. *Alchimia asiatică. Cosmologie și alchimie babiloniană* (1937). Bucharest: Editura Humanitas, 1991.
———. "Folklorul ca instrument de cunoaștere." *Revista fundațiilor regale* 4:4 (1937): 137–52. In Eliade, *Insula lui Euthanasius*, 1943. 28–49.
———. "Ananda Coomaraswamy." *Revista fundațiilor regale* 4:7 (1937): 183–89.
———. "Barabadur, templu simbolic." *Revista fundațiilor regale* 4:9 (1937): 50–68.
———. *Șarpele*. Bucharest: Editura Națională Ciornei, 1937.
———. *Nuntă în Cer*. Bucharest: Editura Cugetarea, 1938.
———. *Fragmentarium* (1939). Bucharest: Editura Humanitas, 1994.
———. "Note și fragmente." *Vremea* 11:536, Bucharest, 1939.
———. *Mitul reintegrării*. Bucharest: Editura Vremea, 1942.
———. *Insula lui Euthanasius* (1943). Bucharest: Editura Humanitas, 1993.
———. *Comentarii la legenda Meșterului Manole*. Bucharest: Editura Publicom, 1943.
———. *Techniques du Yoga*. Paris: Gallimard, 1948.
———. *Le Mythe de l'Éternel Retour*. Paris: Gallimard, 1949.
———. *Traité d'histoire des religions*. Paris: Payot, 1949.
———. "Profesorul Nae Ionescu. 30 de ani de la moarte" (1970). *Împotriva deznădejdii. Publicistica exilului*. Ed. Mircea Handoca. Bucharest: Editura Humanitas, 1992.
———. *La Nostalgie des origins*. Paris: Gallimard, 1971.

———. *Fragments d'un journal*. Paris: Gallimard, 1973.
———. "Die Brücke." *Phantastische Geschichte*. Frankfurt am Main: Insel-Verlag, 1978.
———. *În curte la Dionis*. Bucharest: Cartea Românească, 1981.
———. "Incognito la Buchenwald." *În curte la Dionis*, 1981.
———. "Podul." *În curte la Dionis*, 1981.
———. "Uniforme de general." *În curte la Dionis*, 1981.
———. *Biblioteca maharajahului*. Ed. Mircea Handoca. Bucharest: Editura pentru Turism, 1991.
———. *Drumul spre centru*. Ed. Andrei Pleşu and Gabriel Liiceanu. Bucharest: Editura Univers, 1991.
———. *Taina Indiei*. Ed. Mircea Handoca. Bucharest: Editura Icar, 1991.
———. *Yoga. Problematica filozofiei indiene*. Ed. Constantin Barbu and Mircea Handoca. Craiova: Editura "Mariana," 1991.
———. *Psihologia meditaţiei indiene. Studii despre Yoga*. Ed. Constantin Popescu-Cadem. Bucharest: Editura "Jurnalul literar," 1992.
———. *Jurnal II*. Bucharest: Humanitas, 1993.
———. *Mircea Eliade şi corespondenţii săi*, vol. 1 (A–E), vol. 2 (F–J), vol. 3 (K–P). Ed. Mircea Handoca. Bucharest: Minerva, 1993, 1999, 2003.
———. *Opere* 2. Romane. [*Maitreyi*]. Ed. Mihai Dascal, notes and commentaries by Mihai Dascal and Mircea Handoca. Bucharest: Minerva, 1997.
———. *Misterele şi iniţierea orientală. Scrieri de tinereţe. 1926*. Ed. Mircea Handoca. Bucharest: Editura Humanitas, 1998.
———. *Europa, Asia, America . . . , Corespondenţă*, I, A–H. Ed. and with a foreword by Mircea Handoca. Bucharest: Editura Humanitas, 1999.
———. *Viaţă Nouă, Roman*. Ed. Mircea Handoca. Bucharest: Editura "Jurnalul literar," 1999.
———. *Aristocraţia solilocvială a dialogului. Interviuri şi mărturisiri*, I. Ed. and with a foreword by Mircea Handoca. Editura "Jurnalul literar," Bucharest, 2000.
———. *Diario Portugués (1941–1945)*. Trans. Joaquín Garrigós. Barcelona: Editorial Kairós, 2000.

OTHER WORKS CITED

Ackerman, Robert. *J. G. Frazer, His Life and Work*. Cambridge and New York: Cambridge UP, 1987.
———. *The Myth and Ritual School. J. G. Frazer and the Cambridge Ritualists*. New York and London: Routledge, 1991.
Alexandrescu, Sorin. *Paradoxul român*. Bucharest: Editura Univers, 1998.

Allen, Douglas, *Structure and Creativity: Hermeneutics in Mircea Eliade's Phenomenology and New Directions*. The Hague: Mouton, 1978.
———. *Mircea Eliade et le phénomène religieux*. Paris: Payot, 1982.
———. "Eliade and History." *The Journal of Religion* 4:2 (1988): 545–65.
———. *Myth and Religion in Mircea Eliade*. New York and London: Garland Publishers, 1998.
Alles, Gregory D. "Homo Religiosus." In Eliade, *Encyclopedia of Religion*, 1987. 442–45.
———. "Wach, Eliade, and the Critique from Totality." *Numen* XXXV (1988): 108–38.
Altizer, T. J. J. "The Death of God and the Uniqueness of Christianity." Kitagawa, *The History of Religions: Essays on the Problem of Understanding*. 1967. 119–41.
———. *The Gospel of Christian Atheism*. London: Collins, 1967.
Andolfi, Ferruccio. Review of Eliade, *Mito e Realtà*. Torino: Borla, 1966. *Rivista di Storia e Letteratura Religiosa* 4 (1968): 358–63.
Arcella, Luciano, Paola Pisi, and Roberto Scagno, eds. *Confronto con Mircea Eliade*. Milan: Jaca Book, 1998.
Assmann, Jan. "Cultural and Literary Texts." *Definitely: Egyptian Literature*. Ed. Moers. 1995. 1–15.
Bach, Alice. "Whatever Happened to Dionysus." *Biblical Studies/Cultural Studies*. Ed. J. Cheryl Exum and Stephen D. Moore. Sheffield: Sheffield Academic Press, 1998.
Baillet, Philippe. "Julius Evola et Mircea Eliade (1927–1944): une amitié manquée." *Les Deux Etendards*, Sept.–Dec. 1989.
Baines, John. "Prehistories of Literature: Performance, Fiction, Myth." *Definitely: Egyptian Literature*. Ed. Moers. 1995. 17–41.
Baird, Robert D. *Category Formation and the History of Religions*. The Hague: Mouton, 1971.
Bamberger, Joan. "The Myth of Matriarchy: Why Men Rule in Primitive Society." *Woman, Culture, and Society*. Ed. Michelle Z. Rosaldo and Louise Lamphere. 1974.
Barbosa da Silva, António. *The Phenomenology of Religion as a Philosophical Problem. An Analysis of the Theoretical Background of the Phenomenology of Religion, in General, and of Mircea Eliade's Phenomenological Approach in Particular*. Lund: Gleerup, 1982.
———. *Is There a New Imbalance in Jewish-Christian Relations?: An Analysis of the Theoretical Presuppositions and Theological Implications of the Jewish-Christian Dialogue in the Light of [t]he World Council of Churches' and the Roman Catholic Church's Conceptions of Inter-religious Dialogue*. Uppsala: Uppsala

University, Dept. of Theology, 1992.
Barbour, Ian. *Myths, Models, and Paradigms.* London: SCM Press, 1974.
Barth, Karl. "Rudolf Bultmann—An Attempt to Understand Him." *Kerygma and Myth: A Theological Debate.* Ed. Hans Werner Bartsch. Vol. II. London: SPCK, 1962.
Bausani, A. "Can Monotheism be Taught?" *Numen* X (1963): 167–201.
Beard, Mary. *The Invention of Jane Harrison.* Cambridge: Harvard UP, 2000.
Beauvoir, Simone de. *The Second Sex.* New York: Knopf, 1953.
Berger, Adriana. "Cultural Hermeneutics: The Concept of Imagination in the Phenomenological Approaches of Henry Cobin and Mircea Eliade." *The Journal of Religion* 66:2 (1986): 141–56.
Bergman, Jan. "Mysticism." *Mystische Anklänge in den altägyptischen Vorstellungen von Gott und Welt.* Ed. Sven Samuel Hartman and Carl-Martin Edsman. Based on papers read at the Symposium on Mysticism held at Åbo on 7–9 September 1968. Uppsala: Almqvist and Wiksell, 1970. 67–76.
Berner, Ulrich. "Erforschung und Anwendung religiöser Symbole im Doppelwerk Mircea Eliades." *Symbolon.* Neue Folge. Band 6 (1982): 27–35.
———. "Die Bedeutung der Religionswissenschaft für die gegenwärtige Kultur." *Octogenario. Dankesgabe für Heinrich Karpp.* Düsseldorf: J. Hönscheid, 1988. 229–40.
———. "Concepts of Nature in Greek Religion and Philosophy." *The Invention of Nature.* Ed. Thomas Bargatzky and Rolf Kuschel. Frankfurt am Main and New York: Peter Lang, 1994. 27–45.
———. "Mircea Eliade." *Klassiker der Religionswissenschaft.* Ed. Michaels. 1997. 343–56.
———. "Plutarch und Epikur." *Plutarch: ist "Lebe im Verborgenen" eine gute Lebensregel?, eingeleitet, übersetzt und mit interpretierenden Essays versehen von Ulrich Berner, Bernhard Heininger et al.* Darmstadt: 2000. 117–39.
———. "Religionsphänomenologie und Skeptizismus," *Noch eine Chance.* Ed. Michaels et al. 2001. 369–91.
Bettis, J. D. *Phenomenology of Religion: Eight Modern Descriptions of the Essence of Religion.* London: SCM, 1969.
Bhose, Amita. *Eminescu şi India.* Iaşi: Editura Junimea, 1978.
Bickel, Susanne. *La cosmogonie égyptienne avant le Nouvel Empire, Orbis Biblicus et Orientalis.* Fribourg, Suisse: Éditions universitaires; Göttingen: Vandenhoeck und Ruprecht, 1994.
Bjerke, Øivind Storm. *Edvard Munch. Harald Sohlberg, Landscapes of the Mind.* New York: National Academy of Design, 1995.
Björkman, Gun. "Egyptology and Historical Method." *Orientalia Suecana* 13

(1964): 9–33.

Blacker, Carmen. "Introduction." *Cambridge Women: Twelve Portraits*. Ed. Shils and Blacker. Cambridge: Cambridge UP, 1996.

Bleeker, C. J. "The Future Task of the History of Religions." *Numen* VII (1960): 221–39.

Boers, Hendrikus. *What is New Testament Theology?* Philadelphia: Fortress Press, 1979.

Bolle, Kees W. "History of Religions with a Hermeneutic Oriented toward Christian Theology?" Kitagawa, *The History of Religions: Essays on the Problem of Understanding*. 89–118.

Bordaş, Liviu. "Secretul doctorului Eliade." *Origini. Journal of Cultural Studies* 1 (2002): 72–87.

———. "Une 'correspondance' spirituelle: Mircea Eliade–lettres à Giovanni Papini. 1927–1954." *Origini. Journal of Cultural Studies* 3–4 (2003): 67–73.

———. "Istoria doctorului Honigberger şi secretul unei nuvele eliadeşti." *Origini. Journal of Cultural Studies* 1–2 (2003): 20–30; 3–4 (2003): 129–58; and 1–2 (2004): forthcoming.

Børresen, Kari Elisabeth. *Subordination et Equivalence. Nature et rôle de la femme d'après Augustin et Thomas d' Aquin*. Washington, D.C.: U Press of America, 1981.

———, and Kari Vogt, eds. *Woman's Studies of the Christian and Islamic Traditions, Ancient, Medieval, and Renaissance Foremothers*. Dordrecht, Netherlands: Boston, Kluwer Academic, 1993.

Bousset, Wilhelm. *Kyrios Christos*. Trans. John E. Steely. Nashville: Abingdon Press, 1970.

Braidotti, Rosi. *Patterns of Dissonance*. Trans. Elizabeth Guild. New York: Routledge, 1991.

Brandon, S. G. F. "The Historical Element in Primitive Christianity." *Numen* II (1955): 156–67.

Brauer, Jerald C. "Mircea Eliade and the Divinity School." *Criterion*, Autumn 1985, 23–27.

Bryan, Betsy M. "The Disjunction of Text and Image in Egyptian Art." *Studies in Honor of William Kelly Simpson*—I. Ed. Peter Der Manuelian. Boston: Dept. of Ancient Egyptian, Nubian, and Near Eastern Art, Museum of Fine Arts, 1996. 161–68.

Buchanan, J. "The Total Hermeneutics of Mircea Eliade," *Religious Studies Review* 9:1 (1983): 22–24.

Budge, E. A Wallis. *The Egyptian Book of the Dead*. New York: Dover, 1967.

Bultmann, Rudolf. *Jesus Christ and Mythology*. New York: Charles Scribner's

Sons, 1958.

———. *Existence and Faith, Shorter Writings of Rudolf Bultmann*. Selected, translated, and introduced by Schubert M. Ogden. New York: Meridian Books, 1960.

Bunnin, Nicolas, and E. P. Tsui-James. *The Blackwell Companion to Philosophy*, Malden, MA: Blackwell, 2003.

Bynum, Caroline Walker. *Holy Feast and Holy Fast: The Religious Significance of Food to Medieval Woman*. Berkeley: U of California P, 1987.

Cain, Seymour. "Mircea Eliade: Attitudes toward History." *Religious Studies Review* 6:1 (1980): 13–16.

Calder, William, ed. *The Cambridge Ritualists Reconsidered*. Atlanta: Scholars Press, 1991.

Călinescu, Matei. "Imagination and Meaning." Girardot and Ricketts, *Imagination and Meaning*. 1982. 138–61.

Cave David. *Mircea Eliade's Vision for a New Humanism*. New York and Oxford: Oxford UP, 1993.

———. "Eliade's Interpretation of Sacred Space and its Role towards the Cultivation of Virtue." *Changing Religious Worlds*. Ed. Rennie. 2001. 235–48.

Christ, Carol. "Mircea Eliade and the Feminist Paradigm Shift." *Journal of Feminist Studies in Religion* 5:1 (1991): 75–94.

Christ, Carol P., and Naomi R. Goldenberg, eds. "The Legacy of the Goddess: The Work of Marija Gimbutas." *Journal of Feminist Studies in Religion*, 12:2 (1996).

Cikala, V. Mulago Gwa. "L'homme africain et le sacré." *Traité d'anthropologie du sacré 1—Les origines et le problème de l'homo religiosus*. Ed. Julian Ries. Aix-en-Provence: Edisud, 1995. 255–80.

Cioran, Emil M. "Beginnings of a Friendship." *Myths and Symbols*. Ed. Kitagawa and Long. 1982. 407–14.

———. *Schimbarea la față a României* (1939). Bucharest: Editura Humanitas, 1990.

Clark, Elizabeth. *Ascetic Piety and Women's Faith*. Lewiston, NY: Mellen Press, 1986.

Clay, Diskin. "Lucian of Samosata: Four Philosophical Lives (Nigrinus, Demonax, Peregrinus, Alexander Pseudomantis)." *Rise and Decline of the Roman World*. Ed. Haase and Temporini. 1972. 3406–50.

Cobb, John. "Is Christianity a Religion?" *What is Religion?: An Inquiry for Christian Theology*. Ed. Mircea Eliade and David Tracy. Edinburgh: T and T Clark, 1980.

Constantinescu, Pompiliu. "*Isabel și apele diavolului*." *Vremea*. Bucharest, 3 July

1930.

Croce, Benedetto. *Teoria e Storia della Storiografia*. Bari: Laterza, 1927.

———. Review of Eliade *Le Mythe de l'Éternel Retour: Archétypes et Répétition*. *Quaderni della "Critica"* 15 (1949): 100–102.

Culianu, Ioan P. "L'anthropologie philosophique." Tacou et al., *Cahiers de l'Herne, Mircea Eliade*. Paris: Éditions de l'Herne, 1978.

———. *Mircea Eliade*, 2nd, revised edition. Translated into Romanian by Florin Chirițescu and Dan Petrescu, Bucharest: Nemira, 1998.

———. "Experiență, cunoaștere, inițiere." *Studii românești* I. Trans. Corina Popescu and Dan Petrescu. Bucharest: Nemira, 2000. 227–63.

Dancă, Wilhem. *Mircea Eliade. Definitio sacri: Il sacro come il significativo ed il destino e la sua relazione col metodo storico-fenomenologico nell'opera di Mircea Eliade*. Rome: Gregorian Pontifical University, 1996.

———. *Mircea Eliade. Definitio sacri*. Iași: Editura Ars Longa, 1998.

Davy, M.-M. *Enciclopedia doctrinelor mistice* (1972), vol. I. Timișoara: Editura Armarcord, 1997.

Derchain, Phillipe. "Théologie et littérature." *Ancient Egyptian Literature*. Ed. Loprieno. 1996. 354.

Devi, Maitreyi. *It Does Not Die*. Calcutta: P. Lal, 1976. Republished, Chicago and London: U of Chicago P, 1994/95.

Dietrich, B. C. "Views on Homeric Gods and Religion." *Numen* XXVI:2 (1979): 129–51.

Dirven, Lucinda. "The Author of *De Dea Syria* and his Cultural Heritage." *Numen* XXXXIV (1997): 153–79.

Dodds, E. R. *The Greeks and the Irrational*. Berkeley: U of California P, 1951.

Doniger, Wendy. *Women, Androgynes, and Other Mythical Beasts*. Chicago: U of Chicago P, 1980.

———. *Other Peoples' Myths. The Cave of Echoes*. Chicago: U of Chicago P, 1988.

Dubuisson, Daniel. *Mythologies du XXe Siècle (Dumézil, Lévi-Strauss, Eliade)*. Presses Universitaires de Lille, 1993.

———. "L'ésotérisme fascisant de Mircea Eliade." *Actes de la recherche en sciences socials* 106–107 (1995): 44–51.

Dudley III, Guilford. "Mircea Eliade as the "Anti-Historian" of Religions." *Journal of the American Academy of Religion* 44:2 (1976): 346–59.

———. *Religion on Trial: Mircea Eliade and his Critics*. Philadelphia: Temple UP, 1977.

Durandin, Catherine. *Istoria românilor*. Trans. Liliana Buruiană-Popovici. Iași: Editura Institutului European, 1998.

Durkheim, Émile. "L'Organisation matrimoniale des sociétés Australiennes,"

Année Sociologique, VIII (1903–1904): 118–47.

———. *Elementary Forms of the Religious Life.* London: Allen and Unwin, 1915.

Edmunds, Lowell, ed. *Approaches to Greek Myth,* Baltimore: Johns Hopkins UP, 1990.

Edwards, D. L., ed. *The Honest to God Debate: Some Reactions to the Book* Honest to God. Philadelphia: The Westminster Press, 1963.

Ellinwood, Frank F. *Oriental Religions and Christianity.* London: James Nisbet, 1892.

Ellwood, Robert. *The Politics of Myth: A Study of C.G. Jung, Mircea Eliade, and Joseph Campbell.* Albany: The State U of New York P, 1999.

Empson, William. "Assertion in Words." Tzvetan Todorov et al., *Introduction to Poetics.* Minneapolis: U of Minnesota P, 1981.

Epp, Eldon J., and George W. MacRae, eds. *The New Testament and Its Modern Interpreters.* Atlanta: Scholars Press, 1989.

Erman, Adolf, and Hermann Grapow. *Wörterbuch der ägyptischen Sprache* VI. Berlin: Akademie-Verlag, 1971.

Faivre, Antoine. "L'ambiguità della nozione di sacro in Mircea Eliade." *Confronto con Mircea Eliade.* Ed. Arcella et al. 1998. 363–74.

———. *Theosophy, Imagination, Tradition,* Albany: State U of New York P, 2000.

Fiore, Crescenzo. *Storia sacra e storia profana in Mircea Eliade.* Rome: Bulzoni, 1986.

Foster, John L. "Thought Couplets in Khety's *Hymn to the Inundation.*" *Journal of Near Eastern Studies* 34 (1975): 1–29.

———. "Wordplay in *The Eloquent Peasant*: The Eighth Complaint." *Bulletin of the Egyptological Seminar* 10 (1989–1990): 61–76.

———. "Thought Couplets and the Standard Theory: A Brief Overview." *Lingua Aegyptia* 4 (1994): 139–63.

Frankfort, Henri. *Kingship and the Gods.* Chicago: U of Chicago P, 1948.

Frazer, James George. *The Golden Bough. A Study in Magic and Religion.* Third Edition. London: Macmillan, 1911–15.

Gamwell, Frank I. "Opening Remarks on the Occasion of the Establishment of the Mircea Eliade Chair in the History of Religions." *Criterion* (Autumn 1985): 18–19.

Gandillac, Maurice De. "Le temple dans l'Homme et l'homme dans le monde. Symbolique du temple égyptien." *Cahiers du Sud* 358 (1961): 359–73.

Gaudin, Phillipe, ed. *Les grandes religions (judaisme, christianisme, islamisme, hindouisme, bouddhisme).* Paris: Éditions Gallimard, 1993.

Guilmot, Max. *Le message spirituel de l'Égypte ancienne.* Paris: Hachette, 1970.

Gimbutas, Marija. *The Prehistory of Eastern Europe: Mesolithic, Neolithic, and Copper Age Cultures in Russia and the Baltic Area*. Cambridge: Harvard UP, 1956.

———. *The Language of the Goddess*. San Francisco: Harper and Row, 1989.

Girardot, Norman, and Mac Linscott Ricketts, eds. *Imagination and Meaning: The Scholarly and Literary Worlds of Mircea Eliade*. New York: Seabury Press, 1982.

Goedicke, Hans. "God." *Journal of the Society for the Study of Egyptian Antiquities* 16 (1986): 57–62.

Gonda, Jan. "Vedic Gods and the Sacrifice." *Numen* XXX:1 (1983): 1–34.

Goodenough, E. R. "Religionswissenschaft." *Numen* VI (1959): 77–111.

Goyon, Jean-Claude. *Rituels funéraires de l'ancienne Égypte. Le Rituel d'embaumement, le Rituel de l'ouverture de la bouche et les Livres des respirations*, Littérature ancienne du Proche-Orient 4. Paris: Cerf, 1972.

Grimshaw, Jean. *Feminist Philosophers: Women's Perspectives on Philosophical Traditions*. Brighton, Sussex: Wheatsheaf Books, 1986.

Gross, Rita M. "Androcentrism and Androgyny in the Methodology of History of Religions." *Beyond Androcentrism: New Essays on Women and Religion*. Ed. Rita M. Gross. Missoula: Scholars Press for the American Academy of Religion, 1977.

Grottanelli, Cristiano. "Mircea Eliade, Carl Schmitt, René Guénon 1942." *Interrompere il quotidiano. La costruzione del tempo nell'esperienza religiosa*. Ed. Spineto. Milan: forthcoming.

Guénon, René. *L'Homme et son devenir selon le Vedanta*. Paris: Bossard, 1925.

———. *La crise du monde moderne*. Paris: Bossard, 1927.

———. *Introduction générale à l'étude des doctrines hindoues*. Paris: Les Éditions Véga, 1932.

———. *Formes traditionnelles et cycles cosmiques*. Paris: Gallimard, 1970.

Guilhou, Nadine. "Temps du récit et temps du mythe, des conceptions égyptiennes du temps à travers le *Livre de la Vache Céleste*." *Mélanges Adolphe Gutbub*. Ed. François Daumas. Montpellier: Institut d'égyptologie de l'Université Paul Valéry, 1984. 87–93.

Guilmot, Max. *Le message spirituel de l'Égypte ancienne*. Paris: Hachette, 1970.

Haase, Wolfgang, and Hildegard Temporini, eds. *Rise and Decline of the Roman World*. Berlin and New York: Walter de Gruyter, 1972.

Hannig, Rainer. *Die Sprache der Pharaonen. Großes Handwörterbuch Ägyptisch-Deutsch*. Mainz: P. von Zabern, 1995.

Hansen, H. T. "Mircea Eliade, Julius Evola und die Integrale Tradition." Julius

Evola, *Über das Initiatische: Aufsatzsammlung*. Sinzheim: Frietsch Verlag, 1998. 9–50.

Harrison, Jane. *Homo Sum. Being a Letter to an Anti-Suffragist from an Anthropologist*. Westminster: National Union of Women's Suffrage Societies, 1908.

———. *Rationalism and Religious Reaction*. London: Watts, 1919.

———. *Themis. A Study in the Social Origins of Greek Religion*. London: Merlin Press, 1963. Also reprinted with *Prologomena to the Study of Greek Religion*. New Hyde Park, NY: University Books, 1962.

———. *Ancient Art and Ritual*. New York: Greenwood Press, 1969. Original, New York: H. Holt, 1913.

Hasel, Gerhard. *New Testament Theology: Basic Issues in the Current Debate*. Michigan: Eerdmanns, 1987.

Hegel, G. W. F. "Die Verfassung Deutschlands." *Frühe Schriften* (Werke, 1). Frankfurt am Main: Suhrkamp, 1986.

Hermes Trismegistus. *Corpus Hermeticum*. Trans. D. Dumbrăveanu. Bucharest: Editura Herald, 1999.

Hick, John. *God and the Universe of Faiths*. London: Oneworld, 1993.

Hitchins, Keith. "Desăvârșirea națiunii române." Bărbulescu et al., *Istoria României*. Bucharest: Editura Enciclopedică, 1998.

Horia, Vintilă. "The Forest as Mandala." Kitagawa and Long, *Myths and Symbols*. 1982. 387–95.

Hornung, Erik. *Les dieux de l'Égypte: Le Un et le multiple*. Paris: Editions du Rocher, 1995. Translated by John Baines: *Conceptions of God in ancient Egypt: The One and the Many*. Ithaca: Cornell UP, 1982.

———. *Idea into Image: Essays on Ancient Egyptian Thought*. New York: Timken, 1992.

Hübner, Kurt. *Die Wahrheit des Mythos*. Munich: Beck, 1985.

Idinopulos, Thomas A., and Edward Yonan. *Religion and Reductionism: Essays on Eliade, Segal, and the Challenge of the Social Sciences for the Study of Religion*. Leiden: Brill, 1994.

Ierunca, Virgil. "The Literary Work of Mircea Eliade." *Myths and Symbols*. Ed. Kitagawa and Long. 1982. 343–63.

Ionescu, Nae. "Individualismul englez" (1924). Ionescu, *Neliniștea metafizică*. Ed. Marin Diaconu. Bucharest: Editura Fundației Culturale Române, 1993. 136–45.

———. *Prelegeri de filosofia religiei* (1925). Ed. Marta Petreu. Cluj-Napoca: Editura Biblioteca Apostrof, 1994.

———. *Curs de metafizică* (1928). Ed. Marin Diaconu. Bucharest: Editura

Humanitas, 1991.
———. *Roza Vânturilor. 1926–1933.* Ed. Mircea Eliade. Bucharest: Editura Cultura Națională, 1936.
———. *Curs de istorie a logicii* (1941). Bucharest: Editura Humanitas, 1993.
———. *Neliniștea metafizică.* Ed. Marin Diaconu. Bucharest: Editura Fundației Culturale Române, 1993.
———. *Opere,* vol. VI. Ed. Marin Diaconu and Dora Mezdrea. Bucharest: Editura Crater, 1999.
James, E. O. "The History, Science, and Comparative Study of Religion." *Numen* I (1954): 91–105.
———. "The Religions of Antiquity." *Numen* VII (1960): 137–47.
Jeffner, Anders. "The Relationship between English and German Ways of Doing Philosophy of Religion." *Religious Studies* 15 (1979): 247–56.
Jianu, Ionel. "Ecouri din depărtări." *Rampa.* Bucharest, 10 April 1930: 1.
Johnson, Roger. *Rudolf Bultmann: Interpreting Faith for the Modern Era.* London: Collins, 1987. 22.
Jordan, Louis Henry. *Comparative Religion. Its Genesis and Growth.* Atlanta: Scholars Press, 1986.
Karenga, Maulana. *Ma'at, the Moral Ideal in Ancient Egypt: A Study in Classical African Ethics.* New York: Routledge, 2004.
King, Ursula, ed. "A Hermeneutic Circle of Religious Ideas." *Religious Studies* 17:1 (1981): 565–69.
———. *Turning Points in Religious Studies.* Foreword by Desmond Tutu. Edinburgh: T. and T. Clark, 1990.
———. "Women Scholars and the *Encyclopedia of Religion.*" *Method and Theory in the Study of Religion* 2:1 (1990): 91–97.
———. "A Question of Identity: Women Scholars and the Study of Religion." *Religion and Gender.* Ed. Ursula King. Oxford and Cambridge, MA: Blackwell, 1995.
Kippenberg, Hans G. "Mirrors, Not Windows: Semiotic Approaches to the Gospels." *Numen* XXXXI (1994): 88–97.
Kirk, Geoffrey. *Myth: Its Meaning and Functions in Ancient and Other Cultures.* Berkeley: U of California P, 1970.
Kitagawa, Joseph M., ed. *The History of Religions: Essays on the Problem of Understanding.* Chicago: The U of Chicago P, 1967.
———. "Humanistic and Theological History of Religions with Special Reference to the North American Scene. *Numen* XXVII:2 (1980): 198–221.
———. "Remarks on the Mircea Eliade Chair." *Criterion* (Autumn 1985): 22.

———. "Mircea Eliade." *The Encyclopedia of Religion*, vol. V. New York: MacMillan, 1987. 85.

———, and Charles H. Long, eds. *Myths and Symbols: Essays in Honor of Mircea Eliade*. Chicago: U of Chicago P, 1982.

Kleeman, Faye Yuan. *The Uses of Myth in Modern Japanese Literature: Nakagami Kenji, Ōe Kenzaburō, and Kurahashi Yumiko*. UMI Dissertation Services, 1991.

Kraemer, Hendrik. *Religion and the Christian Faith*. London: Lutterworth Press, 1956.

Kuhn, Thomas. *The Structure of Scientific Revolutions*. Chicago: U of Chicago P, 1962.

Kümmel, Werner G. *The New Testament: The History of the Investigation of Its Problems*. London: SCM Press, 1973.

Laignel-Lavastine, Alexandra. *Cioran, Eliade, Ionescu; L'Oubli du Fascisme*. Paris: Presses Universitaires de France, 2002.

Lang, Andrew. *Letters to Dead Authors*. London and New York: Charles Scribner's Sons, 1891.

———. "Mr. Frazer's Theory of the Crucifixion." *The Fortnightly Review* 69 (1901): 650–62.

Leach, Edmund. *Rethinking Anthropology*. London: U of London, Athlone Press, 1961.

———. "Sermons by a Man on a Ladder," *The New York Review of Books* Oct. 20, 1966: 28–31.

Leclant, Jean. "Espace et temps, ordre et chaos dans l'Égypte pharaonique." *Revue de Synthèses* 55–56 (1964): 217–39.

Lessa, William A., and Evon Z. Vogt. *Reader in Comparative Religion*. New York: Harper and Row, 1958.

Leeuw, Gerardus van der. *Der mensch und die religion. Anthropologischer versuch*. Basel: Verlag Hans zum Falken, 1941.

Lévi-Strauss, Claude. *La pensée sauvage*. Paris: Librairie Plon, 1962. *The Savage Mind*. Chicago: U of Chicago P, 1996.

Lincoln, Bruce. "Theses on Method." *Method and Theory in the Study of Religion* 8 (1996): 225–27.

Long, Charles. "The Significance for Modern Man of Mircea Eliade's Work." *Cosmic Piety, Modern Man and the Meaning of the Universe*. Ed. Christopher Derrick. New York: P. J. Kenedy and Sons, 1967. 131–44.

Loprieno, Antonio (ed.), *Ancient Egyptian Literature. History and Forms*. Probleme der Ägyptologie 10. Leiden and New York: E. J. Brill, 1996.

———. "Defining Egyptian Literature: Ancient Texts and Modern Theories."

Ancient Egyptian Literature. 1996. 39–58.
Lott, Eric J. *Vision, Tradition, Interpretation: Theology, Religion, and the Study of Religion.* Berlin: Mouton de Gruyter, 1987.
Lucian of Samosata. *Alexander the False Prophet* 8. Trans. A. M. Harmon, *Lucian IV.* The Loeb Classical Library. Cambridge: Harvard UP, 1936.
———. *De Dea Syria* 6. Trans. Harold W. Attridge and Robert A. Oden. Missoula: Society of Biblical Literature. Text and Translations. Graeco-Roman Religion Series, 1976.
Lurson, Benoît. "Symétrie axiale et diagonale: deux principes d'organisation du décor de la salle E du temple de Gerf Hussein." *Göttinger Miszellen* 176 (2000): 81–84.
Macquarrie, John, ed. *Contemporary Religious Thinkers: From Idealist Metaphysicians to Existential Theologians.* London: SCM Press, 1968.
Maguire, Daniel. *The Moral Revolution.* San Francisco: Harper and Row, 1986.
Marino, Adrian. *Hermeneutica lui Mircea Eliade.* Cluj-Napoca: Dacia, 1980.
Maritain, Jacques. *Primauté du spirituel.* Paris: Librairie Plon, 1927.
Martin, Jane Roland. "Methodological Essentialism, False Difference, and other Dangerous Traps." *Signs* 19:3 (1994): 630–57.
Martino, Ernesto de. Review of *Le Mythe de l'Éternel Retour. Studi e Materiali di Storia delle Religioni.* Rome 23 (1951): 148–55.
———. "Psychologie et Histoire des Religions, à propos du Symbolisme du 'Centre.'" *Eranos-Jahrbuch* 19 (1951): 247–82.
———. *Il Mondo Magico.* Torino: Universale Bollati Boringhieri, 1973.
Masui, Jacques, ed. *Approches de l'Inde.* Marseille: Les Cahiers du Sud, 1949.
Maw, Martin. *Visions of India: Fulfillment Theology, the Aryan Race Theory, and the Work of British Protestant Missionaries in Victorian India.* Frankfurt: Peter Lang, 1990.
McCutcheon, Russell T. *Manufacturing Religion. The Discourse on Sui Generis Religion and the Politics of Nostalgia.* New York and Oxford: Oxford UP, 1997.
Michaels, Axel, ed. *Klassiker der Religionswissenschaft. Von Friedrich Schleiermacher bis Mircea Eliade.* Munich: C. H. Beck, 1997.
———, Daria Pezzoli-Olgiati, and Fritz Stolz, eds. *Noch eine Chance für die Religionsphänomenologie?* Bern: Studia Religiosa Helvetica. Jahrbuch 6/7, 2001.
Mihăescu, Florin. "Mircea Eliade e René Guénon." *Origini* 150, supplement to *Orion* (Milan) (1997): 15–18.
Miller-McLemore, Bonnie J. "Epistemology or Bust: A Maternal Feminist Knowledge of Knowing." *Journal of Religion* 72 (1992): 229–47.
Moers, Gerald, ed. *Definitely: Egyptian Literature.* Proceedings of the Symposium

"Ancient Egyptian Literature: History and Forms." Los Angeles, March 24–26, 1995. Göttingen: Seminar für Ägyptologie und Koptologie, 1999.

Moi, Toril. *Simone de Beauvoir: The Making of an Intellectual Woman*. Oxford and Cambridge, MA: Blackwell, 1994.

Monastra, Giovanni. "Il rapporto Eliade-Evola. Una pagina della cultura del Novecento," *Diorama letterario* 120 (1988): 17.

Montanari, Enrico. "Eliade e Guénon." *Studi e materiali di storia delle religioni* Rome 61 (1995): 131–49.

Moore, Henrietta L. *Feminism and Anthropology*. Cambridge, UK: Polity Press, 1988.

Muthuraj, J. G. "The Meaning of εθνος and εθνη and Its Significance to the Study of the New Testament." *Bangalore Theological Forum* XXIX (1997): 1–36.

Mutti, Claudio. *Julius Evola sul fronte dell'Est*. Parma: Edizioni all'insegna del Veltro, Parma, 1998. Chapter II republished in an amplified form as Preface–*Evola și România*, in Julius Evola, *Naționalism și asceză*. Trans. Florin Dumitrescu. Alba Iulia and Paris: Fronde, 1998. 11–38.

———. *Eliade, Vâlsan, Geticus e gli altri. La fortuna di Guénon tra i romeni*. Parma: Edizioni all'insegna del Vetro, Parma, 1999. Revised and amplified as, *Guénon în România*. Trans. Elena Pîrvu. Bucharest: Vremea, 2003.

Nakamura, Hajime. *A Comparative History of Ideas*. London and New York: Kegan Paul, 1992.

Nesselrath, Heinz-Günther. "Kaiserzeitlicher Skeptizismus in platonischem Gewand: Lukians 'Hermotimos.'" *Rise and Decline of the Roman World*. Ed. Haase and Temporini. 1972.

———. "Lukian: Leben und Werk." *Lukian, Die Lügenfreunde oder Der Ungläubige*. Ed. Ebner, et al. Darmstadt: 2001 (SAPERE 3), 11–31: 27.

Noica, Constantin. "Notații." *Vremea*. Bucharest. 5 December 1929.

O'Connor, June. "The Epistemological Significance of Feminist Research in Religion." *Religion and Gender*. Ed. Ursula King. 1995.

O'Flaherty, Wendy Doniger. See Doniger, Wendy.

O'Hara, Delia. "Mircea Eliade." *Chicago Magazine* 35:6 (June 1986): 147–51, 177–79.

Ōe Kenzaburō. *Dōjidai Gēmu* (The Game of Contemporaneity). Shinchō-sha, 1979; paperback edition, 1984.

———. *Shōsetsu no Takurami, Chi no Tanoshimi* (Contrivances of Fiction, Pleasures of Knowledge). Shinchō-sha, 1985; paperback edition, 1989.

———. *M/T to Mori no Fushigi no Monogatari* (The Tales of M/T and the "Wonder" of the Forest). Iwanami shoten, 1986; paperback edition, 1990.

Olson, Carl. *The Theology and Philosophy of Eliade*. New York: St. Martin's Press,

1992.

Ore, Katrine. "Mircea Eliade og myte/rite-skolen." *Enhet i Mangfold?* Ed. Ruud and Hjelde. 1998.

Otto, Rudolf. *The Idea of the Holy.* Oxford: Oxford UP, 1923.

———. *Mysticism East and West: A Comparative Analysis of the Nature of Mysticism.* Trans. Bertha L. Bracey and Richenda C. Payne. New York: MacMillan, 1970.

Ouellet, Brigitte. *Divinisation et culte du souverain dans le Proche-Orient ancien.* Unpublished master's thesis at the University of Montreal, 1994.

———. "*Le désillusionné et son ba*" *Le Papyrus de Berlin 3024. Herméneutique d'une expérience mystique.* Unpublished PhD Thesis, Faculty of Theology at the University of Montreal. 2004.

Palit, Roman. "The Grace." *Breath of Grace.* Ed. Pandit. 1973.

Pandit, M. P., ed. *Breath of Grace.* Pondicherry: Dipti Publications, 1973.

Passman, Tina. "Out of the Closet and into the Field: Matriculture, the Lesbian Perspective, and Feminist Classics." *Feminist Theory and the Classics.* Ed. Rabinowitz and Richlin. 1993. 181–208.

Patri, Aimé. "Mircea Eliade nous parle des méthodes de l'ascétisme indou." *Paru* 45 (1948): 49–54.

Penner, H. H. "Language, Ritual, and Meaning." *Numen* XXXII:3 (1983): 1–16.

Peterson, Michael, William Hasker, Bruce Reichenbach, and David Basinger. *Reason and Religious Belief*, 3rd ed. New York: Oxford UP, 2003.

Pezzoli-Olgiati, Daria. "Stadt als heiliger Raum? Drei mesopotamische Beispiele." *Noch eine Chance für die Religionsphänomenologie.* Ed. Michaels, et al. 2001.

Piru, Al. *Panorama deceniului literar românesc 1940–1950.* Bucharest: Editura pentru literatură, 1968.

Pisi, Paola. "I 'tradizionalisti' e la formazione del pensiero di Eliade." Arcella et al., *Confronto con Mircea Eliade.* 1998. 43–133.

Polanski, Tomasz. *Oriental Art in Greek Imperial Literature.* Trier: Bochumer Altertumswissenschaftliches Colloquium. Band 36, 1998.

Preda, Gheorghe. "Viaţa indiană. De vorbă cu Mircea Eliade." *Viaţa literară*, Bucharest 1:30 (June 1933). Reprinted in Eliade, *Aristocraţia solilocvială a dialogului* I, 2000, 21–31.

Quinn, William W. Jr. *The Only Tradition.* Albany: State U of New York P, 1997.

———. "Mircea Eliade and the Sacred Tradition (A Personal Account)." *Nova Religio* 3:1 (1999): 147–53.

Rabinowitz, Nancy Sorkin, and Amy Richlin, eds. *Feminist Theory and the Classics.* New York: Routledge. 1993.

Rastier, François. "Sens et signification." *Protée* 26:1 (1998): 7–18.

Ray, R. A. "Is Eliade's Metapsychoanalysis an End Run Around Bultmann's Demythologization." *Myth and the Crisis of Historical Consciousness*. Ed. L. W. Gibbs and W. T. Stevenson. Missoula, Montana: Scholars Press, 1975. 57–74.

Redford, Donald B. "Historical Sources: Textual Evidence." *The Oxford Encyclopedia of Ancient Egypt*. 104–108. New York: Oxford UP, 2001.

Reeder, Greg. "Ritualized Death and Rebirth: Running the Heb Sed." *KMT: A Modern Journal of Egyptology* 4:4 (1994): 60–71.

Rennie, Bryan. *Reconstructing Eliade: Making Sense of Religion*. Albany: The State U of New York P, 1996.

———, ed. *Changing Religious Worlds. The Meaning and End of Mircea Eliade*. Albany, The State U of New York P, 2001.

———. "Mircea Eliade: A Secular Mystic in the History of Religions?" *Origini. Journal of Cultural Studies* 3–4 (2003): 42–54.

———. "Religion after Religion, History after History. Postmodern Historiography and the Study of Religions." *Method and Theory in the Study of Religion* 15:3 (2003): 68–99.

———. "Mircea Eliade: Further Considerations." *Encyclopedia of Religion* (second edition). New York: MacMillan, 2004.

Reynolds, F. E. "A Tribute to Mircea Eliade." *Criterion* (Autumn 1985): 20–21.

Ricketts, Mac Linscott. "The Nature and Extent of Eliade's 'Jungianism.'" *Union Seminary Quarterly Review* XXV:2 (1970): 211–34.

———. "In Defence of Eliade. Toward Bridging the Communications Gap between Anthropology and the History of Religions." *Religion* 5 (1973): 13–34.

———. *Mircea Eliade et la mort de Dieu*. Tacou, et al., *Cahiers de l'Herne*. 1978.

———. *Mircea Eliade. The Romanian Roots, 1907–1945*, Vol. I–II, Boulder: East European Monographs, 1988.

———. *Former Friends and Forgotten Facts*. Norcross, GA: Criterion, 2003.

Ricoeur, Paul. *De l'interprétation. Essai sur Freud*. Paris: Éditions du Seuil, 1965. *Freud and Philosophy: an Essay on Interpretation*. Trans. Denis Savage. New Haven: Yale UP, 1970.

———. *The Symbolism of Evil*. New York: Harper and Row, 1967.

———. *Le conflit des interprétations. Essais d'herméneutique*. Paris: Éditions du Seuil, 1969. *The Conflict of Interpretations: Essays in Hermeneutics*. Ed. Don Ihde. Evanston: Northwestern UP, 1974.

———. *Introducción a la simbólica del mal*. Buenos Aires: La Aurora. *Le conflict des interprétations*. Paris: Éditions du Seuil, 1969 (third section).

———. *Hermenéutica y Estructuralismo*. Buenos Aires: La Aurora. *Le conflict des interprétations*. Paris: Éditions du Seuil, 1969 (first section).

———. *Teoría de la interpretación. Discurso y excedente de sentido*. Madrid: Siglo XXI. *Interpretation Theory. Discourse and the Surplus of Meaning*. Fort Worth: Texas Christian UP, 1976.

———. *Time and Narrative*. Three Volumes. Chicago: U of Chicago P, 1983, 1985, 1988.

———. "The Phenomenology of Time Consciousness." *The History of Religions: Retrospect and Prospect*. Ed. Joseph Kitagawa. 1985. 13ff.

———. "Poétique et symbolique." *Initiation à la pratique de la théologie—I*. Ed. Bernard Lauret and François Refoulé. Paris: Éditions du Cerf, 1982–1983. 37–61.

———. "From a Hermeneutics of Text to a Hermeneutics of Action." *From Text to Action*. Evanston: Northwestern UP, 1991.

———. *Fe y Filosofía. Problemas del lenguaje religioso*. Buenos Aires: Almagesto-Docencia, 1994.

Ries, Julien. "Archéologie, mythologie, philologie et théologie sur les traces de la pensée indo-européenne archaïque." *L'expression du sacré dans les grandes religions—II*. Louvain-la-Neuve: Centre d'histoire des religions, 1980.

———. "Science des religions et sciences humaines. L'œuvre de Mircea Eliade (1907–1986)." *Revue théologique de Louvain* 17 (1986): 329–40.

———, and Natale Spineto, eds. *Esploratori del pensiero umano. Georges Dumézil e Mircea Eliade*. Milan: Jaca Book, 2000. Also published in French: *Deux explorateurs de la pensée humaine: Georges Dumézil et Mircea Eliade*. Turnout, Belgium: Brepols Publishers, 2003.

Rimmon-Kenan, Shlomith. *Narrative Fiction: Contemporary Poetics*. London and New York: Routledge, 2002.

Robot, Al. "Mircea Eliade scrie romanul generației lui *Întoarcerea din rai*: foame, sex și moarte." *Rampa*, Bucharest, 22 Oct. 1933. Reprinted in Eliade, *Aristocrația solilocvială a dialogului* I, 2000. 56–59.

———. "Cu Mircea Eliade despre el și despre alții." *Rampa*. Bucharest, 5 June 1933. Reprinted in *Aristocrația solilocvială a dialogului* I (2000): 33–51.

Ronen, Ruth. "Fictional Entities, Incomplete Being." *Possible Worlds in Literary Theory*. Cambridge and New York: Cambridge UP, 1994.

Rosaldo, Michelle Z., and Louise Lamphere, eds. *Woman, Culture, and Society*. Stanford: Stanford UP, 1974.

Rudolph, Kurt. "Mircea Eliade and the 'History' of Religions." *Religion* 19 (1989): 101–27.

———. *Geschichte und Probleme der Religionswissenschaft*. Leiden, New York,

Köln: E. J. Brill, 1992.
Ruud, Inger Marie, og Sigurd Hjelde, eds. *Enhet i mangfold? 100 år med religionshistorie i Norge*. Oslo: Tano Aschehoug, 1998.
Said, Edward. *Orientalism*. New York: Vintage Books, 1979.
Saiving, Valerie. "Androcentrism in Religious Studies." *Journal of Religion* 56:2 (1976): 177–97.
Saliba, John A. "Eliade's View of Primitive Man: Some Anthropological Reflections." *Religion* 6 (1976): 150–75.
Schmidt, Wilhelm. *Ursprung der Gottesidee*. Münster: Aschendorff, 1912.
Scott, Bonnie Kime. *Refiguring Modernism*. Bloomington: Indiana UP, 1995.
Sebastian, Mihail. *Journal 1935–1944*, Chicago: Ivan R. Dee, 2000.
Sharma, Arvind, ed. *Women in World Religions*. Albany: State U of New York P, 1987.
Sharpe, Eric J. *Comparative Religion: A History*. LaSalle, IL: Open Court, 1975.
Shils, Edward, and Carmen Blacker, eds. *Cambridge Women: Twelve Portraits*. New York: Cambridge UP, 1996.
Showalter, Elaine. *A Literature of Their Own: British Women Novelists from Brontë to Lessing*. Princeton: Princeton UP, 1977.
Sinha, Debabrata. *Studies in Phenomenology*. The Hague: Martinus Nijhoff, 1969.
Sly, Dorothy. *Philo's Perception of Women*. Atlanta: Scholars Press, 1990.
Smart, Ninian. "Beyond Eliade: The Future of Theory in Religion." *Numen* XXV (1978): 171–83.
———, and D. D. Wallace. "The Encyclopaedia of Religion." *Religious Studies Review* 14:3 (July 1998): 193–206.
Smith, Brian K. "Ritual, Knowledge, and Being." *Numen* XXXIII:1 (1986): 65–89.
Smith, Jonathan Z. "Acknowledgments: Morphology and History in Mircea Eliade's *Patterns in Comparative Religion* (1949–1999)." *History of Religions* 39:4 (2000): 315–51.
Smyth, Edmund J., ed. *Postmodernism and Contemporary Fiction*. London: Batsford, 1991.
Spineto, Natale. "Mircea Eliade e gli archetipi." *Confronto con Mircea Eliade*. Ed. Arcella et al. 1998. 447–63.
———. "Mircea Eliade. Materiali per un bilancio storiografico." Ries and Spineto. *Esploratori del pensiero umano*. 2000. 201–48.
———. "Mircea Eliade and Traditionalism." *Aries* I:1 (2001): 62–87.
Srinivasan, D. "The Religious Significance of Divine Multiple Body Parts in the Atharva Veda." *Numen* XXV:3 (1978): 193–225.
Strenski, Ivan. "Love and Anarchy in Romania: A Critical Review of Mircea

Eliade's Autobiography, Volume One, 1907–1937." *Religion* 12 (1982): 391–403.

———. *Four Theories of Myth in Twentieth-Century History: Cassirer, Eliade, Lévi-Strauss, and Malinowski*. Iowa City: U of Iowa P, 1987.

Swain, Simon. *Hellenism and Empire. Language, Classicism, and Power in the Greek World AD 50–250*. Oxford: Oxford UP, 1996.

Tacou, Constantin, with Georges Banu and Guy Chalvon-Demersay, eds. *Cahiers de l'Herne, Mircea Eliade*. Paris: Éditions de l'Herne, 1978.

Throckmorton, Burton. *The New Testament and Mythology*, London: Darton, Longman, and Todd, 1960.

Tillich, Paul. "The Significance of the History of Religions for the Systematic Theologian." Kitagawa, *The History of Religions: Essays on the Problem of Understanding*. 1967. 242–43.

Tobin, Vincent. "The Egyptian Gods." *Theological Principles of Egyptian Religion*, American University Studies VII/59. 35–56.

Tolcea, Marcel. *Eliade, ezotericul*. Timişoara: Editura Mirton, 2002.

Tristan, Frédérick, Ioan Couliano et al., *Mircea Eliade. Dialogues avec le sacré*. Paris: Éditions N.A.D.P., 1987.

Tucci, Giuseppe. *The Theory and Practice of the Mandala*. Translated from the Italian by Alan Houghton Brodrick—*Teoria e pratica del mandala*. Mineola, NY: Dover, 2001.

Turris, Gianfranco de. "L'"iniziato' e il Profesore. I rapporti 'somersi' fra Julius Evola e Mircea Eliade." Maria Bernardi Guardi, Marco Rossi. *Delle rovine ed oltre, Saggi su Julius Evola*. Rome: Antonio Pellicani Editore, 1995. 219–49.

Ungureanu, Cornel. "Despre căile literaturii," *Orizont*, Timişoara, 25 august 1981.

Uscătescu, George. "Time and Destiny in the Novels of Mircea Eliade." Kitagawa and Long, *Myths and Symbols*. 1982. 397–406.

Varille, Alexandre. "Il faut attaquer les problèmes essentiels de l'égyptologie. Querelle des égyptologues—nouveaux débats." *Mercure de France* 1 (1951): 269–74.

Versnel, Henk. "Myth and Ritual. What's Sauce for the Goose Is Sauce for the Gander: Myth and Ritual, Old and New." *Approaches to Greek Myth*. Ed. Lowell Edmunds. Baltimore: Johns Hopkins UP, 1990.

———. *Inconsistencies in Greek and Roman Religion. Vol. 2: Transition and Reversal in Myth and Ritual*. Studies in Greek and Roman Religion 6. Leiden: Brill, 1990.

Vernus, Pascal. "L'idéologie pharaonique et la singularité historique." *Essai sur la conscience de l'Histoire dans l'Égypte pharaonique*. Bibliothèque de l'École Pratique des Hautes Études, section sciences historiques et philosophiques, vol. 332, 1995. 35–54.

———. "Langue littéraire et diglossie." *Ancient Egyptian Literature*. Ed. Antonio Loprieno. 1996.

Vettori, Vittorio. "A Colloquio con Mircea Eliade. Rivalutazione della categoria del sacro per un nuovo rinascimento mondiale." *L'Osservatore Romano*, Rome, 28–29 November, 1983.

Vulcănescu, Mircea. *Nae Ionescu. Aşa cum l-am cunoscut*. Bucharest: Editura Humanitas, 1992.

Walsem, René Van. "Interpretation of Evidence." *The Oxford Encyclopedia of Ancient Egypt*. Ed. Donald B. Redford. Oxford and New York: Oxford UP, 2001.

Wasserstrom, Steven. *Religion after Religion. Gershom Scholem, Mircea Eliade, and Henry Corbin at Eranos*. Princeton: Princeton UP, 1999.

Werblowsky, R. J. Zwi. "Histories of Religion" *Numen* XXVI:2 (1979): 250–55.

Werner, K. "Symbolism in the Vedas and Its Conceptualisation," *Numen* XXIV:3 (1977): 223–40.

Ziolkowski, Eric J. "Between Religion and Literature: Mircea Eliade and Northrop Frye." *The Journal of Religion* 71:4 (1991): 498–522.

List of Contributors

Ulrich Berner has been lecturer in the history of religions at the universities of Göttingen, Hamburg, Bonn, Bremen, before taking over the chair in *Religionswissenschaft* at Bayreuth University, also in Germany. He has written essays on aspects of Eliade's work (*Saeculum* 1981; *Symbolon* 1982) and on the life and work of Eliade in *Klassiker der Religionswissenschaft*, edited by Axel Michaels (Munich: C. H. Beck, 1997).

Liviu Bordaş studied philosophy and Indology at the University of Bucharest. He has an MPhil with a thesis on the philosophy of Advaita Vedānta. He also studied at the University of Vienna and the University of Rome. He has worked as research fellow at the "Sergiu Al-George" Institute of Oriental Studies, Bucharest. In 1995 he received a scholarship from the Indian government, and until 2001 he continued his Sanskrit studies and research on Indian philosophy at Pondicherry and Delhi Universities. During this period he undertook field research on various Indian religious communities. He was a research fellow of the Center for the Study of Traditional Cultures, in Zalau, Romania from 2001 to 2004 and is currently a fellow at the Romanian Academy in Rome. He is the Editor-in-Chief of the journal of cultural studies "*Origins*," and has a forthcoming book on Eliade, "*The Secret Eliade.*"

César Ceriani Cernadas holds a licentiate in anthropology from the University of Buenos Aires and is currently a graduate student in the Department of Anthropology at the School of Philosophy and Letters of that University. He is a fellow of the National Council for Scientific and Technological Research (CONICET) and has carried out anthropological research in Adventism and Toba Mormonism, focusing in the links between ideology, utopia, and history from an anthropological viewpoint.

Chung Chin-Hong is a professor in the Department of Religious Studies, College of Humanities, Seoul National University. He holds a DMin from San Francisco Theological Seminary, and an STM from United Theological Seminary, Dayton, Ohio. His publications include *Logic of Religious Culture* (SNU Press, 2000), *Cognition and Interpretation of Religious Culture* (SNU Press, 1996), *Understanding Religious Culture* (Seoul: Chongnyonsa, 1995), and *Introduction to the Study of Religion* (Seoul: Chonmangsa, 1980). He has translated Eliade's *Cosmos and History: The Myth of the Eternal Return* into Korean (Seoul: Modern Thought Publishing Co., 1974) and has written, among others, "Soteriological Implications of Literature: On Eliade's *Mantuleasa Street (The Old Man and the Bureaucrats)*" (*The Journal of the Korean Society of Literature and Religion* [1999]: 67–96). Profesor Chung is also a poet and author, having written *Sometimes There Blossom Silver Flowers in the Garden* (a collection of poems—Seoul: Kang, 1997) and *Searching for God, Searching for Human Being* (a traveler's journal) (Seoul: Jipmundang, 1994).

Wilhelm Dancă is a Catholic parish priest in Bucharest. He has a master's degree from Gregorian University in Rome with a thesis on "The human being as symbol in Eliade's Memories" and a PhD, also from Gregorian University with a thesis on "*Definitio sacri*. The sacred as meaning and destiny with regard to the historical-phenomenological method in the work of Mircea Eliade." This was published by Ars Longa, in Iași in 1998. Dr. Danca has also published *Bazele filozofice ale teologiei* (The *Philosophical Foundations of Theology*. Bucuresti: Editura Arhiepiscopiei Romano-Catolice, 1999) and *Introducere în teologia fundamentala* (*Introduction to Fundamental Theology*, Bucurest: Editura Arhiepiscopiei Romano-Catolice, 1999). He has published more than a dozen articles on Eliade in a wide variety of Romanian journals.

Michel Meslin is professor of the history of religions and of the anthropology of religion. He is head of the Research Institute for the Study of Religions at the Sorbonne, Paris. He has dedicated several works to the history of early Christianity (notably on Western Arianism) and on late paganism. His work focuses on the religious representations of ancient civilizations and on traditional religions symbols. He has published *Pour une science des religions* (*Toward a Science of Religions*. Paris: Seuil, 1973) and *L'expérience humaine du divin* (*Human Experience of the Divine*. Paris: Cerf, 1988). More recently, he established the series, les Cahiers d'anthropologie religieuse (Paris: Presses de l'Université de Paris-Sorbonne, 1993).

Joseph Muthuraj is professor of New Testament and chair of the Biblical Studies Department of the United Theological College, Bangalore, India. He is a minister of the Presbyterian Church of South India and holds a PhD in New Testament studies from the Department of Theology of the University of Durham, UK. He has published *A Bibliography of Christian Writings in Tamil in the Libraries of UK and Europe* (Madurai: Tamil Theological Book Club, 1986). He has publish many articles including, "The Meaning of εθνος and εθνη and its significance to the Study of the New Testament," *Bangalore Theological Forum* XXIX:384 (1997): 3–36 and "Re-reading New Testament in India: Some Hermeneutical Explorations," *Asia Journal of Theology* 13 (1999): 14–50. Although he has long worked with the categories of Mircea Eliade, the included article is his first publication on the Romanian historian of religions.

Okuyama Michiaki is assistant professor at Nanzan University and permanent research fellow at the Nanzan Institute for Religion and Culture in Nagoya, Japan. After finishing his doctoral work at the Department of Religious Studies in Tokyo University, he did research at the Institute of Buddhist Studies in Berkeley, Emory, and Princeton. He has translated a number of works related to Eliade into Japanese. These include the Eliade/Couliano *Dictionary of Religions* (Tokyo: Serika Shobō, 1994) and *A History of Religious Ideas III* (co-translator, Tokyo: Chikuma Shobō, 1998). His doctoral dissertation is published (in Japanese) as *Comparison, History, and Interpretation in Eliade's Study of Religion* (Tokyo: Tōsui Shobō, 2000) and earned the ninth Nakamura Hajime Award in 2001.

Katrine Ore is a university teacher at The University of Oslo, Norway, and has a PhD in history of religions with a doctoral thesis on Mircea Eliade: "Gender, Language and Politics in the Writings of Mircea Eliade." Ore has written various articles on Mircea Eliade in Scandinavian books and journals. "Mircea Eliade and the Flight from Modernity: The Fabric of Being. The Fabric of Meaning" (Bergen: 1992); "The Phenomenology of Religion Considered as a Genre of Philosophy. Barbosa da Silvas's Analysis of Eliade's Phenomenological Approach," and, together with Barbosa da Silva. "What is Phenomenology of Religion? A Critical Analysis of the Study of Religion," and "Mircea Eliade and the Myth and Ritual School" (Oslo: 1998).

Brigitte Ouellet holds a PhD in theology and the study of religion with her specialization in Egyptology from the Universities of Montreal and Saint Mary's in Halifax, Nova Scotia. Her PhD thesis is on the Berlin Papyrus 3024, *"the disillusioned man and his* ba: *the hermeneutic of an experience of ontophany."* She describes herself as "crazy about all forms of research, especially in the history and anthropology of religions and the history of ancient Egypt and Mesopotamia." Her master's degree, also from the University of Montreal, is in the history of the ancient Near East with a dissertation on "Divinization and the Cult of the Sovereign in the ancient Near East." She has studied at the Cheops Institute in Paris and teaches Egyptian Hieroglyphics, among other courses. She is the founding president of the Quebec *Society for the Study of Egyptian Antiquities/Société pour l'Étude de l'Égypte Ancienne.* She has published numerous articles and given many presentations on Egyptian antiquities.

Bryan Rennie has a PhD in Religious Studies from the University of Edinburgh, Scotland. He holds the Vira I. Heinz Chair of Religion in the department of Religion, History, Philosophy, and Classics at Westminster College, Pennsylvania. His primary areas of research are the life and work of Mircea Eliade and theory and method in the study of religion. He has published three other books on Eliade: *Reconstructing Eliade: Making Sense of Religion* (SUNY Press, 1996), *Changing Religious Worlds: The Meaning and End of Mircea Eliade* (SUNY Press,

2001) and *Mircea Eliade: A Critical Reader*, which collects significant essays by and about Eliade into a single volume (Equinox Publishers, 2006). He has contributed entries on Eliade to many encyclopedias and dictionaries, including the second edition of the Macmillan Encyclopedia of Religion, originally edited by Eliade. He has also published articles in several journals and edited volumes on Eliade and on other theoretical and methodological considerations in the study of religion. He has delivered papers and organized sessions at the American Academy of Religion and the International Association for the History of Religion, and he has been invited to give presentations on Eliade in Romania, Korea, and at the University of Chicago.

Mac Linscott Ricketts now retired, was full professor and chair of the Department of Philosophy and Religion at Louisburg College in North Carolina. He studied the history of religions under Eliade at Chicago, where he took the MA and PhD degrees with a dissertation on the Native American trickster. He also taught at Duke University. He is the author of numerous articles on Eliade and the two volume *Mircea Eliade: The Romanian Roots* 1907–1945 (New York: Columbia University Press, 1988). With Mary Park Stevenson, Ricketts translated Eliade's major novel, *The Forbidden Forest*, from Romanian into English (University of Notre Dame Press, 1978) and translated Eliade's *Journals*, vols. I and IV, and the *Portuguese Journal* (forthcoming from the State University of New York Press) and his *Autobiography* (vols. I and II).

Natale Spineto has PhDs both from the University of Rome in the history of religions and from the Sorbonne in the anthropology of religions. He taught at the University of Geneva in Switzerland, at the University of Milan in Italy, and is currently conducting research at the University of Turin, Italy. He edited *Mircea Eliade—Raffaele Pettazzoni: L'histoire des religions a-t-elle un sens? Correspondance 1926–1959* (Parigi: Éditions du Cerf, 1994) and has published many articles on Eliade including papers on the "nostalgia for Paradise"; religion and symbol in Eliade; Eliade's comparativism; the experience of light in Eliade's work; Eliade and archetypes; and on Eliade and Ugo Bianchi in a festschrift for Bianchi (Giovanni Casadio, ed., Rome: Il Calamo,

2002). He edited, with Julian Ries, *Deux explorateurs de la pensée humaine. Georges Dumézil et Mircea Eliade* (Brepols: Turnhout, 2003).

Philip Vanhaelemeersch has an MA in Oriental Studies from the Catholic University of Leuven in Belgium (1993) and an MA. in theology, also from Leuven (2000). He holds a Master of Studies in the study of religion and a PhD, both from Oxford. His PhD thesis focuses on the idea of experience (*trăire*) in Romania in the '20s and '30s and the lack of belief common in Eliade's generation. He has published several papers on the 18th-century precursor of Italian historicism and the study of religion, Giambattista Vico, including "Vico: New light on Eliade and his Critics," in *Archæus. Études d'Histoire des Religions* 4:4 (2000): 79–121. He is working on a Romanian anthology on Italian historicism and the study of religion (Benedetto Croce, Adolfo Omodeo, Raffaele Pettazzoni, and Ernesto de Martino) to be published by Polirom in Iași. Dr. Vanhaelemeersch is a research fellow at the Belgian Cultural Academy in Rome.

Pablo Wright has a PhD in anthropology from Temple University and currently is an assistant professor in the Department of Anthropology of the School of Philosophy and Letters at the University of Buenos Aires. He is also Researcher at the National Council for Scientific and Technological Research (CONICET), and directs a research project to study religious heterodoxy in Argentina. He has carried out research in symbolism, cognition, and religion among the Argentine Chaco Toba people.

Name Index

Allen, Douglas, 57, 78, 84, 88
   Structure and Creativity, 78, 84
   Myth and Religion in Mircea Eliade, 57
Alles, Gregory, 174
   "*Homo Religiosus*," 74
Althusser, Louis, 28
Altizer, T. J. J. 74
   The Gospel of Christian Atheism, 74

Barthes, Roland, 28
Berger, Adriana, 97 n.11
Bultmann, Rudolph, 85–88

Campbell, Joseph, 59, 177
Cave, David, 44 n.3, 96 n.2, 97 n.12
Cioran, Emil, 96, 210, 223 n.1
Coomaraswamy, Ananda, 7, 104–05, 121 n.1, 126 n.33, 131–34, 136–42, 146 nn.6 & 11
Corbin, Henri, 104, 144
Croce, Benedetto, 8, 151, 158–65, 310

Dasgupta, Sukumar (Khokha), 120, 125 n.23
Dasgupta, Surendranath, 73, 108–09, 113, 119–20, 127
Descartes, René, 214
Doniger, Wendy, 177
Dubuisson, Daniel, 3, 7, 142
   Mythologies du XXe Siècle, 3
Dumézil, Georges, 1, 49

Eco, Umberto, 48
Eliade, Mircea,
   Aryanism, 77
   as a generalist, 48
   humanism, 88, 94, 97 n.12
   Indian influence on, 73, 101–20, 216–17
   as initiate, 112, 114–16, 118–20
   nationalism, 77–78
   as phenomenologist of religion, 24
   psychic phenomena, etc, interest in, 103, 215–16
   as theologian, 73–78
   critique of theologians, 80–83
   as Western intellectual, 23, 31
   politics, 1
   Works (non-fiction):
   Alchimia asiatic, 215, 218
   Autobiography, 110, 113, 115, 122, 127, 140, 171, 175
   Comentarii la legenda Meşterului Manole, 134, 137–38, 219–20
   Cosmos and History: The Myth of the Eternal Return, 16, 18–21, 26, 48, 88–89, 151–52, 156–57, 161, 237
   Drumul spre centru, 219
   "Folklorul ca instrument de cunoaştere," 133
   Forge and the Crucible, The, 18, 21
   Fragmentarium, 134, 136, 138, 218, 221

Works (non-fiction) *(continued)*
   History of Religious Ideas, 10, 51, 83, 91, 229–30
   Images and Symbols: Studies in Religious Symbolism, 52, 58, 74, 81, 87–88, 155, 158, 191
   "Itinerariu spiritual," 131
   Journals, 147, 152, 155–56, 234–35, 237–38
   "Literary Imagination and Religious Structure," 62
   "Masks: Mythical and Ritual Origins," 176
   "Methodological Remarks on the Study of Religious Symbolism," 64, 81
   Mircea Eliade și corespondencii si, 104, 122, 124
   Mitul reintegrrii, 139, 219
   Myth and Reality, 23, 25–26, 31, 75–76, 232
   Myths, Dreams and Mysteries: the Encounter between Contemporary Faiths and Archaic Realities, 26, 77, 87–88, 93, 190
   Oceanografie, 217–18
   Ordeal by Labyrinth: Conversations with Claude-Henri Rocquet, 22, 49, 113–14, 117, 127–28, 200, 230, 237
   Patañjali and Yoga, 87
   Patterns in Comparative Religion, 15–16, 19, 74–76, 81, 169, 176–77, 189, 191, 193, 195, 230, 235
   "Revolta contra lumii moderne," 132, 135
   Sacred and the Profane: The Nature of Religion, 76, 81, 139, 143, 188, 231
   Shamanism: Archaic Techniques of Ecstasy, 171
   Soliloquii, 220
   "Some notes on *Theosophia Perennis*: Ananda K. Coomaraswamy and Henry Corbin," 140–41
   Symbolism, the Sacred, and the Arts, 76
   Two and the One, The, 48, 76, 92, 198
   Yoga, Essai sur les origines de la mystique indienne, 171, 216
   Yoga, Immortality and Freedom, 91–94, 113
   Zalmoxis, the Vanishing God, 77
(fiction):
   Bengal Nights, 94, 105
   Forbidden Forest, The, 15, 234
   Întoarcerea din rai, 115
   Isabel și apele diavolului, 117
   Lumina ce se stinge, 114, 128 n.41
   "Nineteen Roses," 105
   Nunt în Cer, 1
   Old Man and The Bureaucrats, The, 117
   Șantier. Roman indirect, 110, 115–16, 119
   Șarpele, 233–34
   Secret of Dr. Honigberger, The, 112
   Two Strange Tales, 112
   Viac Nou, Roman, 101, 120
   Youth Without Youth, 105, 129
Evola, Julius, 7, 101–03, 122 n.8, 131–40, 142–44

Faivre, Antoine, 103, 142–43
Foucault, Michel, 28
Frazer, James George, 42, 138, 172–74
Freud, Sigmund, 24, 174, 229

Gadamer, Hans–Georg, 48
Gandhi, Mohendas, 109, 118, 126
Ghose, Aurobindo, 104–06, 108–10, 118–19, 123
Girardot, Norman, 232
   Imagination and Meaning, 232, 234
Gimbutas, Marija, 177–78
Guénon, René, 7, 102–05, 108, 120, 131–34, 137–40, 142–44
   La crise du monde moderne, 132

Harrison, Jane, 170–74, 178
   Autobiography, 171

Name Index

Prologomena to the Study of Greek Religion, 171
Hegel, G. F. W., 153–54, 156–57
Heidegger, Martin, 85, 97 nn.11 & 12, 153–54, 161

Ionescu, Nae, 101, 133, 210–15, 218, 222
Curs de metafizic, 212–15, 218
Isaacson, Jenny, 105–06

Kant, Immanuel, 214, 224
Kitagawa, Joseph, 78

Laignel-Lavastine, Alexandra, 3
Cioran, Eliade, Ionescu, 3
Leeuw, Gerardus Van der, 24, 164, 174–75
Lévi-Strauss, Claude, 28, 30–31, 59
La pensée sauvage, 31
Levinas, Emmanuel, 59
Lucian of Samosata, 5, 38–43

Maitreyi Devi, 108, 112, 115, 120, 125 n. 23
It Does Not Die, 125 n.23
Maritain, Jacques, 214, 224 n.7
Primauté du spirituel, 214
Marx, Karl, 24, 76, 229
McCutcheon, Russell, 45
Manufacturing Religion, 45
Mus, Paul, 133–34, 138

Nietzsche, Friedrich, 24, 213, 229

Otto, Rudolf, 24, 164, 220

Pettazoni, Raffaele, 4, 15, 19, 142, 211, 309, 310

Pisi, Paola, 134, 136–37, 139

Quinn, William W. jr., 141–42
The Only Tradition, 141

Rennie, Bryan, 3, 45, 49, 52
Changing Religious Worlds, 2
Reconstructing Eliade, 3–4, 45, 49, 51–52
Ricketts, Mac Linscott, 3, 37, 133–35, 138, 232
Former Friends and Forgotten Facts, 3
Romanian Roots, The, 131, 133, 135, 138
Ricoeur, Paul, 4, 23–24, 27–33, 48–49, 203
Rimmon-Kenan, Schlomith, 48
Rocquet, Claude-Henri, 105, 117, 128, 230
Rudolph, Kurt, 44 n.5,

Said, Edward, 89–90
Orientalism, 89, 90
Sartre, Jean-Paul, 28
Sebastian, Mihail, 210–11
Journal 1935–1944, 211
Schmidt, Wilhelm, 20
Ursprung der Gottesidee, 20
Scholem, Gerschom, 1, 144
Shivananda, Swami, 112–14, 120
Spinoza, Baruch, 214
Strenski, Ivan, 180 n.1

Tagore, Rabindranath, 105, 118–19
Tillich, Paul, 79–80
Turner, Victor, 28

Wasserstrom, Steven, 7, 45, 143–44
Religion after Religion, 45

Subject Index

Ahistorical, anti–historical, 3, 9, 89, 140, 151, 161, 164, 169, 178, 197, 199
Alchemy, Alchemists, 18, 73, 133–34, 215, 217, 222–23
Androgyne, androgyny, 134–35, 169
Anthropology, 4, 22–23, 32–33, 138, 171, 210, 221, 223, 230
   philosophical, 101
Archaic, man, 5, 38, 40, 42, 87–89
   mentality, 52
   myth, 24, 231
   religion(s), 4, 49, 95, 152–53, 163, 165
   societies, 27, 136–37, 140, 232
   world, 137, 163–64, 244
Archetypes, 16, 18–21, 28, 53–54, 134–37, 139, 153–56, 176–77, 182, 193, 219–20, 222, 231
Aryan race theory, 77, 90–91, 96–97 n.8 & n.13
Axis mundi, 55–56, 134

Bucharest, 103, 109, 112, 116, 120, 210, 277
   university of 1, 305

Camouflage, 10, 26, 104, 112, 129, 244
   of the sacred in the profane, 10, 140, 229–36, 244
   of myth in history, 25
Cannibals, 200
Center, of the world, 76, 134
   symbolism of the, 134–35, 219

Chicago, University of, 1, 15, 113, 141, 229
Coincidentia Oppositorum, 52, 56–57, 139
Cosmic Christianity, 21, 75–78
Cosmogony, cosmogonic, 18, 26, 28, 55, 57, 89, 134–35, 232

Dialectic of the sacred and profane, 8, 52–56, 61, 187–205

Epistemology, epistemological, 180, 187–88, 190, 192, 194–95, 199–201, 20–4
Erlebnis (Romanian *Trăire*), 217, 310
Eschatology, 4, 21, 24, 26, 76–77, 232
Esotericism, esotericists, 7, 104, 108, 128, 132, 134, 140, 142–45
Eternal return, the, 16, 21, 26, 40, 152
Eternity, longing for, 16–17, 20, 152, 156, 163, 219, 238
Existential, 17, 19–20, 22, 26–28, 30, 32–33, 56–57, 85, 139, 178, 188–89, 195, 199–200
Existentialism, 84–89, 154, 157

Folklore, 75–77, 134, 140, 240–41, 255
   Indian, 73
   Romanian, 16
France, 1, 108, 110, 145

Germany, 1, 90, 145, 305

Subject Index

God, 74, 81, 85, 140, 213, 220
  death of, 74, 230
  Egyptian conception of, 53
  experience of, 6, 217, 218–19, 221
  forgetting, 20
  incarnation in Jesus Christ, 76
  relation to humanity, 212
  search for, 211, 213, 222
Goddess(es), 169–73, 176–78, 280 n.3
  Syrian, 38–39, 42

Hermeneutics, 2, 4–6, 8–9, 11, 23–24, 26–28, 30, 32, 39, 43, 47–51, 57, 59–64, 79, 81, 83–85, 94–95, 140, 156, 187, 192, 196–97, 200–01, 203–05, 230
  creative, 8, 11, 39, 83–84, 203, 205
  Eliadean, 5, 47–48, 50, 59–64
  total, 49, 63
Hierophany, hierophanic, 8, 16, 21, 28, 49, 52–54, 56–57, 62, 75–77, 175–76, 190–6, 198–9, 204, 230, 233–6, 243–4
  ontophany, 56–57, 308
Hieros gamos, 169
History, 8, 15, 18–22, 40, 52, 58, 60, 62–5, 76–7, 81, 87–96, 137–8, 151–68, 198, 202, 204, 211, 233–5, 241
  historicism, 3, 8, 61, 88–89, 151–53, 155–58
  historiography, 25, 58, 131, 158–60
  of religions, 1, 5, 37, 42–3, 48–9, 72–3, 78–80, 83, 104, 145, 200, 222, 230
  terror of 21, 33, 77, 117, 161
Homo religiosus, 8, 10, 16, 18, 38, 40, 42, 52, 139, 165, 174–6, 189–90
  Egyptian, 53
Homology, homologies, 2, 49, 52, 62, 89, 93
Human condition, the, 10, 30, 32–33, 80, 88, 219–20

Illud tempus, (*in illo tempore*), 16, 27, 52, 57, 177
India, 1, 3, 6–7, 9, 73–5, 78–9, 83–4, 90–5, 101–5, 108–20, 136, 139, 141, 158, 216, 222, 307

Initiation, initiate, 7, 20, 28, 112, 114–16, 118–20, 139–40, 142–44, 172, 231–32, 234
Italy, 1, 7–8, 144–5, 152, 158, 165, 309–10

Jesus, 76–77, 85–86, 130

Kabbalah, Christian, 7, 144

Marxism, Marxist(s), 76–77, 88–89, 153–54, 157, 165
Media (popular or mass), 27, 30, 232
Melanesian cargo cults, 4, 25
Mesopotamia, 38, 76, 83, 156
Methodology, 6, 37–38, 47–51, 59, 62–63, 65, 72, 81, 83–84, 94, 131, 158, 164, 192, 201–03
Modern:
  art, 25–27, 232
  being/ontology, 29–30
  humanity, 21, 27, 30–31, 41, 47, 64, 86, 88–89, 95, 137, 140, 158, 163, 231–32
  myths, 89, 229
  societies and cultures, 21, 28
  thought, 24, 60, 79, 85–87, 134, 143, 214, 230–32, 236
  [see also World, modern (demythicized)]
Modernism, modernity, 28–29, 31–32, 137, 244
Myth, mythology, 4, 6–7, 10, 16–21, 23–33, 37–43, 49, 52, 54, 56–57, 73–77, 81–82, 84–89, 92–93, 95–96, 112, 126, 160, 162, 171, 173–74, 178, 200, 220, 241–42
  demythicization, demythologization, 27, 29, 85, 87, 165
  survival of myths, 165, 229–32, 235, 240

Nationalism, nationalist, 77–78, 109, 209, 232
Nazism, 77, 230

Subject Index

New Man, the, 132, 147 n.16

Origins, 19, 26
  nostalgia for, 17, 122
  paradise of, 20
  prestige of, 28, 181 n.6
  world of, 4, 18
Paradise, 15, 17, 221
  longing or nostalgia for, 15–16, 231, 234, 309
  of archetypes, 18
Paris, 15, 103, 232
Phenomenology, 9, 15, 21, 24, 48–49, 52, 61–63, 81, 170, 176, 188, 190, 192, 195–98, 201–05, 212, 230
Platonism, Neoplatonism, 22, 136, 175, 220, 222
Positivism, positivist, 6, 91, 94, 110, 137
  antipositivism, 137
Postmodernism, 51
Profane, the, 4, 16–18, 21, 28, 54, 57, 118, 140, 165, 188, 190–91
Psychoanalysis, psychoanalytic, 26, 122

Quest motif, 10

Race, 77, 90, 97 n.13
Reintegration, 15, 17, 117, 134–6, 140, 143–4, 147, 195–6, 198, 234
Resurrection, 76–77, 86
Ritual(s), 16–20, 23, 26–27, 31–32, 39–42, 55, 73, 89, 134, 171, 174, 232
Romania, Romanians, 1, 7, 9, 16, 76–8, 101, 104–05, 108, 110–11, 113, 116, 118–19, 127–28, 132, 143, 145, 209–14, 217, 222, 232
Romanianism, 122, 143

Sacred, The, 4–6, 8–11, 16–22, 23, 25, 27–33, 53, 75–76, 80, 94, 165, 176, 219–20, 234
  center, 135
  irreducibility of, 15, 52–57, 81
  space, 38–40
  as a structure of human consciousness, 15, 188
  tree, 133

Science, 28, 82, 86, 89, 158–60
  occult, 215–17, 222
  of religion(s), 37, 47, 191, 200, 202, 212
Secret, the untellable, 11, 119
Spiritual, spirituality, 9, 20, 84, 87–88, 90, 93, 95, 97 n.12, 110, 115, 128 n.42, 134, 136, 141–44, 160, 209–10, 218–22, 224 n.13, 229
  Archaic, 89, 92, 140
  Hindu, Indian, 79, 90–92, 118
  the primacy of, 117, 211, 214–17
  quest, 73
  reintegration, 140
  Western, 91
Structure(s), 9, 24–25, 76, 198–200, 202, 204
  literary, 63
  religious, 16, 27–31, 48, 50, 52, 62–63, 81, 88, 141, 191, 193–97, 217, 219, 222, 231–32
Svarga Ashram (Rishikesh), 106, 108, 112–13, 127 n.36
Symbol(s), symbolism 10, 15, 18, 26–30, 53–54, 75–76, 81–82, 88–89, 92, 117, 136–39, 142, 173, 193–200, 204, 218, 221–22, 231, 233
  assessment and analysis of, 9, 169
  interpretation of, 24, 33, 52, 85–86, 95
  polysemy of, 134
  symbolic meaning, 9
  symbolic language, 56
  symbolic reality, 203

Tammuz, 38, 44 n.8
Time, 26–8, 87–9, 135, 146, n.11, 151–7, 173, 198, 231, 234, 270
  abolition of, 17–18
  Egyptian, 57–8
  first, 54
  great, 30
  primordial (*urzeit*), 17–18, 161–3, 177
  sacred, 16, 39–40
  sacralization of, 15–22
Traditionalism, 3, 7–8, 103, 133, 135–36, 141

Universals, universalism, 30–33, 51, 74, 76, 79–80, 83, 93, 96, 124, 136, 139, 155–56, 169, 174–79, 196, 198, 215

World(s), 54, 84, 157, 175, 194, 201, 203, 212
  archaic (see Archaic, world)
  being in the, 29, 32, 161–62, 200
  beyond, 219
  center of (see Center)
  construction, 62, 192
  end of, 102
  of essences, 212, 222
  imaginary, 55–56
  inner, 157
  lifeworld, 195, 201 (of *homo religiosus*), 190–01
  of meaning, 32
  modern (demythicized), 10, 25, 29–30, 87, 120, 165, 230–32, 235, 244
  mythical, 4, 18, 38, 86
  renewal, 26
  sacred, 142, sacred in the, 233, 236, 244
  spiritual, 88
  tree, 76
  western, 32
  worldview(s), 5, 37, 41–43, 74, 84, 95

Yoga, 73, 83, 97 n.15, 112, 114, 118–20, 135, 158, 217

www.ingramcontent.com/pod-product-compliance
Lightning Source LLC
Chambersburg PA
CBHW030015240426
43672CB00007B/959